HEAVEN
AND
HELL

Edited by

Joan D. Berbrich

McGRAW-HILL BOOK COMPANY

New York   St. Louis   Dallas   San Francisco   Atlanta

ACKNOWLEDGMENTS

We are indebted to the following for permission to reprint copyrighted material:

AMS Press, Inc. for permission to reprint "How the Devil Redeemed the Crust of Bread" by Leo Tolstoy from *The Complete Works of Count Tolstoy*, translated by Leo Wiener, copyright 1904.

The Estate of Robert Arthur for permission to reprint "Satan and Sam Shay" by Robert Arthur.

Bantam Books, Inc. for permission to reprint "Benjamen Burning" by Joyce Madelon Winslow. Copyright © 1968 by Joyce Madelon Winslow, originally appeared in *Intro #1*, edited by R. V. Cassill. Copyright © 1968 by Bantam Books, Inc.

Richard W. Baron Publishing Co., Inc. for permission to reprint "Stagolee" by Julius Lester from *Black Folktales*. Copyright © 1969 by Julius Lester. Reprinted by permission of the Richard W. Baron Publishing Co., Inc.

Brandt & Brandt for permission to reprint "The Devil and Daniel Webster" by Stephen Vincent Benét from *The Selected Works of Stephen Vincent Benét*. Copyright, 1936, by The Curtis Publishing Company. Copyright renewed © 1964 by Thomas C. Benét, Stephanie B. Mahin, and Rachel B. Lewis. Reprinted by permission of Brandt & Brandt.

Library of Congress Cataloging in Publication Data

Berbrich, Joan D   comp.   New York: McGraw-Hill Book Co.,
Heaven and hell.   1975.

(Patterns in literary art, 15)   268p.
CONTENTS: General introduction.—Heaven and hell and all that: Cynewulf. The last judgment. Parkes, F. E. K. African heaven. Lester, J. Stagolee. Maier, H. What price heaven? Goldin, S. The last ghost. Laurance, A. Chances are. Priestley, J. B. The gray ones. Levertov, D. The dead.—The paths of good and bad intention: France, A. Our lady's juggler. Winslow, J. M. Benjamen burning. Straley, D. B. The Devil grows jubilant. Tolstoy, L. How the Devil redeemed the crust of bread. Beerbohm, M. The happy hypocrite. Davidson, J. A ballad of hell. [etc.]
    1. Heaven—Fiction. 2. Hell—Fiction. [1. Heaven—Fiction. 2. Hell—Fiction. 3. Short stories]
I. Title.   2-10-75
PZ5.B418He   [Fic]   74-8697
ISBN 0-07-004837-1

Editorial Development, Susan Gelles; Editing and Styling, Linda Richmond; Design, Cathy Gallagher; Production, Renee Laniado; Permissions, Laura Mongello

CONTENTS

Acknowledg

GENERAL INTRODUCTION

There are many concepts of an afterlife, but Western thinking has been most influenced by one version: that many years ago a bright archangel named Lucifer was overcome by self-pride and set himself up in opposition to God; that Lucifer's forces attacked the forces of God and on the third day were hurled out of heaven into the abyss; that they landed nine days later in a dark and fearsome pit that became known as hell. And ever since, the forces of God and the devil, of heaven and hell, of good and evil, have been in rivalry for human souls. The conflict and its immediate consequences are best depicted in the great epic poem by John Milton, *Paradise Lost*.

Before that conflict, Milton states, all living things were happy, and all were good. Beauty and brightness illuminated the remotest corners of the world, leaving no shadows in which doubt or fear might lurk. All was serene.

What happened to disrupt this paradise? How did evil start?

Raphael, a messenger from heaven, told Adam and Eve all about it. The serenity lasted, he said, until the day God the Father made a simple but momentous announcement. He proclaimed that henceforth his only Son would be the King of Heaven. All the angels were to obey and worship him. As God finished his speech, Raphael noted that "All seemed well pleased; all seemed, but were not all."

With Christ's rise to power, doubt entered; pride grew; rebellion was born. Satan and a few of his companions resented the Son's dominance, finding his power a lessening of their own. Determined to "win the mount of God," they marshalled forces and prepared for war. The battle roared with the clashing of armor, the raging of chariot wheels, and the hissing of fiery darts in "flaming volleys."

But Satan's cohorts were not content with destruction wrought by sword and arrow, and on the second day they brought cannons that disgorged a "devilish glut, chained thunderbolts and hail of iron globes!" Angels and archangels fell in the ghastly tumult, but spirits (contrary to rumor) are not frail. Quickly they rose; quickly they plucked hills and mountains from their foundations; quickly they hurled them, like mammoth hand grenades, at the still-boasting rebels. For a second time, the rebels retreated.

On the third day the battle order changed. The good angels rested, and the Son of God, alone, went forth to meet the malcontents. With ten thousand thunderbolts, with arrows of lightning, he assailed them, until—truly thunderstruck—they cast themselves from the verge of heaven "to the bottomless pit." The rebels fell for nine days, landing at last in hell, a yawning pit filled with fire and woe and pain.

As his description of the war between heaven and hell came to an end, Raphael turned to Adam and Eve, emphasizing the possible significance of these events for them. Satan envies them, Raphael warned, because newly created and innocent, they enjoy the love of God. Still arrogant, the Fallen Angel can find solace only in revenge—in "getting even" with the Son by enlisting Adam and Eve into his own diabolical crew. Adam and Eve must learn from the example of the rebellious angels; they must "listen not to his temptations."

But as all the world knows, Adam and Eve learned little from Raphael's lecture. They sinned, were exiled from Eden, and were burdened (some would say blessed) with mortality. When confronted by their mortality, by death, even they began to wonder what came next. A heaven for the good? A hell for the wicked? A ghostly land of wanderers? Or just a deep, undreaming sleep?

Heaven
and Hell
and All That

CHAPTER ONE

It must have taken the first thoughtful human only a few seconds to travel from the notion of death to the notion of an afterlife.

There is something in every living being that denies negation. The past is unreal; it was when we were not. The far future is unreal; it will be when we are not. Only the present is real, for it is ours.

To be human is to be the egotistical core of the universe. One's friends are loyal; one's enemies abhorrent; one's beliefs true; one's pains intolerable. One is conscious, minute by minute, of a fingernail torn one-sixteenth of an inch; but starving millions, if they are far enough away, one thinks of only fitfully. Such is the egotism of the individual.

This concern—this all-engrossing concern for self—makes the concept of an afterlife a matter of moment. This body, this personality, this particular brain with its particular memories cannot simply end. Somewhere or somehow the individual self must continue to exist, for without it, it is unthinkable that the world should continue to exist.

Therefore, most people believe there is an afterlife. And people in all ages and all countries have created their own images of life beyond death.

The ancient Greeks and Romans, forever practical, envisioned the afterworld as a sort of dull imitation of life on earth. The great Achilles confided that he would rather be a servant of servants on earth than a respected warrior in Hades.

Plato, in love with the human condition, chose a special kind of reincarnation. Each individual lived, died, was rewarded or punished for a thousand years, and was then given the chance to live again. Only a very few horribly wicked and a very few truly good were not given another chance, for the first would be punished forever, and the latter rewarded forever.

Thus Plato, in a sense, foreshadowed the Christian concept of an afterworld—a concept that came to fruition in the Middle Ages. It was then that the lines were clearly drawn: the good went to heaven, to be eternally happy; the unrepentant wicked went to hell, to be eternally miserable; the majority, being both good and wicked, went to purgatory to be cleansed and made ready for heaven. This Christian concept, Catholic really, had the merit of being widely accepted. People knew rather more about the afterworld than they knew about the other continents. They talked of it easily and with confidence. Priests described it in detail; painters limned specific tortures; writers reached hopelessly for words that would convey pure ecstasy or utter terror.

Hell was dark, lighted only by grim red flames that licked hungrily at sinners' flesh. Demons were skinny, horned, red, with emberlike eyes and diabolical grins. Heaven was light, airy, backed with a soft blue sky. Music permeated the celestial region, and joy was derived from the continuing adoration of God.

So real were heaven and hell in these centuries (800–1500) that related literature and painting became popular art. Cynewulf's poem spoke of the Last Judgment, of the separation of the saved from the damned, and of heaven and hell as geographical places. In miracle and morality plays, the role of the devil grew in importance as audiences delighted in Old Scratch's wild antics. Hieronymus Bosch (1450–1516) and Pieter Brueghel (1520?–1569) created masterpieces on canvas that were graphic enough to appall and obsess six centuries later. Cathedrals rose toward the sky, their slim, tapering spires symbolizing human hands, palm to palm, fingertips straining toward the Highest Good. Stained glass windows, in selfless anonymity, depicted the good and the evil reaping their different harvests; and statues, carved with loving care and total certitude, bedecked cathedral facades, walls, and porticoes. Each Gothic cathedral became not only a communal prayer, but also a communal map to the afterworld.

Such certainty could not last long on this doubtful earth. The

Reformation knocked out purgatory; the Puritans carried hell to such unbelievable lengths that it was rejected by the "damned" masses. The eighteenth century wondered nonchalantly if there were any afterlife at all. Or was the coffee house or theater stall the be-all and end-all?

The nineteenth century, ripped by the jagged edge of Darwin's theory of evolution, turned back to a belief in an afterlife, but one that was more "civilized," more acceptable to the cultured and the literate. The theologian suggested an afterworld in which the good were rewarded by the sight of God and the wicked suffered by being deprived of the sight of God. The new heaven and hell were dull places when compared with their predecessors; but they were comfortable—so comfortable and so dull that they could safely be ignored.

With the advent of Freud and the new psychological perspective, people looked on the now old views and found them boring. A dull hell! A dull heaven! How inane! And what a perfect starting place for the twentieth-century imagination. Now an author could turn heaven into a living library, or an "all-you-can-eat-free" restaurant, or a perpetual fish-fry. Now hell could be portrayed as an overwhelming cacophony or as the silence of utter boredom.

The door was open. Writers began to play with still different ideas. With modern love for the underdog, some suggested that Lucifer was really rather admirable—a brave rebel daring to throw himself against superior forces. Some wondered if hell might be more interesting than heaven. Some puzzled aloud about what would happen if a good man were sent to hell or an evil man to heaven.

By this time strong concepts of heaven and hell were almost gone. Perhaps the afterworld was a gray nothingness paralleling the nothingness of life. Men, such as Thoreau described, who lived lives of quiet desperation yielded to people whose lives, void even of desperation, led only to an afterlife void of all.

Only one step remained—denial. The dead are dead. Period.

Though the progression of concepts of an afterworld has been clear, it has not been total. All of the concepts linger on. All have a place in modern thought and belief. Today, in the closing decades of the twentieth century, one man's concept of heaven may be another's concept of hell.

INTRODUCTION

In the ninth and tenth centuries excitement mounted among the learned, the lords, and the peasants. The year 1000 approached. Surely this would be a cataclysmic year, one that would bring with it the Last Judgment and the immediate coming of the afterlife for all. Soon everyone would know his final, his eternal, destination. Those years of rapt anticipation have special meaning today, for as we approach the year 2000, many people are warning that this truly is the end.

One of the finest Christian poets of the Anglo-Saxon period was Cynewulf. In "The Last Judgment" (one of the *Christ* poems), Cynewulf described Christ's coming and his separation of the saved from the damned. He then went further—he described the demonic horrors awaiting the damned and the pure bliss awaiting the saved.

The Last Judgment

Cynewulf

All heaven and hell shall then be filled
with the sons of men, with the souls of mortal men.
The abyss shall swallow the enemies of God;
the flickering flames shall harass sinners,
workers of injury, and shall not let them depart   5
in joy to any refuge.
The fire shall keep that horde immovable;
it shall vex mankind.
               Foolhardy it seems to me,
that men, creatures with souls endowed,
heed not that their Lord   10
may punish transgressors
in any way whatsoever.
               Then life and death
shall gain their share of souls. The house of torment

shall be full open to perjured spirits;
sin-loving men, with swarthy souls, shall fill it.   15
Then, in retribution for their sins,
the shoal of guilty ones shall be separated,
the base from the holy, unto pernicious death.
There thieves and men of cruelty,
liars and adulterers, shall have no hope of life;   20
and the forsworn shall see their crimes' reward,
grievous and fiercely grim.   Then hell shall take
the crowd of faithless ones, and the Lord shall abandon them
to eternal damnation.   Sinners shall endure
dire racking agony.   Wretched shall he be   25
who sinned full willfully:
on that judgment day, he shall be severed
from his Creator, and doomed to the death below,
among hell's race, yielded to the hot fire,
beneath barriers of flame.   There shall men stretch   30
their limbs, to be bound and to be burned,
and to be scourged, in punishment for sin.
    Then the Holy Spirit, through the might of God,
at the King's command, shall lock the gates of hell—
that worst of torture houses—filled with fire   35
and with countless fiends.   For devils and for men
this torment is most ominous: for it will be a joyless home,
and no one ever will escape from there,
from those cold bonds.   They broke their Lord's command,
the Scriptures' bright teaching.   Now they must abide   40
the livelong night, and, stained with wicked deeds,
forever must they suffer pain without end,
who here despised the bliss of heaven's realm.
    Then shall the chosen carry before Christ
shining treasures; their happiness shall live.   45
With God, at doomsday, shall they have the joy
of life serene, for it shall be granted
to every holy saint in heaven's kingdom.
That is the home that never shall know end,
and there the pure of heart forevermore   50
shall hold their joyous mirth, and praise the Lord,
their life's dear Guardian.   There, clad in light,

clothed in peace, shielded from sorrow,
glorified by joy, radiant with grace,
shall they—loved by the Lord—forever and forever   55
enjoy in bliss the angels' fellowship,
and cherish mankind's Guardian, Father of all,
sovereign preserver of the holy hosts.
    There is angels' song, the bliss of the happy,
and the gracious presence of the Lord,   60
brighter than the sun, for all the blessed ones.
There is the love of the beloved, and life without death's end;
a joyful band of men; youth without age;
the glory of heavenly chivalry; health without pain
for righteous spirits; and for souls sublime,   65
rest without toil. There is day without dark gloom,
ever gloriously bright; bliss without sorrow;
friendship among friends forever without feud;
peace without enmity for the blessed in heaven,
in the communion of saints. Hunger is not there, nor thirst, 70
nor sleep, nor grievous sickness; nor sun's heat,
nor cold, nor care; but there that blissful band,
the fairest of all hosts, shall ever enjoy
their Sovereign's grace; and glory with their King.

FOR DISCUSSION

1.   Cynewulf's description of heaven and hell is traditional. It
was widely accepted in the Middle Ages and is still accepted
by many people today. Divide a sheet of paper in half. Label
one column "Heaven" and one column "Hell." In the first
column, list five characteristics of heaven as given by Cynewulf; in the second column, list five characteristics of hell.

2.   Most people believe that Cynewulf's description of hell is more
graphic and more memorable than his description of heaven.
Do you agree? Why or why not? Why might it be easier to
depict hell than heaven?

3.   Is a newspaper more likely to give front-page treatment to bad
news rather than to good news? Why or why not? What

does your answer to this question combined with your answer to Question 2 suggest about human nature?

4. Cynewulf carefully states that both the punishments of the damned and the rewards of the blessed will endure for eternity. From an earthly point of view, how would you enjoy forever:
   a. "day without dark gloom";
   b. "rest without toil";
   c. "health without pain"?

INTRODUCTION

One thousand years after Cynewulf and halfway across the world from Cynewulf's England, Francis Parkes, another poet, wrote "African Heaven." In this poem, Parkes blends the future afterworld with the present real world, letting each illuminate the other. At a first reading, Parkes's "African Heaven" may seem naive, even charmingly primitive. But a second reading plunges one beyond the naive into the bitterly sophisticated. Parkes, born in Accra, brings to his concept a knowledge of the Africans themselves and of the tourists who invade the land with cocked cameras. The result—in a different country and a different age—is a heaven that bears little resemblance to Cynewulf's.

African Heaven

Francis Ernest Kobina Parkes

Give me black souls,
Let them be black
Or chocolate brown
Or make them the
Color of dust—   5
Dustlike,
Browner than sand.
But if you can
Please keep them black,
Black.   10

Give me some drums;
Let them be three
Or maybe four
And make them black—
Dirty and black: 15
Of wood,

And dried sheepskin,
But if you will
Just make them peal,
Peal.   20

Peal loud,
Mutter.
Loud,
Louder yet;
Then soft,   25
Softer still
Let the drums peal.

Let the calabash
Entwined with beads
With blue Aggrey beads   30
Resound, wildly
Discordant,
Calmly
Melodious.
Let the calabash resound   35
In tune with the drums.

Mingle with these sounds
The clang
Of wood on tin:
Kententsekenken   40
Ken—tse ken ken ken:

Do give me voices
Ordinary
Ghost voices
Voices of women   45
And the bass
Of men.
(And screaming babes?)

Let there be dancers,
Broad-shouldered negroes   50
Stamping the ground
With naked feet

And half-covered
Women
Swaying, to and fro,   55
In perfect
Rhythm
To *"Tom shikishiki"*
And *"Ken,"*
And voices of ghosts   60
Singing,
Singing!

Let there be
A setting sun above,
Green palms   65
Around,
A slaughtered fowl
And plenty of
Yams.

And dear Lord,   70
If the place be
Not too full,
Please
Admit spectators.
They may be   75
White or
Black.

Admit spectators
That they may
See: 80
The bleeding fowl,
And yams,
And palms,
And dancing ghosts.

Odomankoma,   85
Do admit spectators
That they may
Hear:

Our native songs,
The clang of woods on tin   90
The tune of beads
And the pealing drums.

Twerampon, please, please
Admit
Spectators!   95
That they may
Bask
In the balmy rays
Of the
Evening Sun,   100
In our lovely
African heaven!

FOR DISCUSSION

1. After reading this poem once, list the ingredients that the poet demands for his African heaven. Then think about the items on this list. What do they remind you of? Does any one item strike you as different or unexpected?

2. Read the poem a second time. Note the strange alternation of the traditional and the nontraditional ("the calabash" and the "ghost voices"). Note the disturbing repetition of "admit spectators." What kind of heaven is Parkes really describing?

3. One manifestation of irony is in word play, in which one thing is said, but something quite different is implied. Identify three or four examples of irony in this poem. Can you suggest a reason why Parkes chose to use an ironic approach rather than a direct statement to convey his message?

INTRODUCTION

Julius Lester, one of the leading black writers today, looked at the traditional heaven and hell and found them lacking. Blacks are different, Lester seems to insist. Their heritage, their values, their interests are different, and the concepts of heaven and hell created by whites simply will not do.

Stagolee was a real man who first became a legend in a popular song. His story captured the hearts of the masses, and before long, was transformed into a myth for the black city-dweller. Here, in a very modern folktale, is one black view of an afterlife.

Stagolee

Julius Lester

Stagolee was, undoubtedly and without question, the baddest nigger that ever lived. Stagolee was so bad that the flies wouldn't even fly around his head in the summertime, and snow wouldn't fall on his house in the winter. He was bad, jim.

Stagolee grew up on a plantation in Georgia, and by the time he was two, he'd decided that he wasn't going to spend his life picking cotton and working for white folks. Uh-uh. And when he was five, he left. Took off down the road, his guitar on his back, a deck of cards in one pocket and a .44 in the other. He figured that he didn't need nothing else. When the women heard him whup the blues on the guitar he could have whichever one he laid his mind on. Whenever he needed money, he could play cards. And whenever somebody tried to mess with him, he had his .44. So he was ready. A man didn't need more than that to get along with in the world.

By the time Stack was grown, his reputation had spread around the country. It got started one night in one of them honky-tonks down there in Alabama, and Stagolee caught some dude trying to deal from the bottom of the deck. Ol' Stack pulled out his .44 and killed him dead, right there on the spot. Then he moved the dead guy over to the center of the room and used the body as a card table. Another time, something similar happened, and Stack pulled the body over next to him, so a buddy of his, who was kinda short, would have something to sit on. Didn't take long for the word to get around that this was one bad dude! Even white folks didn't mess with Stagolee.

Well, this one time, Stagolee was playing cards with a dude they called Billy Lyons. Billy Lyons was one of them folk who acted like they were a little better than anybody else. He'd had a little education, and that stuff can really mess your mind up. Billy Lyons had what he called a "scientific method" of cardplaying. Stagolee had the "nigger method." So they got to playing, and, naturally, Stagolee was just taking all of Billy Lyons's money, and Billy got mad. He got so mad that he reached over and knocked Stagolee's stetson hat off his head and spit in it.

What'd he do that for? He could've done almost anything else in the world, but not that. Stack pulled his .44, and Billy started copping his plea. "Now, listen here, Mr. Stagolee. I didn't mean no harm. I just lost my head for a minute. I was wrong, and I apologize." He reached down on the ground, picked up Stack's stetson, brushed it off, and put it back on his head. "I didn't mean no harm. See, the hat's all right. I put it back on your head." Billy was tomming like a champ, but Stack wasn't smiling. "Don't shoot me. Please, Mr. Stagolee! I got two children and a wife to support. You understand?"

Stack said, "Well, that's all right. The Lawd'll take care of your children. I'll take care of your wife." And, with that, Stagolee blowed Billy Lyons away. Stagolee looked at the body for a minute and then went off to Billy Lyons's house and told Mrs. Billy that her husband was dead and he was moving in. And that's just what he did, too. Moved in.

Now there was this new sheriff in town, and he had gotten the word about Stagolee, but this sheriff was a sho' nuf' cracker. He just couldn't stand the idea of Stagolee walking around like he was free—not working, not buying war bonds, cussing out white folks. He just couldn't put up with it, so, when he heard that Stagolee had shot Billy Lyons, he figured that this was his chance.

Sheriff told his deputies, said, "All right, men. Stagolee killed a man tonight. We got to get him."

The deputies looked at him. "Well, sheriff. Ain't nothing wrong with killing a man every now and then," said one.

"It's good for a man's health," added another.

"Well," said the sheriff, "that's all right for a white man, but this is a nigger."

"Now, sheriff, you got to watch how you talk about Stagolee. He's one of the leaders of the community here. You just can't come in here and start talking about one of our better citizens like that."

The sheriff looked at them. "I believe you men are afraid. Afraid of a nigger!"

Deputies thought it over for half a second. "Sheriff. Let's put it this way. We have a healthy respect for Stagolee. A long time ago, we struck a bargain with him. We promised him that if he let us alone, we'd let him alone. And everything has worked out just fine."

"Well, we're going to arrest Stagolee," the sheriff said. "Get your guns, and let's go."

The deputies stood up, took their guns, and laid 'em on the shelf. "Sheriff, if you want Stagolee, well, you can arrest him by yourself." And they went on out the door and over to the under-taker's parlor and told him to start making a coffin for the sheriff.

When all the other white folks heard what the sheriff was going to do, they ran over to talk to him. "Sheriff, you can't go around disturbing the peace." But couldn't nobody talk no sense into him.

Now Stagolee heard that the sheriff was looking for him, and, being a gentleman, Stagolee got out of bed, told Mrs. Billy he'd be back in a little while, and went on down to the bar. He'd barely gotten the first drink down when the sheriff came stepping through the door.

He walked over to the bartender. "Barkeep? Who's that man down at the other end of the bar? You know there's a law in this town against drinking after midnight. Who is that?"

Bartender leaned over the counter and whispered in his ear, "Don't talk so loud. That's Stagolee. He drinks when he gets thirsty and he's generally thirsty after midnight."

Sheriff walked over to Stagolee. Stagolee didn't even look

around. Sheriff pulled out his gun. Stack still didn't look around. Sheriff fired a couple of shots in the air. Stagolee poured himself another drink and threw it down. Finally, the sheriff said, "Stagolee, I'm the sheriff, and I'm white. Ain't you afraid?"

Stagolee turned around slowly. "You may be the sheriff, and you may be white, but you ain't Stagolee. Now deal with that."

The sheriff couldn't even begin to figure it out, no less deal with it, so he fell back in his familiar bag. "I'm placing you under arrest for the murder of Billy Lyons."

"You and what army? And it bet' not be the United States Army, 'cause I whupped them already."

"Me and this army," the sheriff growled, jabbing the pistol in Stack's ribs.

Before the sheriff could take another breath, Stagolee hit him upside the head and sent him flying across the room. Stagolee pulled out his gun, put three bullets in him, put his gun away, had another drink, and was on his way out the door before the body hit the floor.

The next day, Stagolee went to both of the funerals to pay his last respects to the sheriff and Billy Lyons, and then he settled down to living with Mrs. Billy. She really didn't mind too much. All the women knew how good-looking Stack was. And he was always respectful to women, always had plenty of money, and, generally, he made a good husband, as husbands go. Stagolee had one fault, though. Sometimes he drank too much. About once a month, Stagolee would buy up all the available liquor and moonshine in the county and proceed to get wasted, and when Stagolee got wasted, he got totally wasted.

The new sheriff waited until one of those nights when Stagolee was so drunk he was staggering in his sleep, and he was lying flat in the bed. If Judgment Day had come, the Lord would have had to postpone it until Stagolee had sobered up. Otherwise, the Lord might've ended up getting Gabriel shot and his trumpet wrapped around his head. When the sheriff saw Stagolee that drunk, he went and got together the Ku Klux Klan Alumni Association, which was every white man in four counties. After the sheriff had assured them that Stagolee was so drunk he couldn't wake up, they broke in the house just as bad as you please. They had the lynching rope all ready, and they dropped it around his neck. The minute that rope touched Stack's neck, he was wide awake and stone cold sober. When white folks saw that, they were falling over each other getting out of there. But Stack was cool. He should've been. He invented it.

"Y'all come to hang me?"

The sheriff said that that was so. Stagolee stood up, stretched, yawned, and scratched himself a couple of times. "Well, since I can't seem to get no sleep, let's go and get this thing over with so I can get on back to bed."

They took him on out behind the jail where the gallows was built. Stagolee got up on the scaffold, and the sheriff dropped the rope around his neck and tightened it. Then the hangman opened up on the trap door, and there was Stack, swinging ten feet in the air, laughing as loud as you ever heard anybody laugh. They let him hang there for a half-hour, and Stagolee was still laughing.

"Hey, man! This rope is ticklish."

The white folks looked at each other and realized that Stack's neck just wouldn't crack. So they cut him down, and Stagolee went back home and went back to bed.

After that, the new sheriff left Stagolee in peace, like he should've done to begin with.

Stagolee lived on and on, and that was his big mistake. 'Cause Stagolee lived so long, he started attracting attention up in Heaven. One day, St. Peter was looking down on the earth, and he happened to notice Stack sitting on the porch picking on the guitar. "Ain't that Stagolee?" St. Peter said to himself. He took a closer look. "That's him. That's him. Why, that nigger should've been dead a long time ago." So St. Peter went and looked it up in the record book, and, sure enough, Stagolee was supposed to have died thirty years before.

St. Peter went to see the Lord.

"What's going on, St. Peter?"

"Oh, ain't nothing shaking, Lord. Well, that's not totally true. I was just checking out earth, and there's a nigger down there named Stagolee who is way overdue for a visit from Death."

"Is that so?"

"It's the truth, Lord."

"Well, we have to do something about that." The Lord

cleared his throat a couple of times and hollered out, "HEY DEATH! HEEEEY, DEATH!"

Now Death was laying up down in the barn catching up on some sleep, 'cause he was tired. Having to make so many trips to Vietnam was wearing him out, not to mention everywhere else in the world. He just couldn't understand why dying couldn't be systematized. He'd tried his best to convince God either to get a system to dying or get him some assistants. He'd proposed that, say, on Mondays, the only dying that would be done would be, say, in France, Germany, and a few other countries. Tuesday it'd be some other countries, and on like that. That way, he wouldn't have to be running all over the world twenty-four hours a day. But the Lord had vetoed the idea. Said it sounded to him like Death just wanted an excuse to eventually computerize the whole operation. Death had to admit that the thought had occurred to him. He didn't know when he was going to catch up on all the paperwork he had to do. A computer would solve everything. And now, just when he was getting to sleep, here come the Lord waking him up.

So Death got on his pale white horse. He was so tired of riding a horse he didn't know what to do. He'd talked to God a few months ago about letting him get a helicopter or something. But the Lord just didn't seem to understand. Death rode on off down through the streets of Heaven, and when folks heard him coming, they closed their doors, 'cause even in Heaven, folks were afraid of Death. And that was the other thing. Death was mighty lonely. Didn't nobody talk to him, and he was getting a little tired of it. He wished the Lord would at least let him wear a suit and tie and look respectable. Maybe then he could meet some nice young angel and raise a family. The Lord had vetoed that idea, too.

"What took you so long, Death?"

"Aw, Lord. I was trying to get some sleep. You just don't realize how fast folks are dying these days."

"Don't tell me you gon' start complaining again."

"I'm sorry, Lord, but I'd like to see you handle the job as well as I do with no help, no sleep, no wife, no nothing."

"Well, I got a special job for you today."

"Can't wait until tomorrow?"

"No, it can't wait, Death! Now hush up. There's a man down in Fatback, Georgia, named Stagolee. You should've picked him up thirty years ago, and I want you to send me a memo on why you didn't."

"Well, I got such a backlog of work piled up."

"I don't want to have to be doing your job for you. You get the lists every day from the Record Bureau. How come you missed this one? If he's escaped for thirty years, who knows who else has been living way past their time. Speaking of folks living past their time, St. Peter, have the librarian bring me all the files on white folks. Seems to me that white folks sho' done outlived their time. Anyway, Death, go on down there and get Stagolee."

Death headed on down to earth. A long time ago, he used to enjoy the ride, but not anymore. There were so many satellites and other pieces of junk flying around through the air that it was like going through a junkyard barefooted. So he didn't waste any time getting on down to Fatback, Georgia.

Now on this particular day, Stagolee was sitting on the porch, picking the blues on the guitar, and drinking. All of a sudden, he looked up and saw this pale-looking white cat in this white sheet come riding up to his house on a white horse. "We ain't never had no Klan in the daytime before," Stagolee said.

Death got off his horse, pulled out his address book, and said, "I'm looking for Stagolee Booker T. Washington Nicodemus Shadrack Nat Turner Jones."

"Hey, baby! You got it down pat! I'd forgotten a couple of them names myself."

"Are you Stagolee Booker T. Wash—"

"You ain't got to go through the thing again. I'm the dude. What's going on?"

"I'm Death. Come with me."

Stagolee started laughing. "You who?"

"I'm Death. Come on, man. I ain't got all day."

"Be serious."

Death looked at Stagolee. No one had ever accused him of joking before. "I *am* serious. It's your time to die. Now come on here!"

"Man, you ain't bad enough to mess with me."

Death blinked his eyes. He'd never run up on a situation like this before. Sometimes folks struggled a little bit, but they didn't refuse. "Stagolee, let's go!" Death said in his baddest voice.

"Man, you must want to get shot."

Death thought that one over for a minute. Now he didn't know how to handle this situation, so he reached in his saddlebags and pulled out his *Death Manual.* He looked up *resistance* and read what it said, but wasn't a thing in there about what to do when somebody threatens you. Then he looked up *guns,* but that wasn't listed. He looked under everything he could think of, but nothing was of any help. So he went back to the porch. "You coming or not, Stagolee?"

Stagolee let one of them .44 bullets whistle past ol' Death's ear, and Death got scared. Death didn't waste no time getting away from there. Before he was sitting in the saddle good, he had made it back to Heaven.

"Lord! You must be trying to get me killed."

"Do what? Get you killed? Since when could you die?"

"Don't matter, but that man Stagolee you just sent me after took a shot at me. Now listen here, Lord, if you want that man dead, you got to get him yourself. I am not going back after him. I knew there was some reason I let him live thirty years too long. I'd heard about him on the grapevine and, for all I care, he can live three hundred more years. I am not going back—"

"O.K. O.K. You made your point. Go on back to sleep." After Death had gone, God turned to St. Peter and asked, "We haven't had any new applications for that job recently?"

"You must be joking."

"Well, I was just checking." The Lord lit a cigar. "Pete, looks like I'm going to have to use one of my giant death thunderbolts to get that Stagolee."

"Looks that way. You want me to tell the work crew?"

The Lord nodded, and St. Peter left. It took 3,412 angels 14 days, 11 hours, and 32 minutes to carry the giant death thunderbolt to the Lord, but he just reached down and picked it up like it was a toothpick.

"Uh, St. Peter? How you spell Stagolee?"

"Lord, you know everything. You're omnipotent, omniscient, omni—"

"You better shut up and tell me how to spell Stagolee."

St. Peter spelled it out for him, and the Lord wrote it on the thunderbolt. Then he blew away a few clouds and put his keen eye down on the earth. "Hey, St. Peter. Will you look at all that killing down there? I ain't never seen nothing like it."

"Lord, that ain't Georgia. That's Vietnam."

The Lord put his great eye across the world. "Tsk, tsk, tsk. Look at all that sin down there. Women wearing hardly no clothes at all. Check that one out with the black hair, St. Peter. Look at her! Disgraceful! Them legs!"

"Lord!"

And the Lord put his eye on the earth and went on across the United States—Nevada, Utah, Colorado, Kansas, Missouri—

"Turn right at the Mississippi River, Lord!"

The Lord turned right and went on down into Tennessee.

"Make a left at Memphis, Lord!"

The Lord turned left at Memphis and went on up through Nashville and on down to Chattanooga into Georgia. Atlanta, Georgia. Valdosta. Rolling Stone, Georgia, until he got way back out in the woods to Fatback. He let his eye go up and down the country roads until he saw Stagolee sitting on the porch.

"That's him, Lord! That's him!"

And the Great God Almighty, the God of Nat Turner and Rap Brown, the God of Muddy Waters and B.B. King, the God of Aretha Franklin and The Impressions, this great God Almighty Everlasting, *et in terra pax hominibus,* and all them other good things, drew back his mighty arm—

"Watch your aim now, Lord."

And unloosed the giant thunderbolt. BOOM!

That was the end of Stagolee. You can't mess with the Lord.

Well, when the people found out Stagolee was dead, you ain't never heard such hollering and crying in all your life. The women were beside themselves with grief, 'cause Stagolee was nothing but a sweet man.

Come the day of the funeral, and Stagolee was laid out in a $10,000 casket. Had on a silk mohair suit and his stetson hat was in his hand. In his right coat pocket was a brand new deck of cards. In his left coat pocket was a brand new .44 with some extra rounds of ammunition and a can of Mace. And by his side was his guitar. Folks came from all over the country to Stack's funeral, and all of 'em put little notes in Stagolee's other pockets, which were messages they wanted Stagolee to give to their kinfolk when he got to Hell.

The funeral lasted for three days and three nights. All the guitar pickers and blues singers had to come sing one last song for Stagolee. All the backsliders had to come backslide one more time for Stagolee. All the gamblers had to come touch Stack's casket for a little taste of good luck. And all the women had to come shed a tear as they looked at him for the last time. Those that had known him were crying about what they weren't going to have any more. And those that hadn't known him were crying over what they had missed. Even the little bitty ones was shedding tears.

After all the singing and crying and shouting was over, they took Stagolee on out and buried him. They didn't bury him in the cemetery. Uh-uh. Stagolee had to have a cemetery all his own. They dug his grave with a silver spade and lowered him down with a golden chain. And they went on back to their homes, not quite ready to believe that Stack was dead and gone.

But you know, it's mighty hard to keep a good man down, and, long about the third day, Stagolee decided to get on up out of the grave and go check out Heaven. Stack just couldn't see himself waiting for Judgment Day. The thought of that white man blowing the trumpet on Judgment Day made him sick to his stomach, and Stagolee figured he was supposed to have his own Judgment Day, anyhow.

He started on off for Heaven. Of course it took him a long time to get there, 'cause he had to stop on all the clouds and teach the little angels how to play Pitty-Pat and Coon-Can and all like that, but, eventually, he got near to Heaven. Now as he got close, he started hearing all this harp music and hymn singing. Stagolee couldn't believe his ears. He listened some more, and then he shrugged his shoulders. "I'm approaching Heaven from the wrong side. This can't be the black part of Heaven, not with all that hymn singing and harp music I hear."

So Stack headed on around to the other side of Heaven, and when he got there, it was stone deserted. I mean, wasn't nobody there. Streets was as empty as the President's mind. So Stack cut on back around to the other side of Heaven. When he got there, St. Peter was playing bridge with Abraham, Jonah, and Mrs. God.

When they looked up and saw who it was, though, they split, leaving St. Peter there by himself.

"You ain't getting in here!" St. Peter yelled.

"Don't want to, either. Hey, man. Where all the colored folks at?"

"We had to send 'em all to Hell. We used to have quite a few, but they got to rocking the church service, you know. Just couldn't even sing a hymn without it coming out and sounding like the blues. So we had to get rid of 'em. We got a few nice colored folks left. And they nice, respectable people."

Stagolee laughed. "Hey, man. You messed up."

"Huh?"

"Yeah, man. This ain't Heaven. This is Hell. Bye."

And Stagolee took off straight for Hell. He was about 2,000 miles away, and he could smell the barbecue cooking and hear the jukeboxes playing, and he started running. He got there, and there was a big BLACK POWER sign on the gate. He rung on the bell, and the dude who come to answer it recognized him immediately. "Hey, everybody! Stagolee's here!"

And the folks came running from everywhere to greet him.

"Hey, baby!"

"What's going down!"

"What took you so long to get here?"

Stagolee walked in, and the brothers and sisters had put down wall-to-wall carpeting, indirect lighting, and, best of all, they'd installed air conditioning. Stagolee walked around, checking it all out. "Yeah. Y'all got it together. Got it uptight!"

After he'd finished checking it out, he asked, "Any white folks down here?"

"Just the hip ones, and ain't too many of them. But they all right. They know where it's at."

"Solid." Stagolee noticed an old man sitting over in a corner with his hand over his ears. "What's his problem?"

"Aw, that's the Devil. He just can't get himself together. He ain't learned how to deal with niggers yet."

Stagolee walked over to him. "Hey, man. Get your pitchfork, and let's have some fun. I got my .44. C'mon. Let's go one round."

22

The Devil just looked at Stagolee real sad-like, but didn't say a word.

Stagolee took the pitchfork and laid it on the shelf. "Well, that's hip. I didn't want no stuff out of you nohow. I'm gon' rule Hell by myself!"

And that's just what he did, too.

FOR DISCUSSION

1. Like Pecos Bill and John Henry and Paul Bunyan, Stagolee is a bigger-than-life character. Mythical anecdotes accumulate quickly around such characters, and Stagolee may be well on his way to becoming a new giant of folklore. In the story, find one mythical anecdote about Stagolee's childhood, one about his adult life, and one about his death. What is the one characteristic shared by all these anecdotes?

2. Lester's descriptions of heaven and hell are, in some respects, similar to Cynewulf's. Yet the attitudes of the two authors are totally different. Find two similarities between Lester's heaven and Cynewulf's, and two similarities between Lester's hell and Cynewulf's. How is Lester's attitude toward heaven and hell different from Cynewulf's? Can you suggest a reason for these differing attitudes?

3. Stagolee finds harp music too soft and bland and seems to be saying that rock and the blues are necessary for happiness. The author also seems to be saying that one's choice of music depends on one's skin color. Many people today would disagree and would insist that one's choice depends on one's age. What do you think? Do you prefer a quiet or noisy background when you work or study? When you think of eternity, would you favor a heaven filled with soft harp music or one jumping with electronically amplified music?

4. In the best folklore tradition, Lester combines the telling of his hero's story with a good many satirical thrusts at contemporary society. The character of Death, for example, fits beautifully into our technological way of life. He sees no reason why dying can't be computerized so that he will have less running

around to do and less paperwork to complete. Find three more examples of incidents or commentary that criticize other aspects of our social structure.

5. The story ends with the devil being deposed as Stagolee takes away his pitchfork. Is this simply the end of an amusing story, or is the author implying more by his conclusion? Explain.

INTRODUCTION

Danny gambled, cheated a bit, and felt at home only when visiting the racetrack or the bookie. Not an admirable character, one would say. As a matter of fact, even Danny didn't consider himself admirable. But his heroic rescue of a small boy sent Danny to heaven.

At first, heaven is exactly as everyone pictures it: angels fly around; St. Peter presides; the saved are somber and dignified. What happens to a scalawag like Danny when he finds himself in such a heaven? He grows bored. St. Peter tries to oblige by creating a racetrack out of clouds, but Danny just grows more bored. If heaven isn't really heaven for Danny, then something must be done. And there's only one logical alternative.

What Price Heaven?

A Play for Radio

Howard Maier

[MUSIC. *In . . . has a bubbling, gay quality . . . and blends into:*
SOUND. *Noise of homeward bound racetrack crowd . . . shouts of touts, sandwich vendors and newsboys.*]

STATION MASTER. (*Calls.*) Stand back from the edge of the platform! New York train'll be in any minute now.

FIRST MAN. Can't come to quick for me. Belmont Park! You can have it! I dropped a bundle—

SECOND MAN. Me, too.

DANNY. (*In quick.*) Ahh, stop gripin', you guys. Whyn't you be like me? Happy, always smiling—

FIRST MAN. Happy. Smiling. Sure—when you beat four out of five races.

SECOND MAN. Lookit this mob. Everybody an' their sister. I'm sweatin'.

DANNY.   Only the losers sweat.

FIRST MAN.   Happy. Smiling—

DANNY.   Okay, okay. Forget it. Only I gotta get a newspaper. Here, you guys, let me past. Now where's that kid? (*Up.*) All right, people, let me through, huh? Comin' through. Sorry, comin' through.

[CAST. *Ad lib adverse criticism as* DANNY *pushes through toward newsboy's voice.*]

FIRST MAN.   (*Calls after him.*) You'll never get through, Danny . . .

DANNY.   Hey, kid! Let's have a paper . . .

FIRST VOICE.   Watch out, you! Watch where you're goin'!

DANNY.   I'm watchin' . . . *you* watch.

SECOND VOICE.   Stop pushing!

WOMAN.   Please . . . Please . . .

DANNY.   (*Calls again.*) Hey, kid . . .

WOMAN.   Please! . . . (*In alarm.*) . . .Oh . . . there! . . . now they've done it—pushed that poor boy off the platform . . . He's down on the tracks!

[CAST. *Ad lib confusion at accident which mounts steadily behind.*]

DANNY.   Dummies! Knockin' the kid off . . . G'wan down and get him.

FIRST VOICE.   Dummy yourself! Why don't *you* get him?

WOMAN.   Oh, please . . . stop arguing! The boy's hurt his ankle.

[SOUND. *Faint train whistle.*]

WOMAN.   (*Up.*) The train! The train's coming! . . . Please, please . . . somebody go down and get him!

DANNY.   Okay, lady—keep your shirt on. I'll get him.

[SOUND. DANNY *jumps down.*]

DANNY.   You all right, kid?

NEWSBOY.   Yeah. Only my ankle—I can't stand . . .

[SOUND. *Up steadily with approaching train.*]

DANNY. Just take it easy . . . don't try to move . . . Uncle Danny'll
hoist you up on the platform . . . Ready? All set?
NEWSBOY. Ahuh.
DANNY. (*Grunts.*) O-kay . . . up we go.

[SOUND. *Train up very strong.*]

DANNY. There you are—safe and sound. (*Calls.*) Hey—one of
you mugs give me a lift.
FIRST VOICE. Hurry!
SECOND VOICE. Quick! Quick!

[CAST. *Ad lib hysteria.* SOUND. *Overpowering train and brakes
grinding right on mike.* WOMAN. *A high piercing scream that tops
everything!* MUSIC. *After long pause . . . a harp motif to establish
heaven and under . . .*]

ST. PETER. Good afternoon, Mr. McGuire.
DANNY. (*Casually.*) How're yah? . . . Hey! What is this? This
nightshirt stuff? Where's my pants?
ST. PETER. Your pants, Mr. McGuire?
DANNY. Yeah—my pants. I had four hundred bucks in my kick
when I left the racetrack. Come on. Let's have my clothes.
ST. PETER. (*Sighing.*) Oh my. So many people are like that when
they first arrive. I wish the boss would get someone else for
this job.
DANNY. Job?—what job?
ST. PETER. (*Ignoring him.*) And anyway I'm more the executive
type. Anyone can open and shut the gates of Heaven—
DANNY. Heaven?—what Heaven? . . . Ahhh, come off that stuff.
Dish out my pants or I yell copper.
ST. PETER. Do you mind stepping over here a second, Mr. McGuire?
That's it . . . just to the edge of this cloud. Now lean over—
careful—there, that's it. Now—what do you see?
DANNY. Well, I'll be—it's Belmont Park! An' there's the railroad
station. I was just on my way home—

ST. PETER. (*Patiently.*) Do you see your pants, Mr. McGuire?

DANNY. (*As if to himself.*) Lookit that crowd at the station . . . and there comes an ambulance down the road like a bat out of—

ST. PETER. (*Sighing.*) Oh, yes—they always do send the wrong wagon . . . Mr. McGuire, do you see your pants?

DANNY. Hey! That's *me* down there on the tracks! An' here comes the docs with the stretcher. Hey—I must be sick.

ST. PETER. (*Gently.*) Not sick, Mr. McGuire—

DANNY. No?

ST. PETER. No, Mr. McGuire—dead . . . But just for the record; so there can be no future complaints. (*Softly insistent.*) *Your pants,* Mr. McGuire? Can you see them?

DANNY. Sure I see them—what would I be doin' layin' all over the railroad tracks without my pants? . . . Hey! What'd you say?

ST. PETER. (*Ignoring question.*) Well, that's that—a fine thing if you'd run to the boss saying I had taken your trousers and stolen four hundred something or other out of your—just what was that word again, Mr. McGuire?

DANNY. (*Absentmindedly.*) Kick. . . . But you said something about somebody or other being dead?

ST. PETER. Not somebody or other—*You,* Mr. McGuire. You're dead.

DANNY. Me? I feel all right— Hey! Wait a minute! Then this must be—

ST. PETER. Heaven.

DANNY. An' you must be—

ST. PETER. St. Peter . . . (*Sighs.*) . . . Oh what a life—the same questions year in and year out. It's a wonder I don't have a nervous breakdown . . . Oh well, here I go again. (*Formal speech.*) Welcome to Heaven, Mr. McGuire. We are extremely happy to have you with us. May I have the honor of presenting you with your wings.

DANNY. (*Pause.*) My wings? But—

ST. PETER. No—don't try to put them on. Just tuck them under your arm . . . That's it. It's a long time since anyone did any flying around here. The guests are all too bored. . . . Shall we go inside?

DANNY.   Yeah. Sure . . . (*Start fading.*) . . .Only I thought that when I died I'd go—

[MUSIC. *Celestial theme up to bridge.*]

ST. PETER.   (*Fades in.*) Well, Mr. McGuire, what do you think of the place?

DANNY.   (*Sarcastically.*) Quite a layout. Must have been quite an architect to think of havin' the same clouds inside as outside . . . only more of them . . . (*Up sharp.*) If you ask me—

ST. PETER.   Shhhh—please, Mr. McGuire, please don't raise your voice. Not even in the slightest way. It's the first law of Heaven.

DANNY.   Some law . . .why?

ST. PETER.   Because any loud noise, or even a voice just a pitch above a conversational tone, disturbs the Gods.

DANNY.   (*Whispers.*) The Gods?

ST. PETER.   That's right. They all live up there in that cloud.

DANNY.   The bright green one, with all the flesh-colored ropes hanging down?

ST. PETER.   That's the one. A little crowded perhaps—but then, if you must be a God, you should be prepared for a little discomfort.

DANNY.   You talk like they were a football team . . . How many Gods you got, Pete?

ST. PETER.   Pete? Pete? Why of course—Pete, a diminutive for Peter. You know—I like it. Pete. Sounds very friendly. You know, no one has ever called me that before, Mr. McGuire.

DANNY.   Think nothing of it. And just call me Danny . . . Now— how about the lowdown on all these Gods of yours?

ST. PETER.   Well, Mr. Mc—I mean Danny—it's like this. Centuries ago, when Heaven was first conceived, there were not so many Gods. But people kept having them. The Chinese had one, and the Hindus another, and the Jews and the Christians and —oh, lots of others. And some people would pray to one, and some to another.

DANNY.   So?

ST. PETER. So, we became sort of crowded up here and had to put them all together in one large cloud.

DANNY. Sort of Macy's basement stuff . . . But what're all those ropes that hang down?

ST. PETER. Ropes? What?— Oh those. They're not ropes, Danny. They're the ears of the Gods.

DANNY. The ears? Long and skinny like that?

ST. PETER. Why surely. You see, after years and years of listening to prayers they have become so attenuated that they almost reach to the earth.

DANNY. You don't tell me.

ST. PETER. I *am* telling you.

DANNY. So they pick up all the prayers, do they? Well, what do they do for the guys that set up the clamoring?

ST. PETER. Nothing.

DANNY. Nothing?

ST. PETER. Well—they listen.

DANNY. Come, come, Pete—no fibbing. I'm on the inside now.

ST. PETER. (*Heatedly.*) Inside or outside—they *just* listen!

DANNY. Ah, ah, Pete—that's not what the rule book says.

ST. PETER. Rule book or *no* rule book—I said they do exactly *nothing!* . . . They're executives.

DANNY. Okay, okay, keep your shirt on, Pete . . .

[SOUND. DANNY *stumbles and falls heavily.*]

DANNY. (*Up loudly.*) . . . Damn this nightshirt! How's a guy supposed to walk in one—

[SOUND. *Whistle . . . from off-mike and approaching at terrific speed.*]

ST. PETER. Shhhh, Danny, shhhh—

DANNY. (*Alarmed . . . as warning whistle approaches mike.*) Hey! Watch it, Pete! Comin' straight at you—a little green cloud. Duck, Pete! Quick!

ST. PETER. Don't be alarmed, Danny. It'll stop. It's only our mail delivery. (*Warning speed sound stops abruptly.*) See? Stopped right in front of my hand. (*Pause.*) Oh, I knew it would happen. It's a letter concerning you, Danny. I'll read it to you . . . (*Reads.*) To Saint Peter, Gatekeeper, First District, Second Assembly. Subject: One Daniel Phineas McGuire. (*Aside.*) Ah, bureaucracy—I tell you, Danny, I'm fed up with it . . . (*Resumes reading.*) Paragraph one: Under the civil penal code, section twelve, paragraph three—this warning is issued to one Daniel Phineas McGuire. If said guest once again breaks the law of Heaven by speaking in any but a normal tone—as put forth in section three, paragraph four—said guest will be subject to punishment. Punishment to be exile . . . And it's signed—Gods number one to two hundred inclusive.

DANNY. (*Whispers.*) Exile? Where? How?

ST. PETER. Over there to your right. See that little black cloud like a puffball, with the long, spiral black chute going down and down?

DANNY. (*Still whispering.*) I see it.

ST. PETER. Well, there are double doors on the top of it, with a sign which says—"To Hell! Beware the Doors!". . . So, you see, when you get a letter like—

DANNY. It's okay, Pete—you don't have to draw me no pictures—I get it.

ST. PETER. (*Dryly.*) Most people do.

[MUSIC. *Bridge.*]

DANNY. (*Fades in.*) Phew! What a joint this Heaven is. What's a guy to do with himself . . . (*Calls.*) . . . Hey, Pete, what're you doin' with your head stuck through the gate? Lookin' for customers?

ST. PETER. Customers? Oh yes—you mean new arrivals.

DANNY. Yeah. Say—mind if I park the carcass and chew the fat a while? All right—don't say it—I'll translate . . . Do you mind if we have a little conversation?

ST. PETER. Why of course not, Danny. How did you like the Gentlemen's Club?

DANNY. A swell bunch of guys. So friendly. Each one a big shot. Each one a snob.

ST. PETER. Now, Danny . . . you must not mind the gentlemen too much. I admit they're a bit quiet.

DANNY. Quiet? Don't exaggerate, Pete. They don't even talk to each other. What do you do for excitement up here?

ST. PETER. Excitement?

DANNY. That's right. You know—horse races. The sport of kings and the racket of heels. Got any horses in Heaven?

ST. PETER. Horses?

DANNY. You know—things with four legs and a tail and a big long head?

ST. PETER. Oh, those. Sure. Plenty of them, over in Horse Heaven. All the most famous of all time.

DANNY. Must be good racing.

ST. PETER. Oh, but they never race. Wouldn't even think of it. That all goes on down there.

DANNY. (*Whispers.*) In Hell?

ST. PETER. Ahuh. You see, long ago, Satan turned that Hell of his into one vast circuit of racetracks—newest gambling gadgets and what not. All the poor lost souls are encouraged to gamble.

DANNY. They are?

ST. PETER. Uhuh. Poor lost souls—they wager hours of frying and boiling against hours of *not* frying and boiling.

DANNY. Well, well, what'd you know. How do they do?

ST. PETER. Badly, very badly. I hear on the best authority that all of them spend most of their time in hot water.

DANNY. (*Thoughtfully.*) It's a shame.

ST. PETER. What's a shame?

DANNY. That we got all the stake horses up here and the Devil's got all the racing down there.

ST. PETER. It is sort of peculiar, isn't it?

DANNY. Peculiar? . . . Look, Pete—how about me getting a gander at these famous nags of ours? . . . Can do?

ST. PETER. Now Danny—I think you're going to be disappointed. . . . Oh, well, it does look as if you were the last guest of the day, so I guess no one can object if I leave a bit early. Come along; we'll fly over to Horse Heaven.

DANNY. Fly over?

ST. PETER. Of course. It's quite a ways, you know . . . Oh, I'm

sorry; I've forgotten that you've never worn your wings . . .
Put them on . . . No, no, not like that . . . stand still . . . now
slip them over your shoulders and sort of wriggle back into
the harness . . .

DANNY. (*Quite loud.*) I'll be—

ST. PETER. Shhh! Remember! . . . Ah, that's better; that's it. Now
just hook it together. That's right; now you've got it.

DANNY. Sort of like a bra.

ST. PETER. A what?

DANNY. A bra . . . like dames wear. You know—women.

ST. PETER. (*Interested.*) They do? Would you mind explaining—

DANNY. (*Impatiently.*) Not now, Pete, not now. One thing at a
time. First horses . . . Now—how do you start this flying
business?

ST. PETER. Just jump up a little. Like this. Then flap your wings.

[SOUND. *Flap of heavy wings.*]

ST. PETER. (*Calls down.*) Come on, Danny. It's quite simple . . .

[SOUND. *Flap of* DANNY's *wings.*]

ST. PETER. That's it; that's just fine. . . .

[MUSIC. *Of celestial quality . . . fade in and keep in background
and over it . . . sound of flapping wings close together.*]

DANNY. (*Hums.*) I got wings; you got wings; all God's chillun got
wings—

ST. PETER. So you like flying, heh, Danny?

DANNY. Who wouldn't? It's like duck soup . . . Here! Watch this!

[SOUND. *Rapid beat of wings simulating zoom of loop-the-loop.*]

DANNY. (*Calls excitedly.*) How'm I doin', Pete?

ST. PETER. (*Alarmed.*) Danny! Stop! If they ever see you—

[SOUND. *Whistling warning sound approaching . . . stops dead on
mike same as before.*]

ST. PETER. (*Tersely.*) They have . . . Well, here we go again. Another directive . . . (*Reads.*) Heaven ordinance number 32321352. I.E.: Stunt flying over the clouds of Heaven strictly forbidden and punishable by exile. . . . See, Danny, what I mean?

[SOUND. *Long pause broken only by the regular flap of both pairs of wings.*]

ST. PETER. Danny?

DANNY. Yeah?

ST. PETER. Danny—how does it—how does it feel to loop-the-loop?

DANNY. Well . . . Look—did you ever put up your last ten bucks, then take the dice and throw a natural?

ST. PETER. No.

DANNY. No? . . . Well then—did you ever have a blonde? You know, about five five, in your arms on the dance floor, say. An' the music playin' soft and low, and her lookin' up into your face outta baby-blue eyes?

ST. PETER. No.

DANNY. No? . . . Then I can't tell you how it feels to loop-the-loop.

ST. PETER. Oh.

DANNY. (*After pause.*) Look, Pete, I was thinking—

ST. PETER. About what, Danny?

DANNY. About me—about me bein' in Heaven.

ST. PETER. What about it?

DANNY. Well, all those guys back in the Club, for instance. They're all big shots, famous guys—Aristotle, Lincoln, Wagner . . . But what I want to know is—is how does a mug like me rate Heaven?

ST. PETER. A mug, Danny?

DANNY. Okay then—a heel, a guy ain't never done nothin' all his life but hang around racetracks. How does he rate Heaven?

ST. PETER. Oh, that—you came in on our other quota.

DANNY. What other quota?

ST. PETER. The hero quota. I think it's number 6123. Something or other about meeting death at the instant of performing some heroic deed.

DANNY. What's all that got to do with me? I ain't no hero.

34

ST. PETER. Remember the little newsboy you saved from being crushed by the train . . . ?

DANNY. You mean that—well, I'll be—

ST. PETER. Here we are, Danny. Horse Heaven. Go ahead. Fly straight through that big orange cloud . . .

[*Flap of wings and background music out.*]

DANNY. (*After pause.*) Holy sufferin' catfish! Pete—do you see what I see? Horses, hundreds of 'em, all dressed up in *tuxedos!* In soup an' fish! High hats and all. Pete—get me out of here quick before I start seein' pink elephants.

ST. PETER. Now take it gently, Danny. They're always like this.

DANNY. Always? You mean horses sit around all dressed up like this, as if they was in the Stork Club, or somethin'? An' sippin' outta little demitassee cups. Don't tell me what they're drinkin' is . . . ?

ST. PETER. Ambrosia—of course it is.

DANNY. (*Groans.*) I knew it; I knew it. Even the horses. It sure puts it on them; they all look pretty high to me.

ST. PETER. High?

DANNY. High in weight. Over 500 pounds overweight, everyone of 'em.

ST. PETER. Yes, I guess they are pretty stout . . . Here, I'll introduce you. (*Up a little.*) Mr. Eclipse; Mr. McGuire . . . (*Aside to Danny.*) Careful, Danny—he's very English; quite standoffish.

DANNY. How are you, Mr. Eclipse? Sure glad to meet you, after all these years of reading about you in the stud books.

[*Note: Throughout, horses speak in a high nasal twang, quite human, but with overtones of a horse's whinny.*]

ECLIPSE. (*Very bored.*) How d'you do.

DANNY. (*Enthusiastically.*) Yes siree, from all I hear you were some punkins in your day. Never thought to meet you in the flesh.

ECLIPSE. How interesting.

DANNY. (*Ire rising.*) What is this, the brush-off—

ST. PETER. (*In quick.*) And, Danny, this is Mr. Star of India; Mr. India—Mr. McGuire. (*Aside to* DANNY.) He's Eclipse's right-hand horse. Careful what you say to him, to any of them for that matter—all very touchy, out of the top drawer, you know . . . (*Up a little.*) And this is Mr. Salvator, Mr. Persimmon, Mr. Lexington and Mr. Broomstick, and—oh yes—Mr. Fair Play.

DANNY. (*Again enthusiastic.*) How'ya, Fair Play? My old man was nuts about your son—Man o' War . . . Thought he was the greatest horse to ever wear plates.

FAIR PLAY. (*Haughtily.*) We've had rumors. Probably a fair performer.

DANNY. (*Angrily.*) You weren't such a hot performer yourself!

ST. PETER. (*In quick.*) Careful, Danny!

DANNY. (*Aside to* PETER.) Look, I don't think I'm going to like this Horse Heaven of yours any better than I did your snob Gentlemen's Club—

ST. PETER. (*Heartily.*) Well, well, gentlemen—what about a race?

[CAST. *Ad lib consternation . . . whispering . . . stamping of shod hooves.*]

ECLIPSE. St. Peter—as our spokesman, I wish to say that we would no more consider racing before such common—

DANNY. (*Still angry.*) Common is it? An' racing is it? Why you're all so fat you couldn't race your way out of a paper bag!

[CAST. *Ad lib indignation.*]

ST. PETER. Now, Danny—

DANNY. All right, all right, I'll be good . . . I'm going for a walk. You want to try and convince them—you stay and convince them. Personally, I think you're wasting your breath on a bunch of snobs.

[CAST. *Ad lib as if insulted and fade.*]

DANNY. (*After long pause.*) Well, well, well—as I live an' breathe —if it ain't my old friend, Larranaga, all dressed up in his soup and fish. You sure look right in the pink of condition, not like these other nags around here. How're'ya, Larranaga? How's tricks?

LARRANAGA. (*A sad woebegone horse, weighted with trouble.*) Tricks are very bad, Mr. McGuire.

DANNY. (*Sympathetically.*) Up here they're all bad . . . When did I see you last, boy?

LARRANAGA. I think at Hialeah Park—

DANNY. Oh, yeah—I remember now.

LARRANAGA. (*Sighs heavily.*) Oh, I wish I had never come to Heaven. All the horses up here high-hat me so.

DANNY. I know just what you mean . . . Hey! Wait a minute. How come you rate Heaven? You were never nothin' more than a—

LARRANAGA. Go ahead and say it, Mr. McGuire. They all do. I was never anything more than a plater—a common, ordinary plater.

DANNY. There, there—at least you didn't run in the last race on the card. You were a high-class selling plater . . . But how come Heaven?

LARRANAGA. Do you recall my death at Hialeah Park, Mr. Mc-Guire?

DANNY. Yeah—I guess so.

LARRANAGA. Well, all the sports writers had it incorrectly. I didn't step in a hole after the finish.

DANNY. No?

LARRANAGA. No. My leg was gone at least fifty feet from the finish, but I persevered and won the race. Remember? Right after crossing the line my leg gave way and I broke my neck. (*Sobs.*) That made me a hero. So here I am. Worse luck. (*Continues to sob heartbrokenly.*)

DANNY. Now take it easy, kid. Keep the old chin up out of the stiff shirt. And don't think I don't know how it is—because I do. (*Start fading.*) Maybe I can sort of fix things. I got sort of an idea . . . you wait here . . .

ST. PETER. (*Fading in.*) Ah, there you are at last, Danny. Well, I have everything arranged. The gentlemen, here, have kindly consented to race.

DANNY. Well, gentlemen, it'll be a pleasure to watch you perform.

Oh, by the way—just bumped into an old friend of mine. Name of Larranaga. You gentlemen know him?

[CAST. *Ad lib sniffs of scorn.*]

DANNY.   I can see that you do. I'd like to see him race.

ST. PETER.   Now, Danny, you're only complicating matters. Four of them are going to race—Diamond Jubilee and Persimmon and Broomstick and Lexington. Sort of an international affair.

DANNY.   (*Stubbornly.*) I don't care; I want my friend Larranaga in it. Make it a five-horse go.

ECLIPSE.   (*Haughtily.*) That's impossible. Why this Larranaga, this bounder, is nothing but a plater.

[CAST. *Ad lib approval.*]

DANNY.   (*Angry.*) So what if he is? You're all so—

ST. PETER.   Gentlemen, gentlemen—we're wasting time. If Mr. Mc-Guire wants his old friend Larranaga to race, then he races!

[CAST. *Ad lib faint protest.*]

ST. PETER.   No, no, gentlemen, I will not listen. (*Authoritatively.*) I have spoken! We will all meet in an hour at the edge of Heaven . . . (*Start fading.*) The matter is settled. Good afternoon, gentlemen . . . Come, Danny . . .

[MUSIC. *Celestial theme in background as before.* SOUND. *Regular, rhythmical flap of wings as before.*]

ST. PETER.   Happy, Danny?

DANNY.   (*In thought.*) What? . . . Oh, sure, sure.

ST. PETER.   What's wrong, Danny? Aren't you interested in your race any more?

DANNY.   (*Heartily.*) Sure, sure thing—it's going to be swell, and thanks. Come on, let's go look over the layout.

ST. PETER.   Layout?

DANNY.   The racetrack.

ST. PETER.   Racetrack?

DANNY. (*Losing patience.*) The place where the horses are going to run.

ST. PETER. But—there is no such place in Heaven.

DANNY. What? No racetrack? Well, we might just as well call off the whole shootin' match then. You just can't have horses—

ST. PETER. Now just a minute, Danny—not so fast. What does one of these racetracks of yours look like? I'll build you one.

DANNY. You'll what?

ST. PETER. I'll build one. You must have noticed the extreme pliability of our architecture up here. (*Soothingly.*) Now just tell me what one of these things you want looks like and I have no doubt I can manage.

DANNY. (*Skeptically.*) Oh you will, will you. . . . First off, you have to have a brown dirt track about a hundred an' fifty feet wide an' two miles around—

ST. PETER. This brown cloud do? See—I'll flatten it out like this and run it in a circle. (*Start fading.*) Then I'll take this green cloud and . . .

[MUSIC. *Background theme builds suddenly in volume and follows into "The Ride of the Valkyrie" furioso.*]

DANNY. (*Calls excitedly over music.*) Attaboy, Pete! It's a beaut! . . . Now another green cloud flat for the infield . . . an' one for the grandstand. . . .

[MUSIC. *Swells to tremendous peak and crashes out.*]

ST. PETER. (*After pause.*) Well—will it do, Danny?

DANNY. It sure will. Stick a couple of mountains back of it and it'd look just like Santa Anita.

ST. PETER. (*Eagerly.*) You want a few mountains?

DANNY. No, no. Thanks. Don't need 'em. They're just scenery for the suckers anyway. (*Pause.*) Ah—here come the horses. Holy mackerel, Pete, don't tell me they're going to race in their tuxedos?

ST. PETER. Why of course. It's traditional here in Heaven . . . like our robes.

DANNY. (*Groans.*) Everything's traditional . . . Say—will you look at those snob horses giving little Larranaga the high-hat!

ST. PETER. I can't see very well . . . I mean, not at a distance . . .
It's all sort of blurred. I'm near-sighted, you know.

DANNY. (*Absentmindedly.*) Too bad . . . oughta wear peepers.

ST. PETER. Peepers?

DANNY. Glasses . . . Never mind—I'll tell you what they're doing
—all the horses are sitting around in a circle—all except poor
Larranaga. He's out in the cold. They're not even talking to
him. (*Up a little.*) Come on, Pete, we'll give them their instructions. . . .

ST. PETER. (*Pause . . . fades in.*) Good afternoon, gentlemen, good
afternoon—nice of you to come.

[CAST. *Horses sniff their disdain.*]

ST. PETER. Mr. McGuire, here, will take over . . .

DANNY. All right now, you horses—pay attention. You—Larranaga, stop fidgetin'. Now listen—you all go down and wait
at the bend. When I raise my hand like this, you start your
post parade. Distance will be two miles. No jockeys. No
weights. St. Peter will throw a little red cloud that breaks
over your heads—that'll be the starting gun. Everybody
understand? . . . Okay, get started then . . .

[SOUND. *Of hooves receding.*]

DANNY. Get goin', Larranaga. What's the matter with you? You're
as nervous as a witch.

LARRANAGA. (*Wails.*) Oh, Mr. McGuire—

DANNY. Don't "Oh, Mr. McGuire" me. Get out there and run. It's
in the bag for you, chum. You're the only one of the lot anywhere near racing condition.

LARRANAGA. But I'm nervous.

DANNY. Then stop being nervous.

LARRANAGA. I can't. Everything in Heaven makes me nervous.

DANNY. Stop stamping an' twitchin' around, I say. You're sweating
up your stiff shirt . . . Now do what I tell you—get out there
and run, and no more nonsense. Remember, I'm betting on
you to cop this heat.

LARRANAGA. Oh, Mr. McGuire, you shouldn't . . . (*Start fading*

. . . *Sound of hooves.*) . . . it only makes my nervousness worse . . .

DANNY. Okay, Pete, we're all set now, I guess. Where are the customers?

ST. PETER. The customers?

DANNY. Sure, customers. Fans. Can't run a horse race without people in the stands.

ST. PETER. Oh yes—yes of course. Yes, yes—we must have customers . . . Just a second now . . . I think I can arrange it . . .

[MUSIC. *Muted bugle call "Assembly" up and under.*]

ST. PETER. (*Proudly.*) See—here come your customers, Danny.

DANNY. (*Low whistle.*) The Gentlemen's Club . . . They don't look none too happy about it though.

ST. PETER. They're not. They hate being disturbed in the middle of the afternoon concert.

DANNY. Well, okay, now we got customers we're ready to go. Where are the bookmakers?

ST. PETER. Bookmakers?

DANNY. Sure, bookmakers . . . pricemakers . . . layers . . . you know—the men who take the bets?

ST. PETER. Oh yes—yes, of course. I'm sorry, Danny, but there is no such thing as a bookmaker in Heaven.

DANNY. (*Bewildered.*) No bookmakers?

ST. PETER. I'm sorry, Danny, terribly sorry.

DANNY. There, there, Pete—never you mind. Don't look so down in the mouth, it ain't your fault . . . (*Excited.*) Tell you what —*I'll* be the bookmaker. How's that? All these gentlemen chumps can bet their money with me.

ST. PETER. Money? Why, Danny, there's no money up here.

DANNY. No money?

ST. PETER. That's right—the gentlemen in the grandstand haven't a penny in their nightgowns.

DANNY. Well then—all I can say is that this is gonna be a floperoo of a race . . . (*Disgustedly.*) Let's call the whole thing off.

ST. PETER. Just a minute, Danny—please, just a minute. Don't be so hasty. I think I can remedy the situation . . . Watch now . . .

[SOUND. *Quick flapping of wings in and out of mike as* ST. PETER *circles audience.*]

DANNY. (*After pause.*) What'd you do now?

ST. PETER. (*Winded.*) I—I gave each gentleman ten gold pieces and told him to wager them with you . . . Look, here they come now.

DANNY. (*In whisper to* PETER.) Pete—you're a swell egg . . . (*Up a little.*) All right, boys, don't crowd. And don't push. Stand in line. You'll all get down. Everybody gets a chance to place their dough on the gee-gee of his choice . . .

[CAST. *Ad lib great betting ado.*]

DANNY. (*Taking bets.*) Eclipse?—Mr. Aristotle . . . he's a hundred to one. Broomstick?—Mr. Lincoln . . . fifty to one and your money back. What's that? No, you don't need a receipt . . . What's that, Mr. Wagner?—oh, Persimmon—he's ten to one . . .

[DANNY AND CAST. *Ad lib betting and gradually fade out.*]

DANNY. (*Aside to* PETER.) Phew!—that's the last of them. These gentlemen of yours, Pete, are certainly fast men with a dollar —especially when it's *your* dollar. . . . Okay, we're all set now. Send 'em to the post.

ST. PETER. (*Pause . . . then.*) I can't see a thing. They're so far away.

DANNY. They're drawin' near the starting post. Gosh, that Larranaga's nervous—jumpin' and mincing around like a two-year-old. Hope he gets a hold of himself. Everything depends on him now.

ST. PETER. Why?

DANNY. Why?—for the simple reason that those snob gentlemen of yours wouldn't wager on anything but the snob horses. So Larranaga's runnin' for the book. For us. You and me. If he wins, we win. If he loses—well, we're overboard and might as well climb the fence, see?

ST. PETER. No—not quite. Do you—

DANNY. Not now, Pete, now now . . . They're at the post. Throw 'em a cloud.

[SOUND. *A soft continuous sputtering with a faint bang.*]

DANNY. They're off an' runnin'! Old fatty Diamond Jubilee broke on top. (*Groans.*) That fool, that Larranaga—
ST. PETER. (*Excited.*) What—what happened?
DANNY. (*Disgusted.*) Larranaga—left flatfooted at the post.
ST. PETER. Is that bad?
DANNY. Bad? . . . Right now I'd sell the entire book for one Hong Kong dollar.
ST. PETER. (*Still excited.*) Never mind that—where are *we?*
DANNY. We? Nowhere. At the post. Up front it's Diamond Jubilee a neck in front of Broomstick, who's two in front of Persimmon with Lexington lapped on—
ST. PETER. But where's Larranaga?
DANNY. Just leavin' the post, that's where he is.
ST. PETER. Can he make up the distance?
DANNY. Not even if he was to put on his wings. Looks like we're sunk, Pete . . . Here they come into the stretch!

[SOUND. *Soft drum of hooves in distance.* CAST. *Ad lib whispering as they root for their horses.*]

DANNY. Broomstick's taken the lead; Diamond Jubilee's droppin' back, he's out of it; the others are comin' bunched. . . .

[CAST. *Ad lib whispered consternation as drum of hooves stops suddenly.*]

DANNY. Well, I'll be—
ST. PETER. (*In quick.*) Tell me! What happened?
DANNY. What happened? I never saw anything like it in my life! Why them four snob horses had the race between 'em—an' the second they hit the stretch they stopped runnin' and sat down and took them little demitassee cups of theirs out of a hunk of cloud and started drinking that ambrosia stuff. (*Groans.*) Some race. Some horses. A regular little tea party right smack in the center of the stretch—

ST. PETER. Where's Larranaga?

DANNY. He's comin'—runnin' like the wind.

ST. PETER. Is he going to stop, too?

[SOUND. *Faint hooves approaching mike.*]

DANNY. Yes, he's going to . . . *No!* . . . He's gone on past . . . he's tearin'—

ST. PETER. (*Very excited.*) Quiet! Quiet! I can see him myself now . . . Oh, look at him run! (*Quite loud.*) Come on, you beauty, run, run, run—

DANNY. (*In sharp.*) Shhhh! Remember where you are.

[SOUND. *Hooves up, on past mike and receding.*]

ST. PETER. Thank you, Danny . . . Oh, look at him come. Oh, you beauty! Look at him move! Isn't he beautiful, Danny? . . . And he's winning; he's winning.

DANNY. Well, that's that, I guess. As crazy a horse race as I ever heard of. But we got one consolation—we took the whole pot, Pete. We're the only winners.

[SOUND. *Off-mike flap of many wings receding in departure.*]

DANNY. Gee, I hate to see the boys go off like that; I've been a loser too many times myself not to know how it feels. Wait—I got an idea . . . (*Up a little.*) Hey, just a second, Mr. Aristotle; you too, Mr. Beethoven. No hard feelings, I hope. Just the breaks of the game. Easy come, easy go, I always say. (*Brightly.*) Hey—I got it! How about a little food? What say we put the feedbag on? Come on—I'm the winner—*I'll* buy dinner for the whole gang!

ST. PETER. Forget it, Danny. No one up here eats food.

DANNY. (*Slowly.*) No food? No drinks? Then what good is all this dough I got loadin' down my nightshirt?

ST. PETER. (*Sadly.*) No good at all, Danny. We never use it up here. (*Hesitantly.*) I—I just thought it would be a lot of fun for you—you wanted the race and everything so much. I'm— I'm sorry, Danny.

DANNY. It's okay, Pete. Forget it. You did your best. Guess I'm just a fool up here . . . Oh, well, might as well dump these no-good gold pieces out then. There they go . . . (*Pause . . . and excitedly.*) Holy mackerel! What a place! They don't even go with a bang—just drop down about ten feet and form a golden cloud . . . What is this? What kind of a place am I in? That's the last straw. I'm getting out of here, and right away. . . . So long, Pete, you've been swell . . .

[SOUND. *Flap of* DANNY's *wings receding.*]

ST. PETER. (*Calls.*) Danny, Danny, where are you going?
DANNY. (*From off mike.*) Never mind where I'm going—I'm going, that's all, and as far as I can get . . . (*Fading.*) . . . Take care of yourself, guy, you got what it takes . . . you're aces in my book, fella . . .
ST. PETER. (*Calls.*) Danny—wait!

[SOUND. *Flap of* PETER's *wings following.*]

ST. PETER. Danny, wait . . . don't be rash . . .

[MUSIC. *Celestial theme as before played as chase music, sustain, then out.* SOUND. *Flap of wings, first one stops, then after interval the other.*]

ST. PETER. (*In fierce whisper.*) Come down off of that cloud, Danny! Have you gone mad! No one has ever been up on that black cloud before. Danny—you so much as talk up there and it's all over. Come down instantly, do you hear, Danny? Come down this instant!
DANNY. (*As if a distance above* PETER's *head.*) Go away, Pete. Go'wan! I don't want you to get mixed up in this thing. I don't want you taking any raps for me.
ST. PETER. Please, Danny—please think it over.
DANNY. (*Firmly.*) I have thought it over. I want to go to Hell; I'll go to Hell. You, you like this place, you stay here . . . Now go away, Pete, and let me alone.
ST. PETER. Danny!

DANNY. Go away!

ST. PETER. Danny! Stop! Oh my—

[DANNY. *Starts singing in very loud off-key voice the opening of "Sweet Adeline."*]

ST. PETER. (*Up and over.*) That does it, sure. That's the end . . . Here, Danny, wait—

DANNY. (*Breaks off singing.*) Go back down, Pete! Don't you come up here! You stay out of this—you're in the clear . . .

ST. PETER. (*Puffing as if climbing cloud.*) Move over . . . Give me your hand . . . There now . . .

[SOUND. *Of rusty iron doors opening slowly.*]

DANNY. The doors to Hell—they're opening! Get out of here Pete!

ST. PETER. (*Calmly.*) Let them open. Here—move over a bit and give a man with a voice a chance.

DANNY. (*Awestruck.*) You wouldn't, would you, Pete?

ST. PETER. I certainly would. . . . Do you mind starting that tune of yours again?

[DANNY AND ST. PETER. DANNY *hesitantly starts song* . . . *After first line* ST. PETER's *bass comes in good and strong* . . . *They achieve a sort of harmony.*]

[SOUND. *Whistling warning from off-mike swells until it tops duet.* MUSIC. *Curtain.*]

FOR DISCUSSION

1. Danny is a simple fellow. His admission to heaven is based on a single act of heroism—a heroism that is almost accidental. So it is not surprising that Danny feels he doesn't really belong. What are some of the things that Danny misses most in the heaven described by Maier?

2. Theologians urge that we remember the difference between spirit and body and remember that it is our spirits that will go

to heaven or hell. Yet Danny and Stagolee are clearly physical beings rather than spirits. Were the two authors unaware of this theological point, or do you think they chose deliberately to ignore it? If the latter, why?

3. From time to time, Maier uses a mocking tone that exposes some of the defects of earthly society. With this in mind, discuss briefly the significance of the following pieces of dialogue.

    a. Talking about the Gods, St. Peter says: "They do exactly *nothing!* . . . They're executives."

    b. After Danny tries "to loop-the-loop," St. Peter receives directive #32321352 announcing, "Stunt flying over the clouds of Heaven strictly forbidden and punishable by exile. . . ."

    c. After winning the stakes, Danny says with growing realization: "No food? No drinks? Then what good is all this dough I got loadin' down my nightshirt?"

INTRODUCTION

If we cannot attain immortality of the body, perhaps we can attain immortality of the mind. That is the premise of this short story by Stephen Goldin. The old-fashioned ghost exists in an afterlife which is "a state of nothingness less substantial than a vacuum, smaller than infinity, larger than thought." This afterlife isolated the human being from his own kind, forced him to be forever alone, to be without truly being. In this story the new ghost exists in a different afterlife. After death the mind becomes an entry in a computer bank and is never again alone. The mind's existence is assured for eternity, except possibly for equipment failures or errors in processing.

The Last Ghost

Stephen Goldin

Eternity is a terrible place to endure alone.

He is the last of his kind, if he is a "he." (Gender is an arbitrary difference. All things are eventually the same—and in eternity, eventually equals always.) He must once have had a name, a handle to his soul, but that was back before the eternity/ instant when he had existed in corporeal form. He tries to think about things as he had known them, and finds he can't. He tries to think about things as they are, and finds he can't quite manage that, either. The will-be is far beyond his powers of contemplation.

He exists (if that's the word) in an everlasting now, as a state of nothingness less substantial than a vacuum, smaller than infinity, larger than thought. Eternity lies as far behind him as it does ahead. He drifts through this lack of anything at infinitely greater than no speed at all. He sees with non-eyes. He hears without ears. He thinks thoughtless thoughts that revolve in circles and make little eddies of emptiness in the not-quite-nothing of his mind.

He searches for
He wants a
He desires some
He loves to
No objects remain within his mental grasp. The words have been corroded by the gentle acid of time. All that's left is the search; the want; the desire; the love.

She began to appear slowly, a flicker at the limits of his nonperception. (Why he considered her a "she" could not be explained. There was just an aspect about her that was complementary to him.) His unthoughts raced in puzzlement. She was a newness in his stale cosmos, where nothing ever changed. He watched her as she took on a form even less substantial than his own. He watched with his crumbling mind at a crossroad, afraid to approach, even more afraid to run from her in fear. (If, that is, there were anyplace to run in eternity.)

She gained awareness suddenly, and started at the alien strangeness of her new environment. The eerie infinitude produced within her a wave of awe commingled with fear. She could, as yet, perceive only herself and the barren continuum around her.

She spoke. (What came out was not sound, but could be interpreted as communication.) "Where am I?"

The action was a simple one. It seemed utterly new to him, but down somewhere among the shards of his memory it was all tantalizingly familiar. He trembled.

She perceived his being, and turned her attention toward him. "What are you? What's happened to me?"

He knew the answers—or rather, he had known them. As it had with everything else, infinity had eaten away at these chunks of information too in what was left of his mind. It had all been so important once. So important! That was why he was what he was, and why he wasn't what he wasn't.

"Please!" she begged him. Hysteria edged her voice. "Tell me!"

Through mists that swirled down dusty corridors of memory, the words came out unbidden. "You are dead."

"No! That's impossible! I can't be!"

Loud silence.

"I can't be," she repeated. "Death was conquered more than five thousand years ago. After our minds were transferred into computer banks, we became immortal. Our bodies may fail, but our minds go on. Nobody dies any more. . . ." Her voice trailed off.

"You are dead," he repeated emotionlessly.

"Are . . . are you a ghost?" she asked.

Though the meaning of the word had been stolen from him, that shred of identity remained. "Yes."

She brooded, and large quantities of non-time elapsed. He waited. He became accustomed to her existence. No longer was she an alien thing in his empty universe. She was now a half-presence, and he accepted her as he had come to accept everything else—without comment.

"I suppose," she said at last, "some sort of equipment failure might have temporarily dislodged my personality pattern from the memory banks. But only temporarily. I'm only half dead so far. As soon as the trouble is fixed, I'll be all right again. I will be all right, won't I?"

He didn't answer. He knew nothing about equipment failures —or had forgotten if he ever had known.

"Equipment failures are supposed to be impossible," she prattled on, trying desperately to convince herself that her comfortable reality would return again. "Still, in thousands of years even a trillion-to-one shot might happen. But they'll fix it soon. They've got to. They must. Won't they? WON'T THEY?"

She stared at her impassive companion with non-eyes widened by panic. "Don't just stand there! Help me!"

Help. That word found a niche somewhere in the haunted cavern of his mind. He was supposed to help . . . to help. . . .

The who, or what, or how he was supposed to help eluded him. That is, if he had ever known.

They drifted on through the void together, side by side, ghost and almost-ghost. The unthoughts of the elder spirit were tangled more than usual, owing to the presence of another after such a lonely period of timelessness. But it was not a bad tangle; in fact, it was rather nice to share the universe with someone else again. She was a pleasant aura beside him in an otherwise insensate world.

50

They had both existed for over five thousand years. He was undoubtedly the older of the pair; but the real difference between them was that, while he had existed alone for so long that solitude had nibbled away at his Swiss cheese mind, she had lived those centuries with other people, other minds—a situation that either cracks one completely or produces near-total stability. The latter was the case with her, and so eventually her initial panic subsided and the clinical attitude she had held for thousands of years returned.

"Well, it appears I'm going to be here for awhile, so I might as well get acquainted with this place. And since you're the only thing around, I'll start with you. Who are you?"

"Dead."

"Obviously." Her non-voice managed to handle even sarcasm nicely. "But don't you have some kind of a name?"

"No."

Just for a moment, she lost her patience. "That's impossible, Gabby. You must have had a name sometime. What was it?"

"I don't . . . I don't . . . I don't . . ." His broken-record attempt to answer was so pathetic that it touched the maternal instincts that she had thought long-dead within her.

"I'm sorry," she said a bit more tenderly. "Let's talk about something else. Where are we?"

"We are . . ."

"Dead," she finished with him. *Oh Lord, help me have patience with him. He's worse than a child.* "Yes, I know that. But I mean our physical location. Does it have a name?"

"No."

Stymied again. Her companion was obviously not inclined to conversation, but her analytical mind felt an urgent need to talk, to try to hold on to her sanity under such adverse conditions. "All right, then, if you don't want to talk, do you mind if I do?"

"No."

So she did. She told him about her earliest life, when she had had a body, and about the things she had done and the children she had had. She spoke of the mind-transferral breakthrough that had finally enabled Man to conquer Death. She told him about the first thousand or so years she had spent in the computer bank when, exhilarated by the thrill of immortality, she had occupied animated robot bodies and engaged in "death-defying" sports and exciting activities. And she related how even this had paled with time, and how she had passed into the current, mature phase of her life, the search for knowledge and wisdom. She told how ships had been built to take these computerized people to the stars, and what strange and wonderful things they had found there.

He listened. Most of it was incomprehensible to him, for the words were either unfamiliar or forgotten. His sievelike mind retained very little of what she said. But he listened, and that was important. He soaked in the experience, the thrill, of another pseudobeing communicating with him.

At last she paused, unable to think of anything else to say. "Would you like to talk now?" she asked.

Something burned within him. "Yes."

"Good," she said. "What would you like to talk about?"

He tried hard to think of something, anything, but once again his brain failed him.

She sensed his difficulty. "Tell me something about yourself," she prompted.

"I am dead."

"Yes, I know that. But what else?"

He thought. What was "himself" that he could tell something about?

"I search for

"I want a

"I desire some

"I love to . . ."

"What, what, what, what?" she insisted. But there was no answer. Frustrated, she continued. "Let's try something else. Does . . . did everyone who died become a ghost like you?"

"Yes."

"Where are they all, then?"

"Gone."

"Gone where?"

"Away."

Almost, she lost her patience again, but her millennia of training saved her. "They *all* went away?"

"Yes."

"All except you?"

"Yes."

"How long has it been?"

"Long."

She hadn't felt closer to crying in nearly five thousand years, both out of sympathy for this pathetic creature and frustration at being unable to solve his riddle. "Why didn't you go with them?"

"I . . . I was left behind."

"Why?"

His answer came much more slowly this time, dredged from the silt at the bottom of his pool of consciousness. "To . . . to . . . to point the way for Those Who Follow."

"You're a guide, then?" she asked incredulously.

"Yes."

"To where?"

"To . . . to . . . away."

"Can you show me where?"

For the first time, sadness was in his voice. "No."

Slowly, very slowly, using all the powers of patience and logical reasoning she had developed over the centuries, she extracted from him the pieces necessary to complete the puzzle. Long ago (how long was indeterminate; time has no meaning in eternity), the ghosts had discovered a new and higher level of existence. All of them had gone over to this new evolutionary state; all except one. One last ghost to show the way up for all the new ghosts who would be coming along.

Only, the mind-transferral breakthrough had changed all that. Suddenly, there were no new ghosts. And the last ghost was left alone. Duty confined him to ghostdom, and solitude condemned him to stagnation.

Her pity exploded like a pink nova, even while some analytical portion of her mind noted that the maternal instinct does not fade through disuse. She cradled his pathetic nonbeing deep within her own shadowy self and whispered words of tender concern.

And suddenly he felt warm with a glow he hadn't felt in eons. His null senses tingled deliciously with the nearness of this glorious other. Happily, he nestled himself against her.

A shock ripped through her. And another. And another. "Oh dear. They're repairing the equipment failure. Soon they'll be fixing the memory circuit, and I'll go back to being alive again."

In the sad stillness that followed, he uttered one word. "Don't."

She was startled. This was the first time he had initiated a thought, the first time he had expressed a preference for something. "What did you say?"

"Don't be alive."

"Why not?"

"I need"

"What?" She could feel herself beginning to fade from this non-place.

"I need"

"Yes? Tell me. Tell me what you need."

"I need"

"WHAT?" She was fading quickly. "I don't have much time left here. Please, tell me what!"

"I need"

She disappeared forever from his non-universe, without a trace.

The last ghost wanders. He is a signpost with nowhere to point. He is a guide with no one to lead. So he drifts on with an empty mind and a half-forgotten, unfulfillable purpose. And occasionally:

I NEED

I NEED

I NEED

As always, the object eludes him.

FOR DISCUSSION

1. As mortals we measure our lives by clock time and by biological time. It is therefore almost impossible for us to comprehend the timelessness of eternity. Now the author has added the dimension of solitude. Can you imagine what would happen to you—to the inner core that makes you, you —if you were to endure eternity alone? Jot down a few of the changes that might occur in you. Then compare your ideas with others'.

2. The "she" of this story had not been alone. She had spent 5,000 years as a part of a multitude: "a situation," notes the author, "that either cracks one completely or produces near-total stability." What kind of person would find "computer immortality" mind-cracking? What kind of person would find it stabilizing?

3. On page 52 "she" describes the sequential process by which she adjusted to the computer bank. Reread this section. Does it parallel at all the sequential process of human life? If humans lived to be 5,000 years old, would the same sort of sequence be operative? Why or why not?

4. At one point in the story the last ghost is called a pseudo-being. What does *pseudo* mean? Is "she" also a psuedo-being? Why or why not?

5. In this story Goldin actually touches on three kinds of an afterlife:
   a.   a ghost in solitude
   b.   an entry in a computer bank
   c.   a ghost who goes on to "a new and higher level of existence"
   Which of the three kinds of an afterlife would you choose (if you had the opportunity) for yourself? Why?

6. Write a paragraph or two that could be added to the story describing what might be meant by "a new and higher level of existence" for the ghosts.

INTRODUCTION

If there is an afterlife, but not in the traditional form, what is it like? Is it simply a place where spirits wander about, chat with each other, and occasionally cast glances of mild curiosity on the earth they once knew so well? Or is it a place where each of us is alone, eternally caught in a world of our own making?

Alice Laurance, in this short story, tries to answer this question. The main character, a young woman, wanders from life into an eerie and terrifying afterlife. Imagine a world beyond death in which there are endless paths but no maps, innumerable forks in the road but no road signs, flickering lights but no indication of their origin. Such an afterlife must be based wholly on chance, an eternity of chance. It is a concept that human reason—if it had the power—would reject.

Chances Are

Alice Laurance

She stood looking down the long empty road and she knew, even as she looked, that it was wrong, for she was lying in the high hospital bed, not standing at all. Yet she was standing, too, looking down the road. There was something forbidding about it—a narrow road cut through high, desolate sand dunes, with a few cattails waving forlornly in a thin breeze—yet she knew in a moment she was going to start down that road. She looked back unhappily, and now she could see herself lying in the bed, the deep stains around her eyes vivid against the pale skin, her dark hair matted and stringy after the fever.

She wanted to say something—something important—or perhaps just to tell them all she loved them, but the words wouldn't form. They were all there: Don, twisting his wedding band the way he did when he was badly upset; Mom, crying; Dad, clearing his throat because men don't cry, and trying to comfort Mom; Aunt

56

Sally, looking helpless; Jan, standing a little apart, the outsider who wasn't family. Mrs. Oliphant was in the next bed; she even loved Mrs. Oliphant, whose baby was fine and healthy, not stillborn like her own. She loved them all. It was good of the hospital to let them all come at once.

As she watched, Don bent over her, saying something, and it made her desperately unhappy that she couldn't catch his words. She turned away, as she would to hide tears, and saw again the long desolate road. She looked down it, trying to see its end and then turned back once more, but Don and the others were gone. There was only a blankness, like a glaring light perceived through closed eyes, forming a barrier she knew she couldn't penetrate. She was already cold and very lonely, and there was nowhere to go but down the road. She looked back once more, hoping the barrier would lift, but it remained in place, and she began to walk, thinking that the dead also have a loss to mourn.

She walked slowly, as if reluctant to leave the place where she'd last seen Don, and for a while she looked around her, curious about the countryside, but it was unvaried, offering no distractions to her thoughts. Her life had not been so very unusual; she'd done nothing memorable, though she'd meant to, and yet, as she walked, she remembered so much.

She remembered the apartment in Queens where she'd grown up. She hadn't thought of it in years, but she could remember the Bo Peep wallpaper that had been on her walls when she was little, and the pastoral scene that had replaced it when she was ten. The wallpaper in the crowded parlor had been a floral pattern, endlessly repeating, but she'd never been very much aware of anything in that room but the huge piano dominating it. Her earliest memories were of listening to her Mother play, and that was appropriate, for the strain of music ran through all her life. She could remember clearly the first time her Mother had lifted her up on the piano bench and guided her tiny fingers over the keys, and the pleasure it had given both of them. She remembered her Mother's attempts to teach her, and then the more formal lessons with Mr. Weinstein; she could still hear his faintly accented voice saying softly, "Again, please. Ah. That is better."

She remembered practicing while her friends were out playing, and never realizing until much later that she wasn't "playing" too.

She remembered her Mother's delight in her ability, and her Father paying for the lessons he couldn't really afford, though she hadn't realized that until later, either. Her Father was a mild, quiet man, undemonstrative, but she could remember his joy when she told him she'd been accepted at Julliard.

A clump of cattails ahead caught her attention, and when she reached them, she saw they marked a faint path that branched off from the main road and would otherwise have been all but unnoticeable. She glanced at the sandy road behind her and saw faint impressions of her own footprints, which the wind blurred even as she watched. She looked at the new path, shivering slightly in the breeze which chilled her only when she paused. The main road was clearly defined, winding in front of her as far as she could see; the other path was little more than the hint of a foot trail that curved around a high dune and vanished. There was no marking, and she understood there were no road signs in this place; you had to find your own way. But how, she suddenly wondered. And to where? She shivered again as she hesitated, and she was suddenly sure that if she started down this road, a barrier would prevent any return to the main road. She paused a moment longer, wondering why she felt safer on one road than on the other, since she had no idea where either led, and then, walking slower than before, she continued down the wider road, troubled by the choice and glancing back frequently, until the clump of cattails vanished from sight.

The countryside was again barren and monotonous, and her thoughts strayed back to memories.

She remembered the years at Julliard—the work, the hours of practice and study, the hours spent selling records in an all-night music shop. She remembered meeting Jan, who became her closest friend—Jan, who could make a violin express all the depths of agony or flights of joy a human being could know; Jan, who knew everything she was feeling without being told because she was feeling it herself. Her breath caught in a sob as she thought of Jan, who would know exactly what music would fit this place, exactly what music would make it comprehensible and tolerable, and she thought automatically of the three recitals she'd given, because Jan had selected the music for them. She'd had a detached feeling about the recitals, though she'd worked hard for them and played well enough. The audiences and critics had been kind, ascribing the flaws to youth and inexperience, but she had known that the real limitations were in talent and perhaps will. Jan had unerringly selected music that made her talent seem greater than it was, but she hadn't wanted a career on the concert stage; she wanted to compose, though even at the outset she'd been uncertain about the dream. The hope was more intense than her confidence.

She remembered moving into her own tiny apartment, meeting the rent and the monthly payments on her piano by giving lessons, while she filled hundreds of notebooks with ideas and snatches of melody. She remembered a procession of small children, mostly rebellious or resentfully well-behaved, trooping to her piano and doggedly pounding out their selections, and she remembered her amusement the day she first heard her voice, in unconscious imitation of Mr. Weinstein, say, "Again, please. Ah. That is better."

Her train of thought broke and she stopped, looking around her slowly. Something had distracted her, but she didn't know what. She looked behind her nervously and saw a clump of cattails she'd passed; they reminded her of the ones marking the side path, and she walked back to the place. Once again there was a path veering off the main road, this one even less defined than the first. As before, the path curved past a dune and was lost to sight. She walked a few feet in one direction and then the other, hoping a change in angle would enlarge her view, but it didn't and the path's end remained hidden behind the dune; to see it she would have to follow the path, and she was certain, as before, that there would be no turning back. The path was again only the suggestion of a trail, and it wasn't enough to lure her. She turned and continued down the main road.

She began to think about Don. She could see him bending over her still form in the hospital bed, speaking words she would never grasp, and again an enormous sense of loss filled her.

She remembered meeting Don, at a party at Shirley Webster's apartment. Strange she could remember Shirley's name; she and Don had tried to remember it a month ago and couldn't. It was Shirley Webster. Neither of them had known her well; she was just a girl who worked in Don's office and had a little brother taking piano lessons. It was such a commonplace introduction and would have meant nothing if, a week later, they hadn't both been standing in line waiting to buy concert tickets. She'd smiled and he'd begun to talk, and he took her to dinner afterwards; they were married a few months later. He was so sure and steady, so endlessly patient and confident and wise, and it still frightened her a little when she thought how easily she might have missed him. Just five minutes difference in time on the day she bought the tickets and he would have meant no more to her than Shirley Webster. He was the only man she'd ever loved; in a fundamental way, she was actually grateful to him simply for being, though she'd never found a way to tell him that. And now she never would.

The desire to see him just once more was so strong in her that she gasped, and she felt a tide of bitterness that, being a ghost, she was condemned to wander this desolate road instead of the earth where Don lived. Why couldn't she will herself back to their house, not to haunt it or to play pranks, but just to look at him once more? She halted and closed her eyes, squeezing them tight in her concentration, but when she opened them she was still on the empty road and she was trembling from the cold wind. Reluctantly, she began to walk again, but memories of Don stayed with her.

He'd been so proud of her music. He would listen for hours as she played, and he invited all his friends in to hear her. He'd encouraged her to compose, never doubting her talent as she herself did, and he'd been so pleased when she'd sold a simple tune to an advertising agency to be used as a jingle and so disappointed when it wasn't used.

And then they'd learned she was going to have a baby, and for both of them all disappointment and unhappiness was erased. For him, the baby was a continuation; for her, a creation. She was certain of very few things, but one of them was that the purpose of life was the creation of something the world had lacked before. She was very far from certain she could fulfill that purpose in music, try as she might. She had worked hard, longer and more grueling hours than any normal job would have required, and with little to show for it. She seemed to lack some central quality that would enable her to complete what she'd started, to turn her fragments into a finished piece of music. She thought of the large box in a closet, filled with the notes she made and, unbidden, one of the fragments of melody ran through her mind. It broke off abruptly where she'd lost the thread and then, without warning, the music resumed, a logical variation following the familiar fragment until she could hear the completed song. She let the music run through her mind again, listening intently, and she knew it was what she'd been striving for, but it was too late. Much too late.

But still, she wanted to write it down, to preserve it in some way, but there was nothing to write on. Almost nothing. She broke off a cattail and marked the notes of the song in the sand, a momentary record. By the time she was finished, the first notes she'd written were blurred by the breeze shifting the sand.

She looked at the fading music and thought again of the baby. She'd wanted him so much, but something had happened. Strange that she couldn't remember what; she could remember so much, but not something as important as that. Perhaps she'd never known. But something had happened and the baby had died. It hadn't even been born at all; it had been taken from her, and something else had been taken from her as well. Not the will to live—she wanted to live, still wanted to. The ability to live had been taken from her, not deliberately or maliciously, but taken all the same, and now she was walking down this long, barren road, going she didn't know where, and so terribly alone.

She watched the wind obliterate her work and then walked on, moving slowly. She wondered how long she'd been walking and found no answer, for there was no way to measure duration here. There seemed to be no night or day; the light remained the same, like early dusk, or afternoon just before a storm. But there was no storm, just faint wind, chilling her when she stopped. For the first time she thought to look at the sky, but there was no sky, just the same curious colorless blank she'd seen when she tried to look back at Don.

She looked back, the road now stretching as far as she could see behind her as well as before her. She could no longer identify the place where she'd written her music, and she couldn't see the two paths that had been the only variety in the scenery.

It suddenly occurred to her to wonder what lay on the other side of the dunes. The presence of cattails usually meant marsh-land, but she had heard neither the roar of the sea nor the lapping of a smaller body of water on the shore. She listened intently again, but the only sound was the sibilant shifting of sand. Uneasily, she turned from the road and attempted to scale one of the dunes, but she could find no foothold in the sand and slipped back each time. She gave up finally, but stood for a moment looking at the dune before she returned to the road and began walking again.

She tried to think about her life, to evaluate it, but she could make no judgment. She'd done nothing terrible, but she'd done nothing wonderful, either. In a way, she'd really done nothing at all. A protest rose up in her—she hadn't been allowed to live long enough, not even thirty years. But did any man, however long he'd lived, think it was long enough? Did any man start down this road without the conviction that the next year denied to him would have been his finest? It seemed to her that no man could travel this road without regret—for things done or undone or left unfinished. For only a suicide chose his moment of death, and suicide without regret was inconceivable. But how could a man prepare? Knowing he could die at any moment, still he needed patience, the patience to study and learn, the patience to work steadily but without haste, risking everything on the chance he'd survive to complete the task. She thought of the music she'd written in the sand and wondered how many others had completed projects in the same way, knowing the terrible futility of it even as they did it.

She couldn't evaluate her life; she didn't even know if it had been happy or sad. The only thing she knew with certainty about life was that she was sorry to leave it.

She began to wonder, again, if there was a God. Incredible that she didn't yet know. She remembered when Don's father had been dying; they'd talked about it, neither of them sure what they thought, and when the old gentleman had died, Don had said, "Well, now he knows." It had seemed a wise remark, and it had told them they believed in something, for total obliteration allows no knowledge; but now the comment did not seem so profound. Perhaps the old man hadn't known—as she didn't know. Perhaps neither of them ever would.

Perhaps God was down one of the paths she'd rejected, if He existed at all. But if He was, how could you know? Perhaps if you didn't find Him, you just continued down the road forever, looking for something you couldn't find and not even knowing what you were seeking. She wondered if you could turn back and take a path passed before, and she stopped, looking behind her. Perhaps you had to dare to take one of the little-used paths to find God. She was about to retrace her steps when she saw a figure far ahead of her in the distance, and she forgot everything else in her desire to reach him. She tried to run, but her feet seemed too heavy; she tried to call out, but the sound was a whisper carried away by the wind. When she finally reached the place, it was deserted—no other person in sight.

The road forked where she stood, splitting into two unmarked paths that looked equally traveled. Both paths wound through high dunes, and both appeared, at first glance, to be simply continuations of the road she'd been following. But then, as her eyes traveled the road to the left, she saw a glow in the distance, like a bright light very far away. The path to the right had no such beacon.

She stood in an agony of indecision, looking down one road and then the other. For a moment the glow seemed to draw her, but she continued to hesitate, afraid to follow either path. She wondered which road the person she'd seen had taken, but there was no indication and she knew it really made no difference; even if she took the same road, by design or chance, she would not overtake him. She longed for someone to advise her; she wanted Don to tell her what to do, but she couldn't wish he was with her. Not here. Her loneliness was intense, but she couldn't wish Don dead, even to join her. And however much she wanted to, there would be no way she could wait for him. The wind would drive her on, in spite of herself.

She looked down the two roads, started to take the road to the left, and then stopped. The glow must have a meaning and the meaning might be God. But she didn't want to see God; she didn't want God to see her. She hadn't known that a moment before, but she knew it now. A man should come to God with some achievement, there should be something he could point to, saying, "I did that." If she'd written her song on paper instead of sand, if her child had lived, she would have taken the road to the left, hoping the glow was God; but as it was, she turned to the right, and a dune immediately blocked her view of the glow. She continued unhappily, pausing every so often to look behind her.

Some time later—it seemed a long time later, but she couldn't be certain—the road again forked into two divergent paths. Once again they were unmarked and looked equally traveled, and again one seemed to lead to a distant glow. She knew she had not some-how worked her way back to the first fork only because this time the glow was to the right. Perhaps it's a second chance, she thought, and then another possible explanation occurred to her. Hell, too, might have a glow. Was Hell the proper destiny for failure? Even if that were true and she accepted it, how could she be certain that this glow and not the first was Hell? There were no guides, and she could see no difference between this glow and the first.

Four times she had come upon alternatives: two small paths and two forks—like pairs of alternatives. Perhaps they indicated some dichotomy between two extremes, a dualism taking different forms. Perhaps several human concepts of what came after life, perhaps all concepts of afterlife, were represented, along with their opposites, by paths or branches in the road. But without guides, how could anyone find his own place? What would happen to a Methodist who happened on Nirvana, or a Buddhist in a Methodist heaven? Did free will mean nothing more than a blind chance, a choice based on nothing at all? But perhaps it wasn't free will at all; perhaps it was a plan much larger than the choice of any single person, so that it didn't matter which road was chosen. Perhaps a Methodist sharing Nirvana was part of the plan.

She remembered her attempts to judge her own life and thought of the word "justice." If there was a plan larger than the individual's choice, then did all men start down this road as equals, regardless of the lives they'd led? But perhaps there were guides —the wind that chilled her each time she paused was a guide, if you thought of it that way. Perhaps she wasn't making choices at all, but acting on some compulsion she didn't recognize. Or per-haps, after all, she was choosing, making her own choices on the basis of the only evidence available.

She wondered what would happen if she rejected all the dif-ferentiated paths. Perhaps the road would simply continue to wind through the dunes until exhaustion forced her to choose some path, or perhaps it was a great circle that would start over, so that she'd eventually return to this spot. But if it wasn't a circle, and if she did continue to refuse alternatives, would she walk forever, facing an infinity of choices, or would she come finally to some oblivion?

She closed her eyes wearily, then opened them and looked once more toward the glow before turning away, taking the road to the left. She walked slowly, expecting and finding side roads and forks, always coming in pairs. They no longer surprised her, but each time she found one she hesitated, uncertain and unhappy, finally choosing what she thought was the continuation of the road she'd been traveling.

Several times she saw figures in the distance, and each time she tried desperately to signal them, even though she knew she would fail. There were no companions here. And then, when she was almost convinced that she would never stop walking this desolate road, the road curved sharply around a high dune, and she came to another fork and saw a figure standing at the divide, hesitating between the alternatives. It was a figure, neither male nor female, and it was only then that she realized her own form was also sexless. She might continue to think of herself in the feminine, but her sex was a memory.

The other person seemed to sense her presence and turned. They looked at each other helplessly, and then both turned away. Neither of them tried to speak, though she was certain the other one was as lonely and unhappy as she. They separated, each taking a different path; her own choice of road dictated by the other's.

The encounter seemed to rob her of the last of her hope; she walked on listlessly, without curiosity or expectations. She continued down the road, wondering apathetically if perhaps there had been some judgment of her she hadn't recognized, and if she was acting out the fate assigned to her with each step. She walked slowly, no longer wanting to see others, until once again the road curved past a dune and she found herself facing a door.

It was a perfectly ordinary door, except that it was set in the middle of the road and was surrounded by the blank barrier. She could not bypass it; she could not scale the dunes to the sides; if she didn't go through it, the only other thing she could do was to turn and go back. To what? The paths she'd already rejected? The blank barrier at the other end of the road? And if she did return to that, what could she expect to find? Nothing. Or another door.

She put her hand on the knob, then hesitated, looking back at the road she'd walked. She was terribly frightened, but she knew what she had to do. God or Hell or oblivion might wait on the other side, but she had to go on. Her hand tightened on the knob; she opened the door and stepped through.

She was blinded by a glaring white light, and she gasped at a sudden smack of flesh against flesh. She heard a baby cry and she smiled. For a split second she knew exactly where she was and understood what had happened, and then he knew nothing at all. A nurse smiled behind her mask as she fastened the identification beads around his chubby little wrist.

FOR DISCUSSION

1. "Her life had not been so very unusual; she'd done nothing memorable, though she'd meant to . . ." These words reflect on the main character's life, but they also foreshadow her concept of the afterworld. In what sense is her concept of an afterworld a natural continuation of her life on earth?

2. "The purpose of life was the creation of something the world had lacked before." These are the words of the main character. Do you agree with her statement? How is this particular belief related to her concept of an afterworld?

3. In the poem "The Road Not Taken," Robert Frost considers the choice a human being must make when confronted by a fork in the road. He suggests that the person with courage and wisdom will take the less-traveled road, and that this action will make "all the difference." How do Frost's ideas throw additional light on the actions of the main character in "Chances Are"?

4. What does the title of this story signify? Is the significance affected by the main character's action at the end of the story when she opens the door? Will her life be any different now? If so, how or why?

5. Theory: *One's afterlife is the inevitable result of one's life on earth.* This theory, valid or not, creates some interesting possibilities. What kind of afterlife is awaiting you? Choose one celebrity. What kind of afterlife is awaiting her or him?

INTRODUCTION

Strip the green from the grass and the blue from the sky. Then strip the color from faces: the white and the black, the yellow and the red faces. Strip all color from everything. Next eliminate the fun, the excitement, the daring, and the hope which make life bearable.

In this horrifying short story, Priestley shows us a world in which the Evil Principle is at work "to turn us into automatic creatures, mass beings without individuality, soulless machines of flesh and blood." Perhaps it is the work of the devil and his demons, with hell taking over the earth. Or perhaps the Gray Ones are just ordinary human beings turning this earth of ours into a cold, efficient, colorless, bureaucratic hell. Think about it the next time a computer mix-up transforms an anticipated baseball game into an exercise in resentment; or the next time you try to straighten out inaccurate billing by writing letter number three to "Dear Computer . . ."

The Gray Ones

J. B. Priestley

"And your occupation, Mr. Patson?" Dr. Smith asked, holding his beautiful fountain pen a few inches from the paper.

"I'm an exporter," said Mr. Patson, smiling almost happily. Really this wasn't too bad at all. First, he had drawn Dr. Smith instead of his partner Dr. Meyenstein. Not that he had anything against Dr. Meyenstein, for he had never set eyes on him, but he had felt that it was at least a small piece of luck that Dr. Smith had been free to see him and Dr. Meyenstein hadn't. If he had to explain himself to a psychiatrist, then he would much rather have one simply and comfortably called Smith. And Dr. Smith, a broad-faced man about fifty with giant rimless spectacles, had nothing forbidding about him, and looked as if he might have been an accountant, a lawyer, or a dentist. His room too was reassuring, with nothing frightening in it; rather like a sitting room in a superior hotel. And that fountain pen really was a beauty. Mr. Patson had already made a mental note to ask Dr. Smith where he had bought that pen. And surely a man who could make such a mental note, right off, couldn't have much wrong with him?

"It's a family business," Mr. Patson continued, smiling away. "My grandfather started it. Originally for the Far East. Firms abroad, especially in rather remote places, send us orders for all manner of goods, which we buy here on commission for them. It's not the business it was fifty years ago, of course, but on the other hand we've been helped to some extent by all these trade restrictions and systems of export licenses, which people a long way off simply can't cope with. So we cope for them. Irritating work often, but not uninteresting. On the whole I enjoy it."

"That is the impression you've given me," said Dr. Smith, making a note. "And you are reasonably prosperous, I gather? We all have our financial worries these days, of course. I know I have." He produced a mechanical sort of laugh, like an actor in a comedy that had been running too long, and Mr. Patson echoed him like another bored actor. Then Dr. Smith looked grave and pointed his pen at Mr. Patson as if he might shoot him with it. "So I think we can eliminate all that side, Mr. Patson—humph?"

"Oh yes—certainly—certainly," said Mr. Patson hurriedly, not smiling now.

"Well now," said Dr. Smith, poising his pen above the paper again, "tell me what's troubling you."

Mr. Patson hesitated. "Before I tell you the whole story, can I ask you a question?"

Dr. Smith frowned, as if his patient had made an improper suggestion. "If you think it might help—"

"Yes, I think it would," said Mr. Patson, "because I'd like to know roughly where you stand before I begin to explain." He waited a moment. "Dr. Smith, do you believe there's a kind of Evil Principle in the universe, a sort of superdevil, that is working hard to ruin humanity, and has its agents, who must really be minor devils or demons, living among us as people? Do you believe that?"

"Certainly not," replied Dr. Smith without any hesitation at all. "That's merely a superstitious fancy, for which there is no scientific evidence whatever. It's easy to understand—though we needn't go into all that now—why anybody, even today, suffering from emotional stress, might be possessed by such an absurd belief, but of course it's mere fantasy, entirely subjective in origin. And the notion that this Evil Principle could have its agents among us might be very dangerous indeed. It could produce very serious antisocial effects. You realize that, Mr. Patson?"

"Oh—yes—I do. I mean, at certain times when—well, when I've been able to look at it as you're looking at it, doctor. But most times I can't. And that, I suppose," Mr. Patson added, with a wan smile, "is why I'm here."

"Quite so," Dr. Smith murmured, making some notes. "And I think you have been well advised to ask for some psychiatric treatment. These things are apt to be sharply progressive, although their actual progress might be described as regressive. But I won't worry you with technicalities, Mr. Patson. I'll merely say that you —or was it Mrs. Patson?—or shall I say both of you?—are to be congratulated on taking this very sensible step in good time. And now you know, as you said, where I stand, perhaps you had better tell me all about it. Please don't omit anything for fear of appearing ridiculous. I can only help you if you are perfectly frank with me, Mr. Patson. I may ask a few questions, but their purpose will be to make your account clearer to me. By the way, here we don't adopt the psychoanalytic methods—we don't sit behind our patients while they relax on a couch—but if you would find it easier not to address me as you have been doing—face to face—"

"No, that's all right," said Mr. Patson, who was relieved to discover he would not have to lie on the couch and murmur at the opposite wall. "I think I can talk to you just like this. Anyhow, I'll try."

"Good! And remember, Mr. Patson, try to tell me everything relevant. Smoke if it will help you to concentrate."

"Thanks, I might later on." Mr. Patson waited a moment, surveying his memories as if they were some huge glittering sea, and then waded in. "It began about a year ago. I have a cousin who's a publisher, and one night he took me to dine at his club— the Burlington. He thought I might like to dine there because it's a club used a great deal by writers and painters and musicians and theater people. Well, after dinner we played bridge for an hour or two, then we went down into the lounge for a final drink before leaving. My cousin was claimed by another publisher, so I was left alone for about quarter of an hour. It was then that I overheard Firbright—you know, the famous painter—who was obviously full of drink, although you couldn't exactly call him drunk, and was holding forth to a little group at the other side of the fireplace. Apparently he'd just come back from Syria or somewhere around there, and he'd picked this idea up from somebody there, though he said it only confirmed what he'd been thinking himself for some time."

Dr. Smith gave Mr. Patson a thin smile. "You mean the idea of an Evil Principle working to ruin humanity?"

"Yes," said Mr. Patson. "Firbright said that the old notion of a scarlet-and-black sulphuric Satan, busy tempting people, was of course all wrong, though it might have been right at one time, perhaps in the Middle Ages. Then the devils were all fire and energy. Firbright quoted the poet Blake—I've read him since—to show that these weren't real devils and their Hell wasn't the real Hell. Blake, in fact, according to Firbright, was the first man here to suggest we didn't understand the Evil Principle, but in his time it had hardly made a start. It's during the last few years, Firbright said, that the horrible thing has really got to work on us."

"Got to work on us?" Dr. Smith raised his eyebrows. "Doing what?"

"The main object, I gathered from what Firbright said," Mr. Patson replied earnestly, "is to make mankind go the way the social insects went, to turn us into automatic creatures, mass beings without individuality, soulless machines of flesh and blood."

The doctor seemed amused. "And why should the Evil Principle want to do that?"

"To destroy the soul of humanity," said Mr. Patson, without an answering smile. "To eliminate certain states of mind that belong essentially to the Good. To wipe from the face of this earth all wonder, joy, deep feeling, the desire to create, to praise life. Mind you, that is what Firbright said."

"But you believed him?"

"I couldn't help feeling, even then, that there was something in it. I'd never thought on those lines before—I'm just a plain businessman and not given to fancy speculation—but I had been feeling for some time that things were going wrong and that somehow they seemed to be out of our control. In theory I suppose we're responsible for the sort of lives we lead, but in actual practice we find ourselves living more and more the kind of life we don't like. It's as if," Mr. Patson continued rather wildly, avoiding the doctor's eye, "we were all compelled to send our washing to one huge sinister laundry, which returned everything with more and more color bleached out of it until it was all a dismal gray."

"I take it," said Dr. Smith, "that you are now telling me what you thought and felt yourself, and not what you overheard this man Firbright say?"

"About the laundry—yes. And about things never going the right away. Yes, that's what I'd been feeling. As if the shape and color and smell of things were going. Do you understand what I mean, doctor?"

"Oh—yes—it's part of a familiar pattern. Your age may have something to do with it—"

"I don't think so," said Mr. Patson sturdily. "This is something quite different. I've made all allowance for that."

"So far as you can, no doubt," said Dr. Smith smoothly, without any sign of resentment. "You must also remember that the English middle class, to which you obviously belong, has suffered recently from the effects of what has been virtually an economic and social revolution. Therefore any member of that class—and I am one myself—can't help feeling that life does not offer the same satisfactions as it used to do, before the War."

"Doctor Smith," cried Mr. Patson, looking straight at him now, "I know all about that—my wife and her friends have enough to say about it, never stop grumbling. But this is something else. I may tell you, I've always been a Liberal and believed in social reform. And if this was a case of one class getting a bit less, and another class getting a bit more, my profits going down and my clerk's and warehousemen's wages going up, I wouldn't lose an hour's sleep over it. But what I'm talking about is something quite different. Economics and politics and social changes may come into it, but *they're just being used.*"

"I don't follow you there, Mr. Patson."

"You will in a minute, doctor. I want to get back to what I overheard Firbright saying, that night. I got away from it just to make the point that I couldn't help feeling at once there was something in what he said. Just because for the first time somebody had given me a reason why these things were happening." He regarded the other man earnestly.

Smiling thinly, Dr. Smith shook his head. "The hypothesis of a mysterious but energetic Evil Principle, Mr. Patson, doesn't offer us much of a reason."

"It's a start," replied Mr. Patson, rather belligerently. "And of course that wasn't all, by any means. Now we come to these agents."

"Ah—yes—the agents." Dr. Smith looked very grave now. "It was Firbright who gave you that idea, was it?"

"Yes, it would never have occurred to me, I'll admit. But if this Evil Principle was trying to make something like insects out of us, it could do it in two ways. One—by a sort of remote control, perhaps by a sort of continuous radio program, never leaving our minds alone, telling us not to attempt anything new, to play safe, not to have any illusions, to keep to routine, not to waste time and energy wondering and brooding and being fanciful, and all that."

"Did Firbright suggest something of that sort was happening?"

"Yes, but it wasn't his own idea. The man he'd been talking about before I listened to him, somebody he'd met in the Near East, had told him definitely all that nonstop propaganda was going on. But the other way—direct control, you might call it—was by the use of these agents—a sort of Evil Fifth Column—with more and more of 'em everywhere, hard at work."

"Devils?" enquired the doctor, smiling. "Demons? What?"

"That's what they amount to," said Mr. Patson, not returning the smile but frowning a little. "Except that it gives one a wrong idea of them—horns and tails and that sort of thing. These are quite different, Firbright said. All you can definitely say is that they're not human. They don't belong to us. They don't like us. They're working against us. They have their orders. They know what they're doing. They work together in teams. They arrange to get jobs for one another, more and more influence and power. So what chance have we against them?" And Mr. Patson asked this question almost at the top of his voice.

"If such beings existed," Dr. Smith replied calmly, "we should

72

soon be at their mercy, I agree. But then they don't exist—except of course as figures of fantasy, although in that capacity they can do a great deal of harm. I take it, Mr. Patson, that you have thought about—or shall we say *brooded over*—these demonic creatures rather a lot lately? Quite so. By the way, what do you call them? It might save time and possible confusion if we can give them a name."

"They're the Gray Ones," said Mr. Patson without any hesitation.

"Ah—The Gray Ones." Dr. Smith frowned again and pressed his thin lips together, perhaps to show his disapproval of such a prompt reply. "You seem very sure about this, Mr. Patson."

"Well, why shouldn't I be? You ask me what I call them, so I tell you. Of course, I don't know what they call themselves. And I didn't invent the name for them."

"Oh—this is Firbright again, is it?"

"Yes, that's what I heard him calling them, and it seemed to me a very good name for them. They're trying to give everything a gray look, aren't they? And there's something essentially gray about these creatures themselves—none of your gaudy, red and black, Mephistopheles stuff about *them*. Just quiet gray fellows busy graying everything—that's them."

"Is it indeed? Now I want to be quite clear about this, Mr. Patson. As I suggested earlier, this idea of the so-called Gray Ones is something I can't dismiss lightly, just because it might have very serious antisocial effects. It is one thing to entertain a highly fanciful belief in some mysterious Evil Principle working on us for its own evil ends. It is quite another thing to believe that actual fellow-citizens, probably highly conscientious and useful members of the community, are not human beings at all but so many masquerading demons. You can see that, can't you?"

"Of course I can," said Mr. Patson, with a flick of impatience. "I'm not stupid, even though I may have given you the impression that I am. This idea of the Gray Ones—well, it brings the whole thing home to you, doesn't it? Here they are, busy as bees, round every corner, you might say."

The doctor smiled. "Yet you've never met one. Isn't that highly suggestive? Doesn't that make you ask yourself what truth there can be in this absurd notion? All these Gray Ones, seeking power over us, influencing our lives, and yet you've never actually come into contact with one. Now—now—Mr. Patson—" And he wagged a finger.

"Who says I've never met one?" Mr. Patson demanded indignantly. "Where did you get that idea from, doctor?"

"Do you mean to tell me—"

"Certainly I mean to tell you. I know at least a dozen of 'em. My own brother-in-law is one."

Dr. Smith looked neither shocked nor surprised. He merely stared searchingly for a moment or two, then rapidly made some notes. And now he stopped sounding like a rather playful schoolmaster and became a doctor in charge of a difficult case. "So that's how it is, Mr. Patson. You know at least a dozen Gray Ones, and one of them is your brother-in-law. That's correct, isn't it? Good! Very well, let us begin with your brother-in-law. When and how did you make the discovery that he is a Gray One?"

"Well, I'd wondered about Harold for years," said Mr. Patson slowly. "I'd always disliked him but I never quite knew why. He'd always puzzled me too. He's one of those chaps who don't seem to have any center you can understand. They don't act from ordinary human feeling. They haven't motives you can appreciate. It's as if there was nothing inside 'em. They seem to tick over like automatic machines. Do you know what I mean, doctor?"

"It would be better now if you left me out of it. Just tell me what you thought and felt—about Harold, for instance."

"Yes, Harold. Well, he was one of them. No center, no feeling, no motives. I'd try to get closer to him, just for my wife's sake, although they'd never been close. I'd talk to him at home, after dinner, and sometimes I'd take him out. You couldn't call him unfriendly—that at least would have been *something*. He'd listen, up to a point, while I talked. If I asked him a question, he'd make some sort of reply. He'd talk himself in a kind of fashion, rather like a leading article in one of the more cautious newspapers. Chilly stuff, gray stuff. Nothing exactly wrong with it, but nothing right about it either. And after a time, about half an hour or so, I'd find it hard to talk to him, even about my own affairs. I'd begin wondering what to say next. There'd be a sort of vacuum between us. He had a trick, which I've often met elsewhere, of deliberately not encouraging you to go on, of just staring, waiting for you to say something silly. Now I put this down to his being a public official. When I first knew him, he was one of the assistants to the Clerk of our local Borough Council. Now he's the Clerk, quite a good job, for ours is a big borough. Well, a man in that position has to be more careful than somebody like me has. He can't let himself go, has too many people to please—or rather, not to offend. And one thing was certain about Harold—and that ought to have made him more human, but somehow it didn't—and that was that he meant to get on. He had ambition, but there again it wasn't an ordinary human ambition, with a bit of fire and nonsense in it somewhere, but a sort of cold determination to keep on moving up. You see what I mean? Oh—I forgot—no questions. Well, that's how he was—and is. But then I noticed another thing about Harold. And even my wife had to agree about this. He was what we called a damper. If you took him out to enjoy something, he not only didn't enjoy it himself but he contrived somehow to stop you enjoying it. I'm very fond of a good show—and don't mind seeing a really good one several times—but if I took Harold along then it didn't matter what it was, I couldn't enjoy it. He wouldn't openly attack or sneer at it, but somehow by just being there, sitting beside you, he'd cut it down and take all the color and fun out of it. You'd wonder why you'd wasted your evening and your money on such stuff. It was the same if you tried him with a football or cricket match, you'd have a boring afternoon. And if you asked him to a little party, it was fatal. He'd be polite, quite helpful, do whatever you asked him to do, but the party would never get going. It would be just as if he was invisibly spraying us with some devilish composition that made us all feel tired and bored and depressed. Once we were silly enough to take him on a holiday with us, motoring through France and Italy. It was the worst holiday we ever had. He killed it stone dead. Everything he looked at seemed smaller and duller and grayer than it ought to have been. Chartres, the Loire country, Provence, the Italian Riviera, Florence, Siena—they were all cut down and grayed over, so that we wondered why we'd ever bothered to arrange such a trip and hadn't stuck to Torquay and Bournemouth. Then, before I'd learned more sense, I'd talk to him about various plans I had for improving the business, but as soon as I'd described any scheme to Harold I could feel my enthusiasm ebbing away. I felt—or he made me feel—any possible development wasn't worth the risk. Better stick to the old routine. I think I'd have been done for now if I hadn't had sense enough to stop talking to Harold about the business. If he asked me about any new plans, I'd tell him I hadn't any. Now all this was long before I knew about the Gray Ones. But I had Harold on my mind, particularly as he lived and worked so close to us. When he became Clerk to the Council, I began to take more interest in our municipal affairs, just to see what influence Harold was having on them. I made almost a detective job of it. For instance, we'd had a go-ahead, youngish Chief Education Officer, but he left and in his place a dull, timid fellow was appointed. And I found out that Harold had worked that. Then we had a lively chap as Entertainments Officer, who'd brightened things up a bit, but Harold got rid of him too. Between them, he and his friend, the Treasurer, who was another of them, managed to put an end to everything that added a little color and sparkle to life round our way. Of course they always had a good excuse—economy and all that. But I noticed that Harold and the Treasurer only made economies in one direction, on what you might call the antigray side, and never stirred themselves to save money in other directions, in what was heavily official, pompous, interfering, irritating, depressing, calculated to make you lose heart. And you must have noticed yourself that we never do save money in those directions, either in municipal or national affairs, and that what I complained of in our borough was going on all over the country—yes, and as far as I can make out, in a lot of other countries too."

Dr. Smith waited a moment or two, and then said rather sharply: "Please continue, Mr. Patson. If I wish to make a comment or ask a question, I will do so."

"That's what I meant earlier," said Mr. Patson, "when I talked about economics and politics and social changes just being used. I've felt all the time there was something behind 'em. If we're doing it for ourselves, it doesn't make sense. But the answer is of course that we're not doing it for ourselves, we're just being manipulated. Take communism. The Gray Ones must have almost finished the job in some of those countries—they hardly need to bother any more. All right, we don't like communism. We must make every possible effort to be ready to fight it. So what happens? More and more of the Gray Ones take over. This is their chance. So either way they win and we lose. We're further along the road we never wanted to travel. Nearer the bees, ants, termites. Because we're being pushed. My God—doctor—can't you feel it yourself?"

"No, I can't, but never mind about me. And don't become too general, please. What about your brother-in-law, Harold? When did you decide he was a Gray One?"

"As soon as I began thinking over what Firbright said," replied Mr. Patson. "I'd never been able to explain Harold before—and God knows I'd tried often enough. Then I saw at once he was a Gray One. He wasn't born one, of course, for that couldn't possibly be how it works. My guess is that sometime while he was still young, the soul or essence of the real Harold Sothers was drawn out and a Gray One slipped in. That must be going on all the time now, there are so many of them about. Of course they recognize each other and help each other, which makes it easy for them to handle us humans. They know exactly what they're up to. They receive and give orders. It's like having a whole well-disciplined secret army working against us. And our only possible chance now is to bring 'em out into the open and declare war on 'em."

"How can we do that," asked Mr. Smith, smiling a little, "if they're secret?"

"I've thought a lot about that," said Mr. Patson earnestly, "and it's not so completely hopeless as you might think. After a time you begin to recognize a few. Harold, for instance. And our Borough Treasurer. I'm certain he's one. Then, as I told you at first, there are about a dozen more that I'd willingly stake a bet on. Yes, I know what you're wondering, doctor. If they're all officials, eh? Well no, they aren't, though seven or eight of 'em are—and you can see why—because that's where the power is now. Another two are up-and-coming politicians—and not in the same party neither. One's a banker I know in the City—and he's a Gray One all right. I wouldn't have been able to spot them if I hadn't spent so much time either with Harold or wondering about him. They all have the same cutting-down and bleaching stare, the same dead touch. Wait till you see a whole lot of 'em together, holding a conference." Then Mr. Patson broke off abruptly, as if he felt he had said too much.

Dr. Smith raised his eyebrows so that they appeared above his spectacles, not unlike hairy caterpillars on the move. "Perhaps you would like a cigarette now, Mr. Patson. No, take one of these. I'm no smoker myself but I'm told they're excellent. Ah—you have a light. Good! Now take it easy for a minute or two because I think you're tiring a little. And it's very important you should be able to finish your account of these—er—Gray Ones, if possible without any hysterical over-emphasis. No, no—Mr. Patson—I didn't mean to suggest there'd been any such over-emphasis so far. You've done very well indeed up to now, bearing in mind the circumstances. And it's a heavy sort of day, isn't it? We seem to have too many days like this, don't we? Or is it simply that we're not getting any younger?" He produced his long-run actor's laugh. Then he brought his large white hands together, contrived to make his lips smile without taking the hard stare out of his eyes, and said finally: "Now then, Mr. Patson. At the point you broke off your story, shall we call it, you had suggested that you had seen a whole lot of Gray Ones together, holding a conference. I think you might very usefully enlarge that rather astonishing suggestion, don't you?"

Mr. Patson looked and sounded troubled. "I'd just as soon leave that, if you don't mind, doctor. You see, if it's all nonsense, then there's no point in my telling you about that business. If it isn't all nonsense—"

"Yes," said Dr. Smith, after a moment, prompting him, "if it isn't all nonsense—"

"Then I might be saying too much." And Mr. Patson looked about for an ashtray as if to hide his embarrassment.

"There—at your elbow, Mr. Patson. Now please look at me. And remember what I said earlier. I am not interested in fanciful theories of the universe or wildly imaginative interpretations of present world conditions. All I'm concerned with here, in my professional capacity, is your state of mind, Mr. Patson. That being the case, it's clearly absurd to suggest that you might be saying too much. Unless you are perfectly frank with me, it will be very difficult for me to help you. Come now, we agreed about that. So far you've followed my instructions admirably. All I ask now is for a little more cooperation. Did you actually attend what you believed to be a conference of these Gray Ones?"

"Yes, I did," said Mr. Patson, not without some reluctance.

"But I'll admit I can't prove anything. The important part may be something I imagined. But if you insist, I'll tell you what happened. I overheard Harold and our Borough Treasurer arranging to travel together to Maundby Hall, which is about fifteen miles north of where I live. I'd never been there myself, but I'd heard of it in connection with various summer schools and conferences and that sort of thing. Perhaps you know it, Dr. Smith?"

"As a matter of fact, I do. I had to give a paper there one Saturday night. It's a rambling Early Victorian mansion, with a large ballroom that's used for the more important meetings."

"That's the place. Well, it seems they were going there to attend a conference of the New Era Community Planning Association. And when I overheard them saying that, first I told myself how lucky I was not to be going too. Then afterwards, thinking it over, I saw that if you wanted to hold a meeting that no outsider in his senses would want to attend, you couldn't do better than hold it in a country house that's not too easy to get at, and call it a meeting or conference of the New Era Community Planning Association. I know if anybody said to me 'Come along with me and spend the day listening to the New Era Community Planning Association,' I'd make any excuse to keep away. Of course it's true that anybody like Harold couldn't be bored. The Gray Ones are never bored, which is one reason why they are able to collar and hold down so many jobs nowadays, the sort of jobs that reek of boredom. Well, this New Era Community Planning Association might be no more than one of the usual societies of busybodies, cranks, and windbags. But then again it might be something very different, and I kept thinking about it in connection with the Gray Ones. Saturday was the day of the conference. I went down to my office in the morning, just to go through the post and see if there was anything urgent, and then went home to lunch. In the middle of the afternoon I felt I had to know what was happening out at Maundby Hall, so off I went in my car. I parked it just outside the grounds, scouted round a bit, then found an entrance through a little wood at the back. There was nobody about, and I sneaked into the house by way of a servants' door near the pantries and larders. There were some catering people around there, but nobody bothered me. I went up some back stairs, and after more scouting, which I enjoyed as much as anything I've done this year,

I was guided by the sound of voices to a small door in a corridor upstairs. This door was locked on the inside, but a fellow had once shown me how to deal with a locked door when the key's still in the lock on the other side. You slide some paper under the door, poke the key out so that it falls onto the paper and then slide the paper back with the key on it. Well, this trick worked and I was able to open the door, which I did very cautiously. It led to a little balcony overlooking the floor of the ballroom. There was no window near this balcony so that it was rather dark up there, and I was able to creep down to the front rail without being seen. There must have been between three and four hundred of them in that ballroom, sitting on little chairs. This balcony was high above the platform, so I had a pretty good view of them as they sat facing it. They looked like Gray Ones, but of course I couldn't be sure. And for the first hour or so, I couldn't be sure whether this really was a meeting of the New Era Community Planning Association or a secret conference of Gray Ones. The stuff they talked would have done for either. That's where the Gray Ones are so damnably clever. They've only to carry on doing what everybody expects them to do, in their capacity as sound conscientious citizens and men in authority, to keep going with their own hellish task. So there I was, getting cramp, no wiser. Another lot of earnest busybodies might be suggesting new ways of robbing us of our individuality. Or an organized covey of masquerading devils and demons might be making plans to bring us nearer to the insects, to rob us of our souls. Well, I was just about to creep back up to the corridor, giving it up as a bad job, when something happened." He stopped, and looked dubiously at his listener.

"Yes, Mr. Patson," said Dr. Smith encouragingly, "then something happened?"

"This is the part you can say I imagined, and I can't prove I didn't. But I certainly didn't dream it, because I was far too cramped and aching to fall asleep. Well, the first thing I noticed was a sudden change in the atmosphere of the meeting. It was as if somebody very important had arrived, although I didn't see anybody arriving. And I got the impression that the *real* meeting was about to begin. Another thing—I knew for certain now that this was no random collection of busybodies and windbags, that they were all Gray Ones. If you asked me to tell you in detail how I knew, I couldn't begin. But I noticed something else, after a minute or two. These Gray Ones massed together down there had now a positive quality of their own, which I'd never discovered before. It wasn't that they were just negative, not human, as they were at ordinary times; they had this positive quality, which I can't describe except as a sort of chilly hellishness. As if they'd stopped pretending to be human and were letting themselves go, recovering their demon natures. And here I'm warning you, doctor, that my account of what happened from then is bound to be sketchy and peculiar. For one thing, I wasn't really well placed up in that balcony, not daring to show myself and only getting hurried glimpses; and for another thing, I was frightened. Yes, doctor, absolutely terrified. I was crouching there just above three or four hundred creatures from some cold hell. That quality I mentioned, that chilly hellishness, seemed to come rolling over me in waves. I might have been kneeling on the edge of a pit of iniquity a million miles deep. I felt the force of this hellishness not on the outside but inside, as if the very essence of me was being challenged and attacked. One slip, a blackout, and then I might wake up to find myself running a concentration camp, choosing skins for lampshades. Then somebody, something, arrived. Whoever or whatever they'd been waiting for was down there on the platform. I knew that definitely. But I couldn't see him or it. All I could make out was a sort of thickening and whirling of the air down there. Then out of that a voice spoke, the voice of the leader they had been expecting. But this voice didn't come from outside, through my ears. It spoke inside me, right in the center, so that it came out to my attention, if you see what I mean. Rather like a small, very clear voice on a good telephone line, but coming from inside. I'll tell you frankly I didn't want to stay there and listen, no matter what big secrets were coming out; all I wanted to do was to get away from there as soon as I could; but for a few minutes I was too frightened to make the necessary moves."

"Then you heard what this—er—voice was saying, Mr. Patson?" the doctor asked.

"Some of it—yes."

"Excellent! Now this is important." And Dr. Smith pointed his beautiful fountain pen at Mr. Patson's left eye. "Did you learn from it anything you hadn't known before? Please answer me carefully."

"I'll tell you one thing you won't believe," cried Mr. Patson.

"Not about the voice—we'll come to that—but about those Gray Ones. I risked a peep while the voice was talking, and what I saw nearly made me pass out. There they were—three or four hundred of 'em—not looking human at all, not making any attempt; they'd all gone back to their original shapes. They looked—this is the nearest I can get to it—like big semitransparent toads—and their eyes were like six hundred electric lamps burning under water, all greeny, unblinking, and shining out of Hell."

"But what did you hear the voice say?" Dr. Smith was urgent now. "How much can you remember? That's what I want to know. Come along, man."

Mr. Patson passed a hand across his forehead and then looked at the edge of this hand with some astonishment, as if he had not known it would be so wet. "I heard it thank them in the name of Adaragraffa—Lord of the Creeping Hosts. Yes, I could have imagined it—only I never knew I'd that sort of imagination. And what is imagination anyhow?"

"What else—what else—did you hear, man?"

"Ten thousand more were to be drafted into the Western Region. There would be promotions for some there who'd been on continuous duty longest. There was to be a swing over from the assault by way of social conditions, which could almost look after itself now, to the draining away of character, especially in the young of the doomed species. Yes, those were the very words," Mr. Patson shouted, jumping up and waving his arms. "Especially in the young of the doomed species. Us—d'you understand—us. And I tell you—we haven't a chance unless we start fighting back now—*now*—yes, and with everything we've got left. Gray Ones. And more and more of them coming, taking charge of us, giving us a push here, a shove there—down—down—down—"

Mr. Patson found his arms strongly seized and held by the doctor, who was clearly a man of some strength. The next moment he was being lowered into his chair. "Mr. Patson," said the doctor sternly, "you must not excite yourself in this fashion. I cannot allow it. Now I must ask you to keep still and quiet for a minute while I speak to my partner, Dr. Meyenstein. It's for your own good. Now give me your promise."

"All right, but don't be long," said Mr. Patson, who suddenly felt quite exhausted. As he watched the doctor go out, he wondered if he had not said either too much or not enough. Too much, he felt, if he was to be accepted as a sensible businessman who happened to be troubled by some neurotic fancies. Not enough, perhaps, to justify, in view of the doctor's obvious scepticism, the terrible shaking excitement that had possessed him at the end of their interview. No doubt, round the corner, Doctors Smith and Meyenstein were having a good laugh over this rubbish about Gray Ones. Well, they could try and make him laugh too. He would be only too delighted to join them, if they could persuade him he had been deceiving himself. Probably that is what they would do now.

"Well, Mr. Patson," said Dr. Smith, at once brisk and grave, as he returned with two other men, one of them Dr. Meyenstein and the other a bulky fellow in white who might be a male nurse. All three moved forward slowly as Dr. Smith spoke to him. "You must realize that you are a very sick man—sick in mind if not yet sick in body. So you must put yourself in our hands."

Even as he nodded in vague agreement, Mr. Patson saw what he ought to have guessed before, that Dr. Smith was a Gray One and that now he had brought two more Gray Ones with him. There was a fraction of a moment, as the three of them bore down upon him to silence his warning forever, when he thought he caught another glimpse of the creatures in the ballroom, three of them now like big semitransparent toads, six eyes like electric lamps burning under water, all greeny, unblinking, shining triumphantly out of Hell. . . .

FOR DISCUSSION

1. Priestley tells us about the Gray Ones instead of about the traditional red demons. In the text find three characteristics of the Gray Ones. Then list three characteristics of traditional demons. Which list is more frightening? Why?

2. The purpose of the Gray Ones is to "wipe from the face of the earth all wonder, joy, deep feeling, the desire to create, to praise life." Describe several of the techniques the Gray Ones use in order to attain this goal.

3. The final step of the Gray Ones, Mr. Patson explained, would

be to drain away the character of "the young of the doomed species." How does it feel to think of human beings as a "doomed species"? If you wanted to drain away the character of the young, how would you go about it?

4.   In this story the reader learns of a new concept of an afterworld. What if—instead of our going to hell—hell comes to us? That is, in brief, what Priestley is suggesting with his theory of the Evil Principle at work on earth. What do you think of this theory? Is it probable? Possible? Take a long, slow look at the world around you. Is it happening right now? Explain.

INTRODUCTION

No consideration of an afterlife is complete if it does not include total denial of any kind of afterlife. Denise Levertov sees death not as a gateway to heaven or hell, but as an ending. There is neither affirmation nor doubt, neither joy nor agony. All that is left is "a heavy thick silence."

The Dead

Denise Levertov

Earnestly I looked
into their abandoned faces
at the moment of death and while
I bandaged their slack jaws and
straightened waxy unresistant limbs and plugged   5
the orifices with cotton
but like everyone else I learned
each time nothing new, only that
as it were, a music, however harsh, that held us
however loosely, had stopped, and left   10
a heavy thick silence in its place.

FOR DISCUSSION

1. What does Levertov mean by "a music, however harsh ... had stopped"? What does it suggest about an afterlife?
2. A poet carefully chooses words for what they imply as well as for what they state. Explain briefly the implied significance of the following words or phrases:
   a. *"Earnestly* I looked."
   b. *"abandoned* faces."

  c. *"slack* jaws."

  d. "I learned *each time* nothing new."

3. Poetry more than prose is dependent on sound. This poem possesses a dull heaviness that is stated in the last line but implied throughout the entire poem by sound as well as diction. For example, there are very few long vowel sounds, and the repeated short vowels contribute to the mood of dullness. List a few other examples of words and phrases that contribute, as sounds, to the overall effect.

The Paths of Good and Bad Intention

CHAPTER TWO

According to theologians, there are two roads to the afterworld: the road to heaven, which is narrow, difficult, and full of obstacles; and the road to hell, which is broad and easy. Choose the road you wish to travel, and you choose also your destination. It sounds absurdly simple, but of course it is not. For to recognize these two roads, one must recognize good and evil. And opinions about good and evil are rarely absolute. Very often what is considered good or evil varies with human nature and values. Over the centuries philosophers have struggled with this problem.

In ancient Greece, Plato talked of Absolute Truth, synonymous with the All Good. He was certain that if we could emerge from the "shadows of the cave" and look clearly at the "sun of knowledge," we would know—and knowing, would understand. Then truth would be within the grasp of all and would be the same for all.

Centuries later Immanuel Kant, an eighteenth-century German philosopher, only half agreed. Objective reality (truth) exists, but each man sees it with different eyes, assimilates it with a different brain, modifies it with different experiences. So what was once the same for all ends by being separate and different for each.

More time passed. The existentialists and the behaviorists added a new dimension. "Act," said the existentialist, "though life is without meaning; act if you would be free." "Act," said the behaviorist, "for you become what you do." Though these two are widely disparate philosophies, there is a haunting similarity in their advice. No longer does man think, pursue truth, then invent procedures that will help him to attain truth or to place himself in harmony with it. Now, without caring about the end, he acts—and in acting, creates truth. We have gone a step further. Not only is truth no longer absolute and the same for all, but it also varies from moment to moment—varies so quickly that the word truth seems an archaism.

This eternal uncertainty as to the nature of truth has made difficult any lasting recognition of good and evil. People have painstakingly built roads to heaven and hell that suited their own cultures and mores. To be ruthless and fearless in war carried an ancient Greek directly to the Elysian fields, but the same behavior would carry a modern pacifist to hell. To steal from the rich to give to the poor made Robin Hood a saint to the oppressed, but the same behavior would make a nineteenth-century tycoon a devil in the eyes of his associates. Few virtues have always been admired; few vices always abhorred.

In our own time the distinction between virtue and vice has been further blurred by our addiction to short-lived fads. Consider the often childish plea for love as a panacea—a hazy, meaningless love based not on knowledge and acceptance, but on popular fashion. Consider the demand for tolerance, a willingness to endure those different from ourselves—to endure, not to understand. Consider the whining cry for instant gratification, a cheap, ersatz happiness. And consider the petulant plaint that no one is responsible for anything, that the "state"—safely impersonal—is responsible for all.

Nor are these constant redefinitions of virtue and vice the only complications faced by the writer who would describe the afterworld. There is a matter of pattern and of intent.

One person may break every moral law, then, just before death, perform a fine and selfless act. Another may lead a good, virtuous life, then, just before death, be guilty of a severe moral lapse. How does one judge each of these? Which road counts—the road of a lifetime, or the road of a moment? Patterns are stubbornly persistent. Could the wicked sinner adapt to a heaven won only by accident? Could the near saint fit into a hell not truly deserved? Would not each be out of harmony with the rest of the pattern?

The matter of intent is even more complex. Suppose one man

attends religious services regularly, obeys the laws of the state, works well at his job, and supports his family without complaint. Such a man should be well on the way to heaven. But what if he does all this not out of love for his fellow human beings and for what is right, but because he is afraid to do otherwise and chooses the safest path? Will his actual good deeds counteract his basic selfishness? Suppose that a second man stumbles through life. He is fired from job after job because time and again he stops to help a sick neighbor, to assist someone with a stalled car, or to right something else that is wrong. He steals at times because he cannot bear to see his neighbor's children starve. His own wife and children suffer. But he always acts with good intentions. Will his intent counteract his actual bad deeds? Suppose that a third man walks a middle course. He is committed neither to good nor evil, but he never gives a penny more than he can easily part with, never gives more of himself than is demanded by the accepted code, never loves enough to be hurt, never cares enough about anything to become vulnerable. What then? Which of these citizens is worthy of a crown, which, of cremation? It is a real problem for the philosophical writer.

Yes, the roads to an afterworld are as tortuous and as unmarked as the great trackless plains once were. And they cannot be safely ignored. Not only are they vitally important to those who believe in a life beyond death, but they are also important to those who do not. For the same roads lead to happiness or despair on earth.

For some, like the Jewish peoples, the continuation of its people is the real afterlife. For others, the afterworld will be here on earth when all human beings have learned to live and work together in a utopia that is no longer a dream. For them, too, the roads have meaning and importance.

If these elusive roads are universally significant, if they are essential to our well-being both here and hereafter, then must they not indeed be based on simple things? In a way, they are. For they are as simple—and as complex—as good and evil, as truth itself.

As one gropes one's own way toward truth, it is easy to understand why the modern writer is both confused and awestruck at the richness of his material. For in our time the roads to heaven and hell are not merely many, they are infinite in number. They are paved, tarred, macadamized, and gold-plated; they wind, stretch, come to dead ends; they intertwine, separate, suddenly merge.

It is a terrifying, puzzling state for human beings trying to live with purpose, but it is a marvelous condition for the writer because his imagination concerning these roads to an afterlife cannot be wilder than the chaotic reality.

INTRODUCTION

One way to reach heaven, or a good life on earth, is to give of one's self. That is easy enough for the artist or the musician who feels that he has something worthy to give, but it is considerably more difficult for the many who possess only a sliver of talent, or none at all. Barnaby believed that he was one of the unfortunate ones. "No gift have I," he sighed. But he had forgotten that the true measure of a gift is in the giver's intent, not in its worldly value.

Our Lady's Juggler
Anatole France

In the days of King Louis there was a poor juggler in France, a native of Compiègne, Barnaby by name, who went about from town to town performing feats of skill and strength.

On fair days he would unfold an old worn-out carpet in the public square, and when by means of a jovial address, which he had learned of a very ancient juggler, and which he never varied in the least, he had drawn together the children and loafers, he assumed extraordinary attitudes, and balanced a tin plate on the tip of his nose. At first the crowd would feign indifference.

But when, supporting himself on his hands face downwards, he threw into the air six copper balls, which glittered in the sunshine, and caught them again with his feet; or when throwing himself backwards until his heels and the nape of the neck met, giving his body the form of a perfect wheel, he would juggle in this posture with a dozen knives, a murmur of admiration would escape the spectators, and pieces of money rain down upon the carpet.

Nevertheless, like the majority of those who live by their wits, Barnaby of Compiègne had a great struggle to make a living.

Earning his bread in the sweat of his brow, he bore rather more than his share of the penalties consequent upon the misdoings of our father Adam.

Again, he was unable to work as constantly as he would have

been willing to do. The warmth of the sun and the broad daylight were as necessary to enable him to display his brilliant parts as to the trees if flower and fruit should be expected of them. In winter time he was nothing more than a tree stripped of its leaves, and as it were dead. The frozen ground was hard to the juggler, and, like the grasshopper of which Marie de France tells us, the inclement season caused him to suffer both cold and hunger. But as he was simple-natured he bore his ills patiently.

He had never meditated on the origin of wealth, nor upon the inequality of human conditions. He believed firmly that if this life should prove hard, the life to come could not fail to redress the balance, and this hope upheld him. He did not resemble those thievish and miscreant merry andrews who sell their souls to the devil. He never blasphemed God's name; he lived uprightly, and although he had no wife of his own, he did not covet his neighbor's, since woman is ever the enemy of the strong man, as it appears by the history of Samson recorded in the scriptures.

In truth, his was not a nature much disposed to carnal delights, and it was a greater deprivation to him to forsake the tankard than the man who bore it. For whilst not wanting in sobriety, he was fond of a drink when the weather waxed hot. He was a worthy man who feared God, and was very devoted to the Blessed Virgin.

Never did he fail on entering a church to fall upon his knees before the image of the Mother of God, and offer up this prayer to her:

"Blessed Lady, keep watch over my life until it shall please God that I die, and when I am dead, ensure to me the possession of the joys of paradise."

Now on a certain evening after a dreary wet day, as Barnaby pursued his road, sad and bent, carrying under his arm his balls and knives wrapped up in his old carpet, on the watch for some barn where, though he might not sup, he might sleep, he perceived on the road, going in the same direction as himself, a monk, whom he saluted courteously. And as they walked at the same rate they fell into conversation with one another.

"Fellow traveller," said the monk, "how comes it about that you are clothed all in green? Is it perhaps in order to take the part of a jester in some mystery play?"

"Not at all, good father," replied Barnaby. "Such as you see me, I am called Barnaby, and for my calling I am a juggler. There would be no pleasanter calling in the world if it would always provide one with daily bread."

"Friend Barnaby," returned the monk, "be careful what you say. There is no calling more pleasant than the monastic life. Those who lead it are occupied with the praises of God, the Blessed Virgin, and the saints; and, indeed, the religious life is one ceaseless hymn to the Lord."

Barnaby replied—

"Good father, I own that I spoke like an ignorant man. Your calling cannot be in any respect compared to mine, and although there may be some merit in dancing with a penny balanced on a stick on the tip of one's nose, it is not a merit which comes within hail of your own. Gladly would I, like you, good father, sing my office day by day, and specially the office of the most Holy Virgin, to whom I have vowed a singular devotion. In order to embrace the monastic life I would willingly abandon the art by which from Soissons to Beauvais I am well known in upwards of six hundred towns and villages."

The monk was touched by the juggler's simplicity, and as he was not lacking in discernment, he at once recognized in Barnaby one of those men of whom it is said in the scriptures: Peace on earth to men of good will. And for this reason he replied—

"Friend Barnaby, come with me, and I will have you admitted into the monastery of which I am prior. He who guided St. Mary of Egypt in the desert set me upon your path to lead you into the way of salvation."

It was in this manner, then, that Barnaby became a monk. In the monastery into which he was received the religious vied with one another in the worship of the Blessed Virgin, and in her honor each employed all the knowledge and all the skill which God had given him.

The prior on his part wrote books dealing according to the rules of scholarship with the virtues of the Mother of God.

Brother Maurice, with a deft hand, copied out these treatises upon sheets of vellum.

Brother Alexander adorned the leaves with delicate miniature paintings. Here were displayed the Queen of Heaven seated upon

Solomon's throne, and while four lions were on guard at her feet, around the nimbus which encircled her head hovered seven doves, which are the seven gifts of the Holy Spirit, the gifts, namely, of Fear, Piety, Knowledge, Strength, Counsel, Understanding, and Wisdom. For her companions she had six virgins with hair of gold, namely, Humility, Prudence, Seclusion, Submission, Virginity, and Obedience.

At her feet were two little naked figures, perfectly white, in an attitude of supplication. These were souls imploring her all-powerful intercession for their soul's health, and we may be sure not imploring in vain.

Upon another page facing this, Brother Alexander represented Eve, so that the Fall and the Redemption could be perceived at one and the same time—Eve the Wife abased, and Mary the Virgin exalted.

Furthermore, to the marvel of the beholder, this book contained presentments of the Well of Living Waters, the Fountain, the Lily, the Moon, the Sun, and the Garden Enclosed of which the Song of Songs tells us, the Gate of Heaven and the City of God, and all these things were symbols of the Blessed Virgin.

Brother Marbode was likewise one of the most loving children of Mary.

He spent all his days carving images in stone, so that his beard, his eyebrows, and his hair were white with dust, and his eyes continually swollen and weeping; but his strength and cheerfulness were not diminished, although he was now well gone in years, and it was clear that the Queen of Paradise still cherished her servant in his old age. Marbode represented her seated upon a throne, her brow encircled with an orb-shaped nimbus set with pearls. And he took care that the folds of her dress should cover the feet of her, concerning whom the prophet declared: My beloved is as a garden enclosed.

Sometimes, too, he depicted her in the semblance of a child full of grace, and appearing to say, "Thou art my God, even from my mother's womb."

In the priory, moreover, were poets who composed hymns in Latin, both in prose and verse, in honor of the Blessed Virgin Mary, and amongst the company was even a brother from Picardy who

sang the miracles of Our Lady in rhymed verse and in the vulgar
tongue.

Being a witness of this emulation in praise and the glorious
harvest of their labors, Barnaby mourned his own ignorance and
simplicity.

"Alas!" he sighed, as he took his solitary walk in the little
shelterless garden of the monastery, "wretched wight that I am, to
be unable, like my brothers, worthily to praise the Holy Mother of
God, to whom I have vowed my whole heart's affection. Alas! alas!
I am but a rough man and unskilled in the arts, and I can render
you in service, blessed Lady, neither edifying sermons, nor treatises
set out in order according to rule, nor ingenious paintings, nor
statues truthfully sculptured, nor verses whose march is measured
to the beat of feet. No gift have I, alas!"

After this fashion he groaned and gave himself up to sorrow.
But one evening, when the monks were spending their hour of lib-
erty in conversation, he heard one of them tell the tale of a religious
man who could repeat nothing other than the Ave Maria. This
poor man was despised for his ignorance; but after his death there
issued forth from his mouth five roses in honor of the five letters of
the name Mary (Marie), and thus his sanctity was made manifest.

Whilst he listened to this narrative Barnaby marveled yet once
again at the loving kindness of the Virgin; but the lesson of that
blessed death did not avail to console him, for his heart overflowed
with zeal, and he longed to advance the glory of his Lady, who is in
heaven.

How to compass this he sought but could find no way, and day
by day he became the more cast down, when one morning he awakened filled full with joy, hastened to the chapel, and remained there
alone for more than an hour. After dinner he returned to the chapel
once more.

And, starting from that moment, he repaired daily to the
chapel at such hours as it was deserted, and spent within it a good
part of the time which the other monks devoted to the liberal and
mechanical arts. His sadness vanished, nor did he any longer groan.

A demeanor so strange awakened the curiosity of the monks.

These began to ask one another for what purpose Brother Barnaby could be indulging so persistently in retreat.

The prior, whose duty it is to let nothing escape him in the behavior of his children in religion, resolved to keep a watch over Barnaby during his withdrawals to the chapel. One day, then, when he was shut up there after his custom, the prior, accompanied by two of the older monks, went to discover through the chinks in the door what was going on within the chapel.

They saw Barnaby before the altar of the Blessed Virgin, head downwards, with his feet in the air, and he was juggling with six balls of copper and a dozen knives. In honor of the Holy Mother of God he was performing those feats, which aforetime had won him most renown. Not recognizing that the simple fellow was thus placing at the service of the Blessed Virgin his knowledge and skill, the two old monks exclaimed against the sacrilege.

The prior was aware how stainless was Barnaby's soul, but he concluded that he had been seized with madness. They were all three preparing to lead him swiftly from the chapel, when they saw the Blessed Virgin descend the steps of the altar and advance to wipe away with a fold of her azure robe the sweat which was dropping from her juggler's forehead.

Then the prior, falling upon his face upon the pavement, uttered these words—

"Blessed are the simple-hearted, for they shall see God."

"Amen!" responded the old brethren, and kissed the ground.

FOR DISCUSSION

1. The juggler "believed firmly that if this life should prove hard, the life to come could not fail to redress the balance. . . ." Many people believe that this philosophy explains apparent injustices. Others, however, believe that it is used to keep the poor from rebelling. Discuss briefly both points of view.

2. Barnaby is poor, uneducated, and alone in the world. Is he therefore a pitiful character? Write a paragraph in which you persuade Barnaby that he actually is a good person and has a fairly rewarding life-style, or write one in which you condemn him and his way of life.

3. What was Barnaby's gift to the Blessed Virgin? What was the prior's gift? Evaluate these two gifts. Is one greater than the other, or are they equal? Explain.

4. This very short story by Anatole France has become a favorite throughout the world. According to this story, what is the surest road to heaven?

5. Read the "Parable of the Talents" in the New Testament. Compare the parable and the short story as to style and message.

INTRODUCTION

To many Jews, there is no afterlife—or rather, the afterlife is here on earth in the continuing existence of the Jewish people as a whole. This end, then, becomes all-important. The child is truly an extension of the parent; the parent lives on in the child. If a child turns away from the religion, a line is broken—and if many such lines are broken, how long will Judaism last?

Benjamen, only six years old, is sensitive to the fears of his elders. Because of this, a Sabbath game becomes a new, frightening road to an afterlife.

Benjamen Burning

Joyce Madelon Winslow

Benjamen A. (for Amos) Israelovitch, six years old, was standing on Delancey Street in Manhattan with his arms raised straight up over his head. The three middle fingers on each hand Benjamen criss-crossed and like this with his arms and six fingers he was standing on Delancey Street. It was Saturday, sundown. There was a Kosher dill pickle smell from the delicatessen and the Spanish music from the tenements above the stores. There were the people out walking and the men talking outside the fish cellar about what tomorrow's business would be like if it was like last year this time, God forbid! The men wore yamalkas and mezuzahs and pais. The women you could not see—they stayed inside. The Spanish, Puerto Ricans, beat rugs against the walls of the buildings from inside their windows, cleaning for tomorrow. The house must be clean for after church. Their women you heard yelling for a child mostly. The Jewish women you wondered where they were.

In front of the iron grating of Katz's dry goods stall, locked against thieves on the Sabbath, Arnie Frankel played with seven other boys. Arnie was seven, the oldest, he could be the Rabbi. Jared was only a week younger but he couldn't be the Rabbi; the

Cantor he could be. So he was the Cantor and sang the responses and Arnie got to lead the congregation or scold the boys for not knowing their Hebrew lesson. Michael, David, Micah, Jon, David S. and E-li, as he was called, were the congregation sometimes and sometimes the bad pupils. Right now they were the congregation.

"Benjamen, come on and play," Eli called.

"E-li, you're not supposed to yell in Schul," Arnie scolded.

"Don't call me E-li. Call me right."

The Rabbi made a face at Eli. "Hey, Benjamen," the Rabbi called. "Come here. You can help make a minyan."

Benjamen didn't answer. He was thinking of Aunt Reisa and Uncle Art's when he was there a whole weekend alone.

The Rabbi asked again. "Benjamen, come here."

"Can't," Benjamen answered, looking at his fingers. "I'm not through yet."

"What are you doing?"

"I'm burning."

"Why?"

" 'Cause I'm a Havdalah candle."

Arnie nodded, and turned back to his congregation. He started davening, and they all followed, rocking back and forth on their heels chanting. They said the Sh'ma, the Hatzi-Kaddish, and the Adoration. They did the reading from the Torah, the Kiddish, and heard a brief sermon from Jared on singing louder and coming to Schul on time, and finished the service with three verses of Ayn Kelohenu and a benediction from Arnie. Then the women started coming to collect their sons for bed—tomorrow would be a big day. They'd have to get up early to go visit Aunt Reisa and Uncle Art in the country, or Cousins Harry and Hope on the Island, or go with Marion and the boys to the shore.

"Say good night, Cantor," Jared's mother said. She was proud of his game. Someday, for real, who knows? "Benjamen," she said, "your mother wants you home now, too. What's with the hands, Benjamen?"

"I'm a Havdalah candle."

"Ah, yes, three wicks, very good, Benjamen, just like a real Havdalah candle. Did you help your mother light hers at sundown?"

"Paul did it. I watched him."

"Good boy. It will burn all night while you sleep and tomorrow when you wake up it will be a puddle of wax. Come. Your mother sent me to get you. Stop playing Havdalah candle now and come home."

Benjamen politely followed Jared's mother home, his arms raised up over his head, his six middle fingers crossed. She looked back at him. "Benjamen, are you still playing Havdalah candle?"

"I *am* a Havdalah candle. I'm not through burning."

"Mmm. Well, burn on the way home. Hurry up." She walked briskly, looking back over her shoulder every so often at Benjamen burning, at Jared, glad he was a Cantor and not a candle. God bless Benjamen he was such a serious little boy. Oh well, don't butt in where you're not asked.

At home, Benjamen's mother was helping him into pajamas. Benjamen had not lowered his arms once.

"Benjamen, you would help me get this shirt off if you would please untwist your wick," his mother asked.

"I can't. The flame would go out."

"Benjamen, I've almost had it with this Havdalah candle game. Stop burning and take off that shirt *now*. And then get into the bathroom so you can wash up before you go to bed."

"Would you brush my teeth?"

"Benjamen! Harold! Harold, would you come in here and tell your son to behave and mind his mother. Benjamen, I want you to put your arms down at once and get into pajamas and brush your teeth, or no trip to the country tomorrow. Do you hear me?"

"I'm not through burning," Benjamen snuffled.

"All right. Burn. Burn. You can go into bed with your playclothes on and burn all night, but don't expect to visit Aunt Reisa tomorrow." She went out of the room muttering, "Just like his brother at his age, thought he was a Kiddush cup and drank everything in the house. What are we raising here, a pulpit or a family?" Benjamen kicked off the covers, maneuvered between them and fell asleep.

Mrs. Israelovitch came in later to tuck him in and saw Benjamen fast asleep with his arms raised high above his head, the three middle fingers on each hand criss-crossed. At eleven P.M., just before she went to bed, she checked on him. He was asleep, still burning. At six A.M. just before she started breakfast she looked in. Same.

Benjamen got up at six-thirty, ran to the front door, got the funny sheets out of the Sunday paper, ran into his parents' bedroom and plopped onto his father's stomach.

"Umph!" said Mr. Israelovitch.

"Morning," kissed Benjamen. "Read me Dagwood first."

Mr. Israelovitch rubbed his face, kissed his son. "Well, so you stopped burning? Your mother will be happy."

"The flame went out early this morning. For a while I thought it would never go out."

"Neither did we. What happened, your arms got tired?"

"No, the candle burned to the bottom. You know about Havdalah candles. What does this say?"

"It says, Alexander, tell Cookie breakfast is ready and we better eat or we'll never get to Aunt Reisa's and Uncle Art's."

"It does not," Benjamen laughed. Then pouted, "Can I go?"

"We'll have to ask your mother."

Mr. Israelovitch and Benjamen went into the kitchen where Mrs. Israelovitch was laying out lox, bagels, whitefish, cream cheese, Muenster cheese, and onion rolls on the table. Benjamen's older brother, Paul, ten, got up early to beat the line at the delicatessen. He'd also gotten some halvah, chocolate, for Aunt Reisa, like his mother said.

"Can I go to Aunt Reisa's?" Benjamen asked his mother.

"You'll have to ask your father."

"Can I?"

"Will you stop burning the next time your mother asks you?"

"I wanted to but I couldn't. I couldn't. The flame wouldn't go out till it burned away and I wasn't finished burning yet."

"Benjamen," his mother said, "you must learn the difference between a game and being Benjamen. Candles do not eat breakfast. You could have stopped burning."

"I wasn't playing a game. I *was* a Havdalah candle. Honest."

"Benjamen," his mother said . . .

"Oh, Mom, let him go," Paul said. "Benjamen, you won't be a Havdalah candle anymore, will you?"

"I don't think so."

"OK. Just tell Mom you're sorry and let's eat, huh?"

"I'm sorry."

"OK," said his mother. "This time OK. But not again."

That night in the car on the way back from Aunt Reisa's, about sundown, Benjamen quietly lifted both arms above his head, his palms together.

"Put your arms down before they see you," Paul whispered fiercely.

"I can't."

"Benjamen, you promised Mom you wouldn't be a Havdalah candle anymore."

"I'm not."

"Well, then what are you doing with your arms, anyway," whispered Paul who hated to see his brother hit because he was usually hit for something, too, afterwards.

"I'm burning," Benjamen explained out loud.

"You're *what?*" Mrs. Israelovitch exclaimed, turning around.

"Benjamen," his father tried, "there are no Havdalah candles on Sunday. Saturday only."

"I'm not a Havdalah candle. I'm a Yarzeit candle."

"If you think you're going to burn for twenty-four hours like this, you're wrong," his mother yelled. "Harold, stop the car at once. I am going to finish this burning once and for all."

"Don't hit him," pleaded Paul.

"I can't help it," Benjamen cried. "I just can't help it. God said I have to burn."

"*God* said," Mr. Israelovitch said slowly. "When did God say this?"

"Just now. He tells me to burn at sundown and I don't know what I am till then."

"All right, Benjamen," said his father. "You may burn. We won't try to stop you. If God said, that's all there is to it. Esta, this is something for the Rabbi, not us. Go to the Rabbi tomorrow."

Mrs. Israelovitch explained to the Rabbi Monday.

"Thank God he thinks he is a candle and not a bush," the Rabbi consoled.

"He doesn't have enough fingers to be a bush. I'm telling you, Rabbi, I don't know what to do. All night long he burned. For all I know, he's at home still burning. Breakfast he didn't eat."

"He'll live."

"Wash up he didn't do."

"A little dirt never hurt."

"To school he didn't go."

"What! He didn't go to school?! That's not good. That's no-ot good! Why didn't he go to school?"

Mrs. Israelovitch threw up her hands. "Because he's burning!"

Mr. Israelovitch closed the cosmetics store early to come home and hear what the Rabbi said.

"He said don't worry."

"What don't worry with my son in there burning. He doesn't eat or go to school today and I'm not supposed to worry?"

"He says it will pass."

"What did he say about God telling him?"

"He said be glad that's all He asked."

Benjamen burned till just before sundown, then came out of his room and ate three cheese blintzes, a plate of macaroni salad, a plate of potato salad, a pickle, a glass of chocolate milk and some strudel. Then some more chocolate milk. His mother fed, looked worried, was quiet. The Rabbi said to humor it, it would go away.

"More?" his father asked gently. Benjamen shook his head.

"Where's Paul?"

"At Jared's watching the color television. Benjamen, how, ah, how do you feel?"

"Fine."

"Nothing hurts?"

"No. Can I go to Jared's?"

"*May* I go to Jared's," his mother corrected.

"May I go to Jared's?"

His father looked lovingly at him. "Ah, Benjamen, Benjamen. The youngest is supposed to be the easiest. Benjamen, a question. Will you burn anymore?"

"Harold!"

"Forgive me, Esta, I cannot ignore. Benjamen, do you like this burning? It hurts me so to see you not eat or go to school, and be so unhappy."

"I *have* to," he yelled and ran out the front door, slamming it hard. A little later Paul called to say Benjamen said to say he was at Jared's, too, and he was sorry for slamming the door. They'd be home after Cisco Kid.

Wednesday and Thursday went by. Benjamen walked to school with Paul, and walked back with him. They played after school, Benjamen winning two steelies and four cat's-eyes, Paul winning at stickball from Peter Bashkin who claimed gutter balls don't count. Mr. Israelovitch smoked his pipe after dinner, Mrs. Israelovitch massaged his shoulders. They discussed the day's business, the boys, and wondered why they could find the time to work and write their eldest, Alan, at the college and he could let two weeks go by and not a word.

"When he wants money, *then* we hear," Mr. Israelovitch puffed.

"He's a good boy, he's busy," Mrs. Israelovitch said. She defended him, but still, she thought a letter would be nice. She would write and tell him to write his father at once.

"Wait till I tell Reisa about the Yarzeit candle," Mrs. Israelovitch said. "She may have some ideas about this."

"First you better explain to her what is a Yarzeit candle."

"Harold! My own sister raised in my mother's house knows a Yarzeit candle."

"Hmm? Then she's forgotten maybe, like she forgets to keep Kosher and to pray in the Schul and to keep the head covered. What is Arthur, a pagan he prays without his head covered? We get a little money, a little acceptance, a home in the high-falootin' neighborhood, and so soon we forget!"

"So soon we forget? So soon we forget? *You* forget you're talking about my only sister? And while we're on the subject of forgetting, did you forget a little common courtesy at supper? Since when do you go to someone's house and eat off their table and then throw it up to their faces that the food you are eating isn't good enough for you because it isn't Kosher? You knew they weren't Kosher before you sat down! You had to yell at them in front of Benjamen?"

"I didn't want to eat there in the first place! Who made me eat there? If I had my way, we wouldn't have gone at all."

"She's my sister and I wanted to see her. You'd begrudge me

my own sister? And it does Benjamen no harm to run in a little grass for a change, to play with their dog. Where in the city can he play with a dog?"

"He likes dogs? I'll take him to the pound."

"Harold, don't pick up just one word. You're stubborn as a mule. They have not been blessed with children and they are very good to Benjamen."

"You call it good to Benjamen when Arthur takes him to their Temple, it should burn, and they wear no yamalkas? This you call good? We send him to Hebrew School and teach him here so he can go there and pray without a yamalka? Next you'll let him eat pork at their table!"

"They wouldn't serve him pork!"

"Aach! Just because there's a mezuzah on their door you don't call that a Jewish home. A cat can have kittens, it doesn't make it a mother."

"They're Jewish the way they think Jewish is. She's my sister, Harold, and I love her."

"Esta, I love your sister dearly, and her husband, he's a good man, but Jewish the way Jewish is they are not. Jewish you light the candles and break chalah and pray with the head covered. You don't drink a glass wine, then take the empty glass and call it a glass wine. You leave out the wine, it's an empty glass only. Esta, no more do I want Benjamen visiting that pagan. He doesn't need this."

"Harold, you're getting entirely too carried away. What is this 'no more'? You don't make bad relations between my sister and me because you don't like their Temple. No one asked you to go to their Temple. So we won't let Benjamen visit their Temple anymore, it upsets you so. Everytime they talk about their Temple or their young Rabbi you give such a look you scare him half to death."

"Esta, I said no more and I mean it. And I want no consulting with her on this burning. We can handle this ourselves without their help, and not another word said!"

They kissed and made up before they went to sleep because they promised they would never go to sleep angry. But a honeymoon it was not.

Friday, when Mr. and Mrs. Israelovitch came home from Schul, Paul met them at the door crying.

"What's the matter?"

"I can't make him stop," Paul cried. "He was crying all night and he won't stop."

Mr. and Mrs. Israelovitch ran into the bedroom. Benjamen was on his bed with his train and silky blanket, all cried out. Up in the air he held five fingers, and four fingers.

"Nine fingers? What has nine candles, Benjamen?"

"One is the Shamos."

"A menorah," his father slumped. "Are you going to burn eight days and nights, Benjamen?"

"He can't burn for eight days, he'll starve to death," his mother said. "Benjamen, enough! Enough!"

His father sat on the bed next to Benjamen and looked like he would cry.

"I *have* to," whispered Benjamen.

"When did you start burning, Benjamen?"

No answer.

"A little after you left," Paul cried.

"Benjamen, you're making your brother cry. *Please* stop burning," his father pleaded.

"I can't."

"Why can't you?" his mother asked.

"God said I have to." Benjamen tried to cry but he was too tired out. He hiccuped crying.

His father sighed. "Go to sleep, Benjamen." He lifted him up, tucked him in, kissing him good night with a hug. He shepherded his family out of the room. "He's never burned for more than a day. Tomorrow he'll forget he was a menorah and will eat supper again." He put his hand on Paul's head. "Don't worry, Paul. It'll be all right." Paul went to bed troubled, but not worried. Mother and Father were home. Everything would be all right.

But everything was not all right. Benjamen ate nothing Saturday. Nothing on Sunday. Despite pleading. Despite threats. Despite crying.

The supper table Monday night was lonesome again. Only

three people where four should be. Mrs. Israelovitch put silverware at Benjamen's place, but he was not there. She would keep putting silver though. The day I don't put silver is the day I give up and die, she thought. Mr. and Mrs. Israelovitch and Paul stayed within their places. They did not spread out more comfortable over Benjamen's part of the table. Benjamen's part of the table was for Benjamen, no two ways about it.

"You'll pass the salt, please?" Mrs. Israelovitch asked.

It was passed.

There was a lot of sighing and dipping the bread into the natural gravy, and eating and as for talking not much. Paul never heard before the cup into the saucer make such a loud noise. He was very frightened.

After supper, Paul snuck some gefilte fish with a carrot slice in to Benjamen. If his mother caught him he'd get hit: "It hurts me as much as it hurts you," she said. "He'll get so hungry, he'll eat, you'll see and everything will be all better. Trust me." Paul waited till his parents left Benjamen's room and were talking in the living room.

"Benjamen, I'll feed you some fish," Paul said. "Open your mouth."

"I don't want any."

"You *love* gefilte fish. Come on, please eat some fish."

"I don't want any. I don't want anything. Just leave me alone." Benjamen was sitting on his bed with his silky blanket, nine fingers up in the air.

"Aren't you hungry? I'll get you some candy. Don't you even want some candy?"

"No." Benjamen was very white, very quiet, very unhappy.

"Oh Benjamen, what's the matter?" Paul sat down next to him and put his arm around him. Benjamin did not flinch away like he usually did when someone got mushy. Benjamen looked very little, very different.

"I've got to keep burning," he whispered. "If the flame goes out we die."

"We won't die," Paul promised.

"Because I'm keeping it burning," Benjamen said.

Paul picked up the carrot with the fork and held it close to

Benjamen. "Carrot?" He talked like Mrs. Israelovitch. "A nice piece carrot, Benjamen?"

Benjamen shook no.

"*Please* eat the carrot. Just the carrot."

Benjamen shook no.

Paul cried almost. He didn't know what to do, what to do. All of a sudden he screamed, "NO!" He stabbed the fish with the fork and flung it, plate, carrot, fork, everything crash to the floor screaming, "Awful fish! I hate you fish!"

Mr. Israelovitch came running in. He scooped Paul up, held him tight.

"I hate you fish," Paul sobbed. "I hate you fish!"

'I know," Mr. Israelovitch soothed. He looked at Mrs. Israelovitch standing worried in the doorway. "It's all right shanevelt, it's all right." Later in the week Benjamen let Paul feed him some rye bread and butter, but Paul only. From his mother and father he would eat nothing.

On the fifth day the doctor came and worried over Benjamen. He knew the Israelovitches well. He'd seen the children through measles, German measles, chicken pox, scarlet fever, a nail in the foot, a broken nose, and the polio scare. He knew how they were doing in school, he celebrated with the family bar mitzvah, and his own daughter Nancy was in college with their oldest, Alan. This with Benjamen worried him. He was thinking how to say what he thought to Harold and Esta.

"Nu?" Mrs. Israelovitch said.

"Esta, there are some things we need a different kind medicine."

"I don't care how much it costs," Mr. Israelovitch said. "Get it."

The doctor tried again. "There are some things there are no shots, no pills." He stopped. How to go on? He knew this family, he loved and understood them. Understood? Felt, more like. His own grandparents raised his parents this way and it was a good way, they were good people. But change, even for their own good, they did not do. "There are some things," he said to the anxious, unblinking eyes, "we help by talking, listening."

"I try to talk to him, doctor," Mrs. Israelovitch said. "Me he won't answer."

"Of course," the doctor said. She had given him an opportunity. "You know some times you get angry, you don't know why and you talk to a friend, a complete stranger in the market, maybe? You talk, you feel better. Maybe Benjamen would talk to a stranger, someone new who knows special how to understand him?" He waited. They did not understand yet. He'd have to do this the best he could so Benjamen could be helped. "I have a friend," he continued, "who is very good with children, with this kind of problem like Benjamen is having."

"You know other children who burn?" Mrs. Israelovitch asked.

"Not always burn, but don't talk, don't eat. Deep down inside is something bothering them."

"This is a personal friend?"

"A man I trust," the doctor said. "A very good doctor downtown."

"Oh *ho!*" Mr. Israelovitch exclaimed. The doctor cringed slightly. "Comes the dawn! I know what it is you're saying. A doctor with the couches, yes? A what do you call him—a *headshrinker!*" He pounced on the word. "A headshrinker! No! No son mine goes to a headshrinker."

The doctor nodded sadly. He knew it. No changing. There was only one thing he could say here, the question that always commanded attention, respect and consideration. "Harold, what can it hurt to try?"

Mr. Israelovitch was shaking his head back and forth, back and forth.

"We'll discuss it," Mrs. Israelovitch said firmly. They started discussing the second the doctor walked out the door.

"I don't know, I just don't know," Mrs. Israelovitch began. "My mother, may she rest in peace, never had this problem with us. Did we do something wrong? Alan, God bless him, is a healthy, smart boy. Paul is a good boy. What did we do wrong with Benjamen?"

"What is this with the headshrinker?" Mr. Israelovitch said. "Did we ever go to headshrinkers? We got a good hit, no more problem. Or we went to the Rabbi and we did what he said. No couches, no books on raising the children. My father couldn't read the English if he had such a book. Now, so different. Who's changed, I ask you? The children or the parents?"

"Maybe it's the only thing to do," Mrs. Israelovitch sighed. "For the first time I can't help mine own child." She began to cry. "I can't help mine own child. What kind mother am I?"

"Maybe I expected too much?" Mr. Israelovitch said sadly. "Alan, God bless him, was always saying I expect so much from him he was afraid to bring home a bad mark."

"We never expected all A's. Just the best they can do. They knew we never got angry if it is the best they can do. Is it too much to expect the best from your children?"

"We should thank God we got two healthy sons. With two such sons it's only fair there are problems with the third. Who else has two such boys? Oh, Benjamen. Oh, my little one."

"Now what was good is bad. It used to be you heard drink more milk. Drink more milk. No more. Is bad for the skin. It used to be eggs was good for you—good for the shine on the hair. Now no more. Is bad for the heart. And butter. If mine mother, may she rest in peace, cooked with butter it was a luxury it was so expensive, so delicious. Now, no! Margarine they say to use. I'm telling you, first the milk, then the eggs, then the butter is all bad. The next thing you know, they'll say your own parents is no good for you!"

"They said it! What do you think the doctor was saying? Who goes to a headshrinker? Someone who hates his parents!"

"No! Someone who hates his parents?"

"What do you think—someone is going to pay fifty dollars to tell a headshrinker he is happy at home? What do you think the doctor was saying before?"

"He thinks Benjamen hates us? Oi Gottenu! It should come to this!" She started to sob into her handkerchief, rocking back and forth, back and forth in the rocker. Mr. Israelovitch wept inside.

Benjamen burned till the menorah burned out. He grew feverish. He didn't seem to hear when you spoke to him, he didn't cry, he never smiled. He stayed in his room and sat still with his silky blanket. He seemed to be waiting for something.

Alan flew home Saturday. He'd never heard his mother so upset. He knew the story from letters, now from the phone. His mother had half-cried, half-laughed it, trying to minimize it for him

Benjamen saying over and over in a fever he was going to keep the flame alive, going to burn forever going to be the Eternal Light over and over he says this, Alan, he has 104° fever, he is in Mt. Sinai Hospital your father is beside himself God help us he is so sick over and over he says he is the Eternal Light God says he must burn forever I don't know what all this is maybe you better come home—.

Alan, Paul, Mr. and Mrs. Israelovitch, Jared's mother and the doctor sat at a table in the doctors' dining room of the hospital, no one touching his coffee. Paul was quiet, still. Alan was stunned. Yesterday he was listening to a lecture in sociology. Today he had just seen his little brother in a hospital bed packed with ice, the doctor shaking his head back and forth, back and forth, and the nurse looking with compassion at his mother. The Rabbi had already left to see other patients. He told Alan to pray, to be a strength for his poor parents, for Paul. Alan looked at Paul. I wonder how much he understands of this, he thought. I wonder how it will affect him. My God! he thought. Benjamen! He hardly knew him. He was away at the University for two of Benjamen's growing-up years. He got pictures Benjamen drew for him while he was at school, he sent Benjamen little presents, he didn't even know his own brother. How selfish to take and take. While he was dating girls Benjamen was burning inside, burning up with something while he was sure his mother's letters exaggerated, while he laughed over her spelling errors.

"What kind of a God lets this happen?" he burst out. "What kind of a God lets a little boy—"

"Sha!" Mr. Israelovitch commanded. "You do not speak of God in such a tone."

"It's natural to want to blame," Mrs. Israelovitch soothed. "Sha, Alan, my baby, my precious baby." She hugged Paul to her, covering him with tears, he was the closest to her. Jared's mother got up and put her arms around Mrs. Israelovitch. She sobbed against Jared's mother. Paul edged away.

"Why did he have to burn? Why did he have to burn?" Mrs. Israelovitch sobbed.

"He said God told him," Mr. Israelovitch said hoarsely. "I don't understand. I never heard such a thing."

Paul was restless. He wanted to run. He wanted to cry. He wanted to be home eating supper all of them together. He wanted to sit on his father's lap. He didn't like this. He felt like he had to run.

"He said we would all die if he stopped burning," Paul said.

"What's this?" said his father. "When did he say this?" They all listened carefully.

Paul was frightened. Maybe he shouldn't have told. "He said it when I took him the fish."

"What else did he say?"

"Nothing."

"Where does he get an idea like this?" Mrs. Israelovitch said.

"Who knows where children get ideas?" Jared's mother said. "They get an idea in their heads, it takes forever to find out from where."

"We would all die if he stopped burning," the doctor said. He thought. He tapped the table.

"Paul," the doctor said, "do you know what he meant?"

Paul shook his head. He started to cry.

"Mom, let's get him home," Alan said. "Let's all go home. There's nothing we can do here." He wanted to get out of the hospital smell, the doctors getting their supper in the hospital. Maybe he could bring a toy or a stuffed animal to Benjamen tomorrow. Maybe he could understand all this if he were at home, he never did enough for Benjamen.

"I'm staying," his mother said. "What if the fever breaks, if he wants to see me? I stay here all night if I have to." Her voice got louder. "You come home from the college, you right away give orders."

"No, no, I just—"

"Don't just me. Who sent you to college? Who scrimped so you could go to school to take girls to shows? And you don't even write a letter to your father once a week who waits to hear from you. You know how he loves you."

"Mom, I'm sorry. I—"

"I'm sorry. I'm sorry. You think that settles everything?" She wiped the corner of her eye. "You get some new ideas you think you know everything, you use God's name in vain in front of us you forget you are Alan Israelovitch, you forget where you come from like my sister, God bless her. Next you'll forget the Sabbath, you'll forget to keep Kosher, you'll forget everything like you forget your own parents. Maybe sending you to the college wasn't such a smart idea. Maybe we made a mistake with you, Alan, letting you have so much. I swore I'd never say this in front of your father but I'm saying it. All this new, you forget your own home. I didn't go to college, Alan, but I still know more about life than you."

"I never forgot you, Mom, believe me, I never forgot you."

"Not even a letter once a week that's asking too much."

"I'm sorry about the letters. I didn't realize—"

"Big shot! New ideas."

"There's nothing wrong with new ideas."

"Oh, no?"

"No! There's nothing wrong with change if it makes you better!"

"So now we're no good, eh? Your family made you, Alan. Your family you run to when you are in trouble or lonely. The old family you don't think is so bad then."

"The old family is fine. But new ideas, new ideas let you see more. Mom, I never knew what was going on in the world till I went to college. I thought the world began and ended with Delancey Street. Other people aren't so different, you know? They just have different ways of saying the same things."

"You mean to tell me," Mr. Israelovitch said with remarkable control, "you are no different from Reisa, Art, from forgetting the Sabbath, the Covenant? This is what I get after all these years of trying to teach you—"

"I knew you'd get back to them. It always gets back to them, doesn't it? Well, there's nothing wrong with them. They're different. OK. But it's what they want, the way they want to live. So let them. We live the way we live. The whole world doesn't have to do what you do just because you think it's right. Who are you anyway?"

There was a silence. Alan swallowed. Drank some cold coffee. He wasn't going to take it back. He was tired of being different, of fighting prejudice, other ideas. They had to know sooner or later.

"Alan," the doctor said, "we're all very emotional and excited here. Maybe you owe your father an apology?"

"I'm sorry," Alan said.

"Ach!" Mr. Israelovitch turned away, disgusted, defeated, sick at his heart. "I can see it all happening before mine own eyes. Our way of life is dying with our own children. With mine own generation, all the Jews will be dead. My own son doesn't keep up the faith, God help us!"

The doctor leaned forward as Mr. Israelovitch was speaking.

"Harold," he said quickly, "did you ever say that in front of Benjamen?"

"Say what?"

"All the Jews will be dead."

"I don't know."

"Oh, Dad, you always say that whenever you talk about Reisa and Art."

"Maybe I did. You remember that, eh? Too bad you don't remember as well the other things I've been trying to teach you."

"Mr. Freund says something like that all the time," Paul said.

"What does he say?" the doctor asked.

"He says the flame will go out if we don't keep the faith strong. He says it when we give the wrong answer."

"Oh, my God," Mrs. Israelovitch breathed. "I understand." She shuddered. "A pox be on my house."

Mr. Israelovitch was stricken. He mumbled something, at first incredulous, horrible, then louder, "I've killed my own son? Esta, forgive me. I've killed my own son?"

"Bite your tongue. He isn't dead." She put her hand over her heart, rocking back and forth, back and forth in the cold hospital chair.

Upstairs, Benjamen dreamed of candles, tall candles of red, yellow, orange, bright gold candles and all the candles were people, Mr. Freund, Aunt Reisa and Uncle Art, Paul, his mother and father all gloriously burning, big tall, strong flames, thousands of red flames, swirls and arcs of hot, fiery light in front of Katz's delicatessen, candle smells and black smoke, hotter, all the people melting into hot puddles of wax, his father dripping hot melted faces of flame to his feet the hiss of sliding wax bodies mirrors and mirrors of blinding heat a wall of fire he was surrounded by blue-hot flame yellow spots running exploding run Benjamen run! Benjamen plunging through the wall of fire, sickening heat, fire in his hands and feet. Upstairs Benjamen kept burning till the flame went out.

FOR DISCUSSION

1. Benjamen is only six years old. Does this make it easier for the reader to accept his belief that he is a candle? Can you remember any time in your own childhood when something that started out as a game suddenly became frighteningly real? Why is a child more likely than an adult to undergo this kind of transformation?

2. Mr. Israelovitch and Mr. Freund often said "the flame will go out if we don't keep the faith strong." What did this mean to the two adults? What did it mean to Benjamen?

3. This concept of an afterlife in Judaism is unique among religions, but the concept itself is not unusual. To what extent does almost every parent seek immortality in a child? What are some of the ways in which this desire is manifested? How is the conflict between Alan and his parents partly the result of this same desire?

INTRODUCTION

"The devil's snare does not catch you unless you are first caught by the devil's bait," wrote St. Ambrose in the fourth century. Sixteen hundred years have passed since Ambrose wrote, but there is a good deal of truth still in his words. We human beings are such perverse creatures that we are fascinated by that which leads us to destruction.

Here a modern poet tries his hand at describing "devil's bait up-to-date." Since the automobile is the major and best-loved symbol of the twentieth century, it is fitting that it should become the devil's latest irresistible lure.

The Devil Grows Jubilant
Daniel B. Straley

As merriment bubbled from within
The Devil sat up with a gleeful grin,
For his statisticians him had told
Tipsy drivers had increased tenfold.
Then with nimble thumb his spouse he woke   5
And the cheering tidings to her broke.

"Though the flowing bowl has been man's curse,
Since the auto age it has gorged the hearse,
And the twain have scourged the world with crime
That will flourish more with the tick of time.   10
Thus, my dear, for us there'll be no dearth
For they spawn crime among the youth of earth."

The yawning wife in the brimstone heat
About her chin drew the spark-holed sheet
And patted her wave in helldom style,   15
Dutifully listening all the while,

Then with drowsy smile and approving cough
On the wings of slumber she drifted off,
But the Devil, pleased with his year-end catch,
Jubilantly began new schemes to hatch.   20

FOR DISCUSSION

1. This particular poem is one of a series called *Said the Devil to His Wife.* Much of the fun of the poem lies in its *anthropomorphic* treatment of the devil. (*Anthropomorphic* means attributing human behavior and conduct to nonhuman things or creatures.) In the poem find three anthropomorphic descriptive phrases that contribute to the humor.

2. According to Straley, what is the newest road to hell? This poem was written in 1944. Is there a new, newest road to hell today? List a few possibilities.

3. This poem, as you no doubt realize, is written in rhyming couplets. Try writing an original poem, also in rhyming couplets, based on one of the new roads to hell listed in your answer to question two.

INTRODUCTION

Count Leo Tolstoy, often considered the greatest novelist of Russia, was a man of passion. Converted in mid-life to a personal religion, this aristocrat turned away from nobles and intellectuals. He found evil easy to recognize: it lay in money, in alcohol, in tobacco. Excess of any kind was to be avoided.

Writing should be stripped to its essentials, asserted Tolstoy the artist; life should be stripped to its essentials, asserted Tolstoy the preacher. In this fablelike short story, the excesses—the non-essentials of life—lead the peasant down the path to hell.

How the Devil Redeemed the Crust of Bread

Leo Tolstoy

A poor peasant went out to plow, without having had his breakfast, and took with him from home a crust of bread. The peasant turned over the plow and untied the beam, which he put under a bush; here he also placed his crust of bread, which he covered with his caftan.

The horse grew tired, and the peasant was hungry. The peasant stuck fast the plow, unhitched the horse and let it go to graze, and himself went to his caftan, to have his dinner. He raised the caftan, but the crust was not there; he searched and searched for it, and turned his caftan around and shook it, but the crust was gone. The peasant marveled.

"This is remarkable," he thought. "I have not seen anyone, and yet somebody has carried off the crust of bread."

But it was a little devil who, while the peasant had been plowing, had carried off the crust; he sat down behind a bush to hear how the peasant would curse and scold him, the devil.

The peasant looked a bit dejected.

"Well," he said, "I shall not starve. Evidently the one who carried it off needed it. May he eat it to his health!"

And the peasant went to the well, drank some water, rested himself, caught the horse, hitched it up, and began once more to plow.

The little devil felt sad because he had not led the peasant into sin, and went to the chief devil to tell him about it.

He appeared before the chief devil and told him how he had carried off the peasant's crust, and how the peasant, instead of cursing, had told him to eat it to his health. The chief devil grew angry.

"If the peasant has in this business got the better of you," he said, "it is your own fault,—you did not know any better. If the peasants, and the women, after them, take such a notion, we shall have a hard time of it. This matter cannot be left in such a shape. Go," he said, "once more to the peasant, and earn the crust. If in three years you do not get the better of the peasant, I will bathe you in holy water."

The little devil was frightened. He ran down upon the earth, and began to think how he might redeem his guilt. He thought and thought, and finally thought it out. He turned into a good man, and hired himself out as a laborer to the peasant. He taught the peasant in a dry year to sow in a swamp. The peasant listened to his hired hand and sowed the grain in the swamp. The other peasants had all their grain burned up by the sun, but the poor peasant's corn grew thick, tall, and with full ears. The peasant had enough to eat until the next crop, and much corn was left. In the summer the hired hand taught the peasant to sow on the uplands. It turned out to be a rainy summer. The corn of the other peasants fell down and rotted and made no ears, but this peasant's corn on the uplands was heavy with ears. The peasant had now even more corn left, and he did not know what to do with it.

The hired hand taught the peasant to mash the grain and brew liquor. The peasant brewed some liquor, and began to drink himself and to give it to others. The little devil came to his chief, and began to boast that he had earned the crust. The chief devil went to look for himself.

He came to the peasant, and saw that the peasant had invited some rich men, to treat them to liquor. The hostess was carrying the liquor around to the guests. As she walked around, her foot caught in the table, and she spilled a glass. The peasant grew angry, and scolded his wife.

How the Devil Redeemed the Crust of Bread   121

"Devil's fool," he said. "Is this slops that you, with your clumsy hands, spill such precious liquor on the ground?"

The little devil nudged his chief.

"Watch him!" he said. "Now he will regret his crust."

The host scolded his wife, and began himself to carry the liquor around. A poor peasant, who had not been invited, came back from his work. He greeted the company and sat down, watching the people drink the liquor; as he was tired he wanted to have a drink himself. He sat and sat, and swallowed his spittle,—but the host did not offer him any; he only muttered:

"Where will a man get enough liquor for the whole lot of you?"

This, too, pleased the chief devil; but the little devil boasted:

"Wait, it will be worse than that."

The rich peasants had a glass, and so had the host. They began to flatter one another and to praise one another, and to speak oily, deceptive words. The chief devil listened to that, too, and was glad of it.

"If this drink will make them so foxy, and they will deceive one another," he said, "they will be in our hands."

"Wait," said the little devil, "and see what is coming; let them drink another glass. Now they wag their tails to one another, like foxes, and want to deceive one another, but look, they will soon be like fierce wolves."

The peasants had another glass, and their words became louder and coarser. Instead of oily speeches, they began to curse and to get angry with one another, and they fell to, and mauled one another's noses. The host, too, took a hand in the fight. And he was also beaten.

The chief devil saw this, too, and was glad.

"This," he said, "is nice."

But the little devil said:

"Wait, it will be better yet! Let them have a third glass. Now they are like mad wolves, but let them have a third glass, and they will become like swine."

The peasants had a third glass. They went completely to pieces. They muttered and yelled, they did not know themselves what, and paid no attention to one another. They began to scatter, some going away by themselves, and some by twos and threes; they all fell down and wallowed in the street. The host went out to see them off, and he fell with his nose in the gutter, and he became all soiled and lay there like a pig, grunting.

This pleased the chief devil even more.

"Well," he said, "you have invented a fine drink, and you have earned the crust. Tell me how you made this drink. It cannot be otherwise than that you have first let into it some fox blood,—and this made the peasant as sly as a fox. And then you let in some wolf blood,—and this made him as fierce as a wolf. And finally you poured in some pig blood, and this made him a pig."

"No," said the little devil, "that was not the way I did. All I did was to let him have more corn than he needed. That beast blood has always lived in him, but it has no chance so long as he gets barely enough corn. At that time he was not sorry even for the last crust, but when he began to have a surplus from his corn, he began to think of how he might have his fun from it. And I taught him the fun of drinking liquor. And when he began to brew God's gift into liquor for his fun, there arose in him his fox, wolf, and pig blood. Let him now drink liquor, and he will always be a beast."

The chief praised the little devil, forgave him for the crust of bread, and made him a captain.

FOR DISCUSSION

1. The little devil first tried to lead the peasant to sin by stealing his crust of bread. How did he hope the peasant would react? How did the peasant actually react?
2. In his second attempt to lead the peasant astray, what technique did the little devil use? What was the result of this second attempt?
3. According to Tolstoy, life should be stripped to its essentials. How does this story reflect this attitude of the author?
4. According to Tolstoy, writing should be stripped to its essentials. How does this story illustrate this rule?
5. Tolstoy seems to be saying that excess is the shortest road to hell. Do you agree or disagree? Explain.

INTRODUCTION

Max Beerbohm was one of the more imaginative writers of the early twentieth century. In this short story, he began with a character named, rather surprisingly, Lord George Hell. His Lordship is, of course, "greedy, destructive, and disobedient," and possesses all possible vices. What would happen, Beerbohm wonders, if Lord George Hell pretended to be Lord George Heaven? The answer, as the story evolves, is a prophecy of B. F. Skinner's philosophy. It was Skinner, the behavioral psychologist, who said that "we become what we do." By accident, Lord George learns much the same thing. His actions set his feet firmly on the path to heaven.

The Happy Hypocrite

Max Beerbohm

None, it is said, of all who reveled with the Regent, was so wicked as Lord George Hell. I will not trouble my little readers with a long recital of his great naughtiness. But it were well they should know that he was greedy, destructive, and disobedient. I am afraid there is no doubt that he often sat up at Carlton House until long after bedtime, playing at games, and that he generally ate and drank more than was good for him. His fondness for fine clothes was such that he used to dress on weekdays quite as gorgeously as good people dress on Sundays. He was thirty-five years old and a great grief to his parents.

And the worst of it was that he set such a bad example to others. Never, never did he try to conceal his wrongdoing; so that, in time, everyone knew how horrid he was. In fact, I think he was proud of being horrid. Captain Tarleton, in his account of *Contemporary Bucks*, suggested that his Lordship's great candor was a virtue and should incline us to forgive some of his abominable faults. But, painful as it is to me to dissent from any opinion, expressed by one who is now dead, I hold that candor is good only when it reveals good actions or good sentiments, and that, when it reveals evil, itself is evil, even also.

Lord George Hell did, at last, atone for all his faults, in a way that was never revealed to the world during his lifetime. The reason of his strange and sudden disappearance from that social sphere, in which he had so long moved and never moved again, I will unfold. My little readers will then, I think, acknowledge that any angry judgment they may have passed upon him must be reconsidered and, it may be, withdrawn. I will leave his Lordship in their hands. But my plea for him will not be based upon that candor of his, which some of his friends so much admired. There were, yes! some so weak and so wayward as to think it a fine thing to have a historic title and no scruples. "Here comes George Hell," they would say, "How wicked my lord is looking!" Noblesse oblige, you see, and so an aristocrat should be very careful of his good name. Anonymous naughtiness does little harm.

It is pleasant to record that many persons were inobnoxious to the magic of his title and disapproved of him so strongly that, whenever he entered a room where they happened to be, they would make straight for the door and watch him very severely through the keyhole. Every morning when he strolled up Piccadilly they crossed over to the other side in a compact body, leaving him to the companionship of his bad companions on that which is still called the "shady" side. Lord George was quite indifferent to this demonstration. Indeed, he seemed wholly hardened, and when ladies gathered up their skirts as they passed him he would lightly appraise their ankles.

I am glad I never saw his Lordship. They say he was rather like Caligula, with a dash of Sir John Falstaff, and that sometimes on wintry mornings in St. James's Street young children would hush their prattle and cling in disconsolate terror to their nurses' skirts as they saw him come (that vast and fearful gentleman!) with the east wind ruffling the rotund surface of his beaver, ruffling the fur about his neck and wrists, and striking the purple complexion of his cheeks to a still deeper purple. "King Bogey" they called him in the nurseries. In the hours when they too were naughty, their nurses would predict his advent down the chimney or from the linen-press, and then they always "behaved." So that, you see, even the unrighteous are a power for good, in the hands of nurses.

It is true that his Lordship was a nonsmoker—a negative virtue, certainly, and due, even that, I fear, to the fashion of the day—but there the list of his good qualities comes to abrupt conclusion. He loved with an insatiable love the town and the pleasures of the town, whilst the ennobling influences of our English lakes were quite unknown to him. He used to boast that he had not seen a buttercup for twenty years, and once he called the country "a Fool's Paradise." London was the only place marked on the map of his mind. London gave him all he wished for. Is it not extraordinary to think that he had never spent a happy day nor a day of any kind in Follard Chase, that desirable mansion in Herts, which he had won from Sir Follard Follard, by a chuck of the dice, at Boodle's, on his seventeenth birthday? Always cynical and unkind, he had refused to give the broken baronet his "revenge." Always unkind and insolent, he had offered to install him in the lodge—an offer which was, after a little hesitation, accepted. "On my soul, the man's place is a sinecure," Lord George would say; "he never has to open the gate for me." So rust had covered the great iron gates of Follard Chase, and moss had covered its paths. The deer browsed upon its terraces. There were only wild flowers anywhere. Deep down among the weeds and water lilies of the little stone-rimmed pond he had looked down upon, lay the marble faun, as he had fallen.

Of all the sins of his Lordship's life surely not one was more wanton than his neglect of Follard Chase. Some whispered (nor did he ever trouble to deny) that he had won it by foul means, by loaded dice. Indeed no cardplayer in St. James's cheated more persistently than he. As he was rich and had no wife and family to support, and as his luck was always capital, I can offer no excuse for his conduct. At Carlton House, in the presence of many bishops and cabinet ministers, he once dunned the Regent most arrogantly for 5,000 guineas out of which he had cheated him some months before, and went so far as to declare that he would not leave the house till he got it; whereupon His Royal Highness, with that unfailing tact for which he was ever famous, invited him to stay there as a guest, which, in fact, Lord George did, for several months. After this, we can hardly be surprised when we read that he "seldom sat down to the fashionable game of Limbo with less than four, and sometimes with *as many as seven* aces up his sleeve." We can only wonder that he was tolerated at all.

At Garble's, that nightly resort of titled rips and roysterers, he usually spent the early part of his evenings. Round the illuminated garden, with La Gambogi, the dancer, on his arm and a Bacchic retinue at his heels, he would amble leisurely, clad in Georgian costume, which was not then, of course, fancy dress, as it is now. Now and again, in the midst of his noisy talk, he would crack a joke of the period, or break into a sentimental ballad, dance a little or pick a quarrel. When he tired of such fooling, he would proceed to his box in the tiny alfresco theater and patronize the jugglers, pugilists, play-actors and whatever eccentric persons happened to be performing there.

The stars were splendid and the moon as beautiful as a great camellia one night in May, as his Lordship laid his arms upon the cushioned ledge of his box and watched the antics of the Merry Dwarf, a little, curly-headed creature, whose debut it was. Certainly Garble had found a novelty. Lord George led the applause, and the Dwarf finished his frisking with a pretty song about lovers. Nor was this all. Feats of archery were to follow. In a moment the Dwarf reappeared with a small, gilded bow in his hand and a quiverful of arrows slung at his shoulder. Hither and thither he shot these vibrant arrows, very precisely, several into the bark of the acacias that grew about the overt stage, several into the fluted columns of the boxes, two or three to the stars. The audience was delighted. *"Bravo! Bravo Saggitaro!"* murmured Lord George, in the language of La Gambogi, who was at his side. Finally, the waxen figure of a man was carried on by an assistant and propped against the trunk of a tree. A scarf was tied across the eyes of the Merry Dwarf, who stood in a remote corner of the stage. *Bravo* indeed! For the shaft had pierced the waxen figure through the heart or just where the heart would have been, if the figure had been human and not waxen.

Lord George called for port and champagne and beckoned the bowing homuncle to his box, that he might compliment him on his skill and pledge him a bumper of the grape.

"On my soul, you have a genius for the bow," his Lordship cried with florid condescension. "Come and sit by me, but first

let me present you to my divine companion the Signora Gambogi—
Virgo and Sagittarius, egad! You may have met on the Zodiac."

"Indeed, I met the Signora may years ago," the Dwarf replied,
with a low bow. "But not on the Zodiac, and the Signora perhaps
forgets me."

At this speech the Signora flushed angrily, for she was indeed
no longer young, and the Dwarf had a childish face. She thought
he mocked her; her eyes flashed. Lord George's twinkled rather
maliciously.

"Great is the experience of youth," he laughed. "Pray, are you
stricken with more than twenty summers?" "With more than I can
count," said the Dwarf. "To the health of your Lordship!" and
he drained his long glass of wine. Lord George replenished it,
and asked by what means or miracle he had acquired his mastery
of the bow.

"By long practice," the little thing rejoined; "long practice on
human creatures." And he nodded his curls mysteriously.

"On my heart, you are a dangerous boxmate."

"Your Lordship were certainly a good target."

Little liking this joke at his bulk, which really rivaled the
Regent's, Lord George turned brusquely in his chair and fixed his
eyes upon the stage. This time it was the Gambogi who laughed.

A new operetta, *The Fair Captive of Samarcand,* was being
enacted, and the frequenters of Garble's were all curious to behold
the new debutante, Jenny Mere, who was said to be both pretty
and talented. These predictions were surely fulfilled, when the
captive peeped from the window of her wooden turret. She looked
so pale under her blue turban. Her eyes were dark with fear;
her parted lips did not seem capable of speech. "Is it that she is
frightened of us?" the audience wondered. "Or of the flashing
scimitar of Aphoschaz, the cruel father who holds her captive?"
So they gave her loud applause, and when at length she jumped
down, to be caught in the arms of her gallant lover, Nissarah, and,
throwing aside her Eastern draperies, did a simple dance, in the
convention of Columbine, their delight was quite unbounded. She
was very young and did not dance very well, it is true, but they
forgave her that. And when she turned in the dance and saw her
father with his scimitar, their hearts beat swiftly for her. Nor were
all eyes tearless when she pleaded with him for her life.

Strangely absorbed, quite callous of his two companions, Lord George gazed over the footlights. He seemed as one who was in a trance. Of a sudden, something shot sharp into his heart. In pain he sprang to his feet and, as he turned, he seemed to see a winged and laughing child, in whose hand was a bow, fly swiftly away into the darkness. At his side was the Dwarf's chair. It was empty. Only La Gambogi was with him, and her dark face was like the face of a fury.

Presently he sank back into his chair, holding one hand to his heart, that still throbbed from the strange transfixion. He breathed very painfully and seemed scarce conscious of his surroundings. But La Gambogi knew he would pay no more homage to her now, for that the love of Jenny Mere had come into his heart.

When the operetta was over, his love-sick Lordship snatched up his cloak and went away without one word to the lady at his side. Rudely he brushed aside Count Karaloff and Mr. Fitz-Clarence, with whom he had arranged to play hazard. Of his comrades, his cynicism, his reckless scorn—of all the material of his existence—he was oblivious now. He had no time for penitence or diffident delay. He only knew that he must kneel at the feet of Jenny Mere and ask her to be his wife.

"Miss Mere," said Garble, "is in her room, resuming her ordinary attire. If your Lordship deign to await the conclusion of her humble toilet, it shall be my privilege to present her to your Lordship. Even now, indeed, I hear her footfall on the stair."

Lord George uncovered his head and with one hand nervously smoothed his rebellious wig.

"Miss Mere, come hither," said Garble. "This is my Lord George Hell, that you have pleased who by your poor efforts this night will ever be the prime gratification of your passage through the roseate realms of art."

Little Miss Mere who had never seen a lord, except in fancy or in dreams, curtseyed shyly and hung her head. With a loud crash Lord George fell on his knees. The manager was greatly surprised, the girl greatly embarrassed. Yet neither of them laughed, for sincerity dignified his posture and sent eloquence from its lips.

"Miss Mere," he cried, "give ear, I pray you, to my poor words, nor spurn me in misprision from the pedestal of your beauty, genius, and virtue. All too conscious, alas! of my presumption in the same, I yet abase myself before you as a suitor for your adorable hand. I grope under the shadow of your raven locks. I am dazzled in the light of those translucent orbs, your eyes. In the intolerable whirlwind of your frame I faint and am afraid."

"Sir—" the girl began, simply.

"Say 'My Lord,' " said Garble, solemnly.

"My lord, I thank you for your words. They are beautiful. But indeed, indeed, I can never be your bride."

Lord George hid his face in his hands.

"Child," said Mr. Garble, "let not the sun rise e'er you have retracted those wicked words."

"My wealth, my rank, my irremediable love for you, I throw them at your feet." Lord George cried, piteously. "I would wait an hour, a week, a luster, even a decade, did you but bid me hope!"

"I can never be your wife," she said, slowly. "I can never be the wife of any man whose face is not saintly. Your face, my lord, mirrors, it may be, true love for me, but it is even as a mirror long tarnished by the reflection of this world's vanity. It is even as a tarnished mirror. Do not kneel to me, for I am poor and humble. I was not made for such impetuous wooing. Kneel, if you please, to some greater, gayer lady. As for my love, it is my own, nor can it ever be torn from me, but given, as true love needs to be given, freely. Ah, rise from your knees. That man, whose face is wonderful as the faces of the saints, to him I will give my true love."

Miss Mere, though visibly affected, had spoken this speech with a gesture and elocution so superb, that Mr. Garble could not help applauding, deeply though he regretted her attitude towards his honored patron. As for Lord George, he was immobile, a stricken oak. With a sweet look of pity, Miss Mere went her way, and Mr. Garble, with some solicitude, helped his Lordship to rise from his knees. Out into the night, without a word, his Lordship went. Above him the stars were still splendid. They seemed to mock the festoons of little lamps, dim now and guttering in the garden of Garble's. What should he do? No thoughts came; only his heart burnt hotly. He stood on the brim of Garble's lake, shallow and artificial as his past life had been. Two swans slept on its surface. The moon shone strangely upon their white, twisted necks.

Should he drown himself? There was no one in the garden to prevent him, and in the morning they would find him floating there, one of the noblest of love's victims. The garden would be closed in the evening. There would be no performance in the little theater. It might be that Jenny Mere would mourn him. "Life is a prison, without bars," he murmured, as he walked away.

All night long he strode, knowing not whither, through the mysterious streets and squares of London. The watchmen, to whom his figure was most familiar, gripped their staves at his approach, for they had old reason to fear his wild and riotous habits. He did not heed them. Through that dim conflict between darkness and day, which is ever waged silently over our sleep, Lord George strode on in the deep absorption of his love and of his despair. At dawn he found himself on the outskirts of a little wood in Kensington. A rabbit rushed past him through the dew. Birds were fluttering in the branches. The leaves were tremulous with the presage of day, and the air was full of the sweet scent of hyacinths.

How cool the country was! It seemed to cure the feverish maladies of his soul and consecrate his love. In the fair light of the dawn he began to shape the means of winning Jenny Mere, that he had conceived in the desperate hours of the night. Soon an old woodman passed by, and, with rough courtesy, showed him the path that would lead him quickest to the town. He was loth to leave the wood. With Jenny, he thought, he would live always in the country. And he picked a posy of wild flowers for her.

His *rentrée* into the still silent town strengthened his Arcadian resolves. He, who had seen the town so often in its hours of sleep, had never noticed how sinister its whole aspect was. In its narrow streets the white houses rose on either side of him like cliffs of chalk. He hurried swiftly along the unswept pavement. How had he loved this city of evil secrets?

At last he came to St. James's Square, to the hateful door of his own house. Shadows lay like memories in every corner of the dim hall. Through the window of his room a sunbeam slanted across his smooth, white bed, and fell ghastly on the ashen grate.

It was a bright morning in Old Bond Street, and fat little Mr. Aeneas, the fashionable mask-maker, was sunning himself at the door of his shop. His window was lined as usual with all kinds of masks—beautiful masks with pink cheeks, and absurd masks with protuberant chins; curious faces copied from old tragic models; masks of paper for children, of fine silk for ladies, and of leather for working men; bearded or beardless, gilded or waxen (most of them, indeed were waxen), big or little masks. And in the middle of this vain galaxy hung the presentment of a Cyclop's face, carved cunningly of gold, with a great sapphire in its brow.

The sun gleamed brightly on the window and on the bald head and varnished shoes of fat little Mr. Aeneas. It was too early for any customers to come and Mr. Aeneas seemed to be greatly enjoying his leisure in the fresh air. He smiled complacently as he stood here, and well he might, for he was a great artist, and was patronized by several crowned heads and not a few of the nobility. Only the evening before, Mr. Brummell had come into his shop and ordered a light summer mask, wishing to evade for a time the jealous vigilance of Lady Otterton. It pleased Mr. Aeneas to think that his art made him the recipient of so many high secrets. He smiled as he thought of the titled spendthrifts, who, at this moment, *perdus* behind his masterpieces, passed unscathed among their creditors. He was the secular confessor of his day, always able to give absolution. A unique position!

The street was as quiet as a village street. At an open window over the way, a handsome lady, wrapped in a muslin peignoir, sat sipping her cup of chocolate. It was La Signora Gambogi, and Mr. Aeneas made her many elaborate bows. This morning, however, her thoughts seemed far away, and she did not notice the little man's polite efforts. Nettled at her negligence, Mr. Aeneas was on the point of retiring into his shop, when he saw Lord George Hell hastening up the street, with a posy of wild flowers in his hand.

"His Lordship is up betimes!" he said to himself. "An early visit to La Signora, I suppose."

Not so, however. His Lordship came straight towards the mask shop. Once he glanced up at the Signora's window and looked deeply annoyed when he saw her sitting there. He came quickly into the shop.

"I want the mask of a saint," he said.

"Mask of a saint, my lord? Certainly!" said Mr. Aeneas, briskly. "With or without halo? His Grace the Bishop of St. Aldreds always wears his with a halo. Your Lordship does not wish for a halo? Certainly! If your Lordship will allow me to take the measurement—"

"I must have the mask today," Lord George said. "Have you none ready-made?"

"Ah, I see. Required for immediate wear," murmured Mr. Aeneas, dubiously. "You see, your Lordship takes a rather large size." And he looked at the floor.

"Julius!" he cried suddenly to his assistant, who was putting finishing touches to a mask of Barbarossa which the young king of Zürremburg was to wear at his coronation the following week. "Julius! Do you remember the saint's mask we made for Mr. Ripsby, a couple of years ago?"

"Yes, sir," said the boy. "It's stored upstairs."

"I thought so," replied Mr. Aeneas. "Mr. Ripsby only had it on hire. Step upstairs, Julius, and bring it down. I fancy it is just what your Lordship would wish. Spiritual, yet handsome."

"Is it a mask that is even as a mirror of true love?" Lord George asked gravely.

"It was made precisely as such," the mask-maker answered. "In fact it was made for Mr. Ripsby to wear at his silver wedding, and was very highly praised by the relatives of Mrs. Ripsby. Will your Lordship step into my little room?"

So Mr. Aeneas led the way to his parlor behind the shop. He was elated by the distinguished acquisition to his clientele, for hitherto Lord George had never patronized his business. He bustled round his parlor and insisted that his Lordship should take a chair and a pinch from his snuffbox, while the saint's mask was being found.

Lord George's eye traveled along the rows of framed letters from great personages, which lined the walls. He did not see them though, for he was calculating the chances that La Gambogi had not observed him, as he entered the mask shop. He had come down so early that he thought she would be still abed. That sinister old proverb, *La jalouse se lève de bonne heure*, rose in his memory. His eye fell unconsciously on a large, round mask made of dull silver, with the features of a human face traced over its surface in faint filigree.

"Your Lordship wonders what mask that is!" chirped Mr. Aeneas, tapping the thing with one of his little finger nails.

"What is that mask?" Lord George murmured, absently.

"I ought not to divulge, my lord," said the mask-maker. "But I know your Lordship would respect a professional secret, a secret of which I am pardonably proud. This," he said, "is a mask for the sun-god, Apollo, whom heaven bless!"

"You astound me," said Lord George.

"Of no less a person, I do assure you. When Jupiter, his father, made him lord of the day, Apollo craved that he might sometimes see the doings of mankind in the hours of night time. Jupiter granted so reasonable a request, and when next Apollo had passed over the sky and hidden in the sea, and darkness had fallen on all the world, he raised his head above the waters that he might watch the doings of mankind in the hours of night time. But," Mr. Aeneas added, with a smile, "his bright countenance made light all the darkness. Men rose from their couches or from their revels, wondering that day was so soon come, and went to their work. And Apollo sank weeping into the sea. 'Surely,' he cried, 'it is a bitter thing that I alone, of all the gods, may not watch the world in the hours of night time. For in those hours, as I am told, men are even as gods are. They spill the wine and are wreathed with roses. Their daughters dance in the light of torches. They laugh to the sound of flutes. On their long couches they lie down at last and sleep comes to kiss their eyelids. None of these things may I see. Wherefore the brightness of my beauty is even as a curse to me and I would put it from me.' And as he wept, Vulcan said to him, 'I am not the least cunning of the gods, nor the least pitiful. Do not weep, for I will give you that which shall end your sorrow. Nor need you put from you the brightness of your beauty.' And Vulcan made a mask of dull silver and fastened it across his brother's face. And that night, thus masked, the sun-god rose from the sea and watched the doings of mankind in the night time. Nor any longer were men abashed by his bright beauty, for it was hidden by the mask of silver. Those whom he had so often seen haggard over their daily tasks, he saw feasting now and wreathed with red roses. He heard them laugh to the sound of flutes, as their daughters danced in the red light of torches. And when at length they lay down upon their soft couches and sleep kissed their eyelids, he sank back into the sea and hid his mask under a little rock in the bed of the sea. Nor have men ever known that Apollo watches them often in the night time, but fancied it to be some pale goddess."

134

"I myself have always thought it was Diana," said Lord George Hell.

"An error, my lord!" said Mr. Aeneas, with a smile. "*Ecce signum!*" And he tapped the mask of dull silver.

"Strange!" said his Lordship. "And pray how comes it that Apollo has ordered of *you* this new mask?"

"He has always worn twelve new masks every year, inasmuch as no mask can endure for many nights the near brightness of his face, before which even a mask of the best and purest silver soon tarnishes, and wears away. Centuries ago, Vulcan tired of making so very many masks. And so Apollo sent Mercury down to Athens, to the shop of Phoron, a Phoenician mask-maker of great skill. Phoron made Apollo's masks for many years, and every month Mercury came to his shop for a new one. When Phoron died, another artist was chosen, and, when he died, another, and so on through all the ages of the world. Conceive, my lord, my pride and pleasure when Mercury flew into my shop, one night last year, and made me Apollo's warrant-holder. It is the highest privilege that any mask-maker can desire. And when I die," said Mr. Aeneas, with some emotion, "Mercury will confer my post upon another."

"And do they pay for your labor?" Lord George asked.

Mr. Aeneas drew himself up to his full height, such as it was. "In Olympus, my lord," he said, "they have no currency. For any mask-maker, so high a privilege is its own reward. Yet the sun-god is generous. He shines more brightly into my shop than into any other. Nor does he suffer his rays to melt any waxen mask made by me, until its wearer doff it and it be done with." At this moment Julius came in with the Ripsby mask. "I must ask your Lordship's pardon, for having kept you so long," pleaded Mr. Aeneas. "But I have a large store of old masks and they are imperfectly cataloged."

It certainly was a beautiful mask, with its smooth, pink cheeks and devotional brows. It was made of the finest wax. Lord George took it gingerly in his hands and tried it on his face. It fitted *à merveille.*

"Is the expression exactly as your Lordship would wish?" asked Mr. Aeneas.

Lord George laid it on the table and studied it intently. "I wish it were more as a perfect mirror of true love," he said at length. "It is too calm, too contemplative."

"Easily remedied!" said Mr. Aeneas. Selecting a fine pencil, he deftly drew the eyebrows closer to each other. With a brush steeped in some scarlet pigment, he put a fuller curve upon the lips. And, behold! it was the mask of a saint who loves dearly. Lord George's heart throbbed with pleasure.

"And for how long does your Lordship wish to wear it?" asked Mr. Aeneas.

"I must wear it until I die," replied Lord George.

"Kindly be seated then, I pray," rejoined the little man. "For I must apply the mask with great care. Julius, you will assist me!"

So, while Julius heated the inner side of the waxen mask over a little lamp, Mr. Aeneas stood over Lord George gently smearing his features with some sweet-scented pomade. Then he took the mask and powdered its inner side, quite soft and warm now, with a fluffy puff. "Keep quite still, for one instant," he said, and clapped the mask firmly on his Lordship's upturned face. So soon as he was sure of its perfect adhesion, he took from his assistant's hand a silver file and a little wooden spatula, with which he proceeded to pare down the edge of the mask, where it joined the neck and ears. At length, all traces of the "join" were obliterated. It remained only to arrange the curls of the lordly wig over the waxen brow.

The disguise was done. When Lord George looked through the eyelets of his mask into the mirror that was placed in his hand, he saw a face that was saintly, itself a mirror of true love. How wonderful it was! He felt his past was a dream. He felt he was a new man indeed. His voice went strangely through the mask's parted lips, as he thanked Mr. Aeneas.

"Proud to have served your Lordship," said that little worthy, pocketing his fee of fifty guineas, while he bowed his customer out.

When he reached the street, Lord George nearly uttered a curse through those sainted lips of his. For there, right in his way, stood La Gambogi, with a small, pink parasol. She laid her hand upon his sleeve and called to him softly by his name. He passed her by without a word. Again she confronted him.

"I cannot let go so handsome a lover," she laughed, "even though he spurn me! Do not spurn me, George. Give me your posy of wild flowers. Why, you never looked so lovingly at me in all your life!"

"Madam," said Lord George, sternly, "I have not the honor to know you." And he passed on.

The lady gazed after her lost lover with the blackest hatred in her eyes. Presently she beckoned across the road to a certain spy.

And the spy followed him.

Lord George, greatly agitated, had turned into Piccadilly. It was horrible to have met this garish embodiment of his past on the very threshold of his fair future. The mask-maker's elevating talk about the gods, followed by the initiative ceremony of his saintly mask, had driven all discordant memories from his love-thoughts of Jenny Mere. And then to be met by La Gambogi! It might be that, after his stern words, she would not seek to cross his path again. Surely she would not seek to mar his sacred love. Yet, he knew her dark, Italian nature, her passion for revenge. What was the line in Virgil? *Spretaeque*—something. Who knew but that somehow, sooner or later, she might come between him and his love?

He was about to pass Lord Barrymore's mansion. Count Karoloff and Mr. FitzClarence were lounging in one of the lower windows. Would they know him under his mask? Thank God! they did not. They merely laughed as he went by, and Mr. Fitz-Clarence cried in a mocking voice, "Sing us a hymn, Mr. What-ever-your-saint's-name-is!" The mask, then, at least, was perfect. Jenny Mere would not know him. He need fear no one but La Gambogi. But would not she betray his secret? He sighed.

That night he was going to visit Garble's and to declare his love for the little actress. He never doubted that she would love him for his saintly face. Had she not said, "That man whose face is wonderful as are the faces of the saints, to him I will give my true love"? She could not say now that his face was as a tarnished mirror of love. She would smile on him. She would be his bride. But would La Gambogi be at Garble's?

The operetta would not be over before ten that night. The clock in Hyde Park Gate told him it was not yet ten—ten of the morning. Twelve whole hours to wait, before he could fall at Jenny's feet! "I cannot spend that time in this place of memories," he thought. So he hailed a yellow cabriolet and bade the jarvey drive him out to the village of Kensington.

The Happy Hypocrite   137

When they came to the little wood where he had been but a few hours ago, Lord George dismissed the jarvey. The sun, that had risen as he stood there thinking of Jenny, shone down on his altered face, but, though it shone very fiercely, it did not melt his waxen features. The old woodman, who had shown him his way, passed by under a load of faggots and did not know him. He wandered among the trees. It was a lovely wood.

Presently he came to the bank of that tiny stream, the Ken, which still flowed there in those days. On the moss of its bank he lay down and let its water ripple over his hand. Some bright pebble glistened under the surface, and, as he peered down at it, he saw in the stream the reflection of his mask. A great shame filled him that he should so cheat the girl he loved. Behind that fair mask there would still be the evil face that had repelled her. Could he be so base as to decoy her into love of that most ingenious deception? He was filled with a great pity for her, with a hatred of himself. And yet, he argued, was the mask indeed a mean trick? Surely it was a secret symbol of his true repentance and of his true love. His face was evil, because his life had been evil. He had seen a gracious girl, and of a sudden his very soul had changed. His face alone was the same as it had been. It was not just that his face should be evil still.

There was the faint sound of someone sighing. Lord George looked up, and there, on the further bank, stood Jenny Mere, watching him. As their eyes met, she blushed and hung her head. She looked like nothing but a tall child, as she stood there, with her straight, limp frock of lilac cotton and her sunburnt straw bonnet. He dared not speak; he could only gaze at her. Suddenly there perched astride the bough of a tree, at her side, that winged and laughing child, in whose hand was a bow. Before Lord George could warn her, an arrow had flashed down and vanished in her heart, and Cupid had flown away.

No cry of pain did she utter, but stretched out her arms to her lover, with a glad smile. He leapt quite lightly over the little stream and knelt at her feet. It seemed more fitting that he should kneel before the gracious thing he was unworthy of. But she, knowing only that his face was as the face of a great saint, bent over him and touched him with her hand.

"Surely," she said, "you are that good man for whom I have

waited. Therefore do not kneel to me, but rise and suffer me to kiss your hand. For my love of you is lowly, and my heart is all yours."

But he answered, looking up into her fond eyes, "Nay, you are a queen, and I must needs kneel in your presence."

And she shook her head wistfully, and she knelt down, also, in her tremulous ecstasy, before him. And as they knelt, the one to the other, the tears came into her eyes, and he kissed her. Though the lips that he pressed to her lips were only waxen, he thrilled with happiness, in that mimic kiss. He held her close to him in his arms, and they were silent in the sacredness of their love.

From his breast he took the posy of wild flowers that he had gathered.

"They are for you," he whispered, "I gathered them for you, hours ago, in this wood. See! They are not withered."

But she was perplexed by his words and said to him, blushing, "How was it for me that you gathered them, though you had never seen me?"

"I gathered them for you," he answered, "knowing I should soon see you. How was it that you, who had never seen me, yet waited for me?"

"I waited, knowing I should see you at last." And she kissed the posy and put it at her breast.

And they rose from their knees and went into the wood, walking hand in hand. As they went, he asked the names of the flowers that grew under their feet. "These are primroses," she would say. "Did you not know? And these are ladies' feet, and these forget-me-nots. And that white flower, climbing up the trunks of the trees and trailing down so prettily from the branches, is called Astyanax. These little yellow things are buttercups. Did you not know?" And she laughed.

"I know the names of none of the flowers," he said.

She looked up into his face and said timidly, "Is it worldly and wrong of me to have loved the flowers? Ought I to have thought more of those higher things that are unseen?"

His heart smote him. He could not answer her simplicity.

"Surely the flowers are good, and did not you gather this posy for me?" she pleaded. "But if you do not love them, I must not. And I will try to forget their names. For I must try to be like you in all things."

"Love the flowers always," he said. "And teach me to love them."

So she told him all about the flowers, how some grew very slowly and others bloomed in a night; how clever the convolvulus was at climbing, and how shy violets were, and why honeycups had folded petals. She told him of the birds, too, that sang in the wood, how she knew them all by their voices. "That is a chaffinch singing. Listen!" she said. And she tried to imitate its note, that her lover might remember. All the birds, according to her, were good, except the cuckoo, and whenever she heard him sing she would stop her ears, lest she should forgive him for robbing the nests. "Every day," she said, "I have come to the wood, because I was lonely, and it seemed to pity me. But now I have you. And it is glad."

She clung closer to his arm, and he kissed her. She pushed back her straw bonnet, so that it dangled from her neck by its ribbons, and laid her little head against his shoulder. For a while he forgot his treachery to her, thinking only of his love and her love. Suddenly she said to him, "Will you try not to be angry with me, if I tell you something? It is something that will seem dreadful to you."

"*Pauvrette*," he answered, "you cannot have anything very dreadful to tell."

"I am very poor," she said, "and every night I dance in a theater. It is the only thing I can do to earn my bread. Do you despise me because I dance?" She looked up shyly at him and saw that his face was full of love for her and not angry.

"Do you like dancing?" he asked.

"I hate it," she answered, quickly. "I hate it indeed. Yet— tonight, alas! I must dance again in the theater."

"You need never dance again," said her lover. "I am rich and I will pay them to release you. You shall dance only for me. Sweetheart, it cannot be much more than noon. Let us go into town, while there is time, and you shall be made by bride, and I your bridegroom, this very day. Why should you and I be lonely?"

"I do not know," she said.

So they walked back through the wood, taking a narrow path which Jenny said would lead them quickest to the village. And, as they went, they came to a tiny cottage, with a garden full of flowers. The old woodman was leaning over its paling, and he nodded to them as they passed.

"I often used to envy the woodman," said Jenny, "living in that dear little cottage."

"Let us live there, then," said Lord George. And he went back and asked the old man if he were not unhappy, living there alone.

"'Tis a poor life here for me," the old man answered. "No folk come to the wood, except little children, now and again, to play, or lovers like you. But they seldom notice me. And in winter I am alone with Jack Frost. Old men love merrier company than that. Oh! I shall die in the snow with my faggots on my back. A poor life here!"

"I will give you gold for your cottage and whatever is in it, and then you can go and live happily in the town," Lord George said. And he took from his coat a note for two hundred guineas, and held it across the palings.

"Lovers are poor, foolish derry-docks," the old man muttered. "But I thank you kindly, sir. This little sum will keep me cosy, as long as I last. Come into the cottage as soon as can be. It's a lonely place and does my heart good to depart from it."

"We are going to be married this afternoon, in the town," said Lord George. "We will come straight back to our home."

"May you be happy!" replied the woodman. "You'll find me gone when you come."

And the lovers thanked him and went their way.

"Are you very rich?" Jenny asked. "Ought you to have bought the cottage for that great price?"

"Would you love me as much if I were quite poor, little Jenny?" he asked her after a pause.

"I did not know you were rich when I saw you across the stream," she said.

And in his heart Lord George made a good resolve. He would put away from all his worldly possessions. All the money that he had won at the clubs, fairly or foully, all that hideous accretion of gold guineas, he would distribute among the comrades he had impoverished. As he walked, with the sweet and trustful girl at his side, the vague record of his infamy assailed him, and a look of pain shot behind his smooth mask. He would atone. He would shun no sacrific that might cleanse his soul. All his fortune he would put from him. Follard Chase he would give back to Sir Follard. He would sell his house in St. James's Square. He would keep some little part of his patrimony, enough for him in the wood, with Jenny, but no more.

"I shall be quite poor, Jenny," he said.

And they talked of the things that lovers love to talk of, how happy they would be together and how economical. As they were passing Herbert's pastry shop, which as my little readers know, still stands in Kensington, Jenny looked up rather wistfully into her lover's ascetic face.

"Should you think me greedy," she asked him, "if I wanted a bun? They have beautiful buns here!"

Buns! The simple word started latent memories of his childhood. Jenny was only a child, after all. Buns! He had forgotten what they were like. And as they looked at the piles of variegated cakes in the window, he said to her, "Which are buns, Jenny? I should like to have one, too."

"I am almost afraid of you," she said. "You must despise me so. Are you so good that you deny yourself all the vanity and pleasure that most people love? It is wonderful not to know what buns are! The round, brown, shiny cakes, with little raisins in them, are buns."

So he bought two beautiful buns, and they sat together in the shop, eating them. Jenny bit hers rather diffidently, but was reassured when he said that they must have buns very often in the cottage. Yes! he, the famous toper and gourmet of St. James's, relished this homely fare, as it passed through the insensible lips of his mask to his palate. He seemed to rise, from the consumption of his bun, a better man.

But there was no time to lose now. It was already past two o'clock. So he got a chaise from the inn opposite the pastry shop, and they were swiftly driven to Doctors' Commons. There he purchased a special license. When the clerk asked him to write his name upon it, he hesitated. What name should he assume? Under a mask he had wooed this girl, under an unreal name he must make her his bride. He loathed himself for a trickster. He had vilely stolen from her the love she would not give him. Even now, should he not confess himself the man whose face had frightened her, and go his way? And yet, surely, it was not just that he, whose soul was transfigured, should bear his old name. Surely George Hell was dead, and his name had died with him. So he dipped a pen in the ink and wrote "George Heaven," for want of a better name. And Jenny wrote "Jenny Mere" beneath it.

An hour later they were married according to the simple rites of a dear little registry office in Covent Garden.

And in the cool evening they went home.

In the cottage that had been the woodman's they had a wonderful honeymoon. No king and queen in any palace of gold were happier than they. For them their tiny cottage was a palace, and the flowers that filled the garden were their couriers. Long and careless and full of kisses were the days of their reign.

Sometimes, indeed, strange dreams troubled Lord George's sleep. Once he dreamt that he stood knocking and knocking at the great door of a castle. It was a bitter night. The frost enveloped him. No one came. Presently he heard a footstep in the hall beyond, and a pair of frightened eyes peered at him through the grill. Jenny was scanning his face. She would not open to him. With tears and wild words he beseeched her, but she would not open to him. Then, very stealthily, he crept round the castle and found a small casement in the wall. It was open. He climbed swiftly, quietly through it. In the darkness of the room some one ran to him and kissed him gladly. It was Jenny. With a cry of joy and shame he awoke. By his side lay Jenny, sleeping like a little child.

After all, what was a dream to him? It could not mar the reality of his daily happiness. He cherished his true penitence for the evil he had done in the past. The past! That was indeed the only unreal thing that lingered in his life. Every day its substance dwindled, grew fainter yet, as he lived his rustic honeymoon. Had he not utterly put it from him? Had he not, a few hours after his marriage, written to his lawyer, declaring solemnly that he, Lord George Hell, had forsworn the world, that he was where no man would find him, that he desired all his worldly goods to be distributed, thus and thus, among these and those of his companions? By this testament he had verily atoned for the wrong he had done, had made himself dead indeed to the world.

No address had he written upon this document. Though its injunctions were final and binding, it could betray no clue of his hiding place. For the rest, no one would care to seek him out. He, who had done no good to human creature, would pass unmourned out of memory. The clubs, doubtless, would laugh and puzzle over his strange recantations, envious of whomever he enriched. They would say 'twas a good riddance of a rogue and soon forget him. But she, whose prime patron he had been, who had loved him in her vile fashion, La Gambogi, would she forget him easily, like the rest? As the sweet days went by, her specter, also, grew fainter and less formidable. She knew his mask indeed, but how should she find him in the cottage near Kensington? *Devia dulcedo latebrarum!* He was safe hidden with his bride. As for the Italian, she might search and search—or had forgotten him, in the arms of another lover.

Yes! Few and faint became the blemishes of his honeymoon. At first, he had felt that his waxen mask, though it had been the means of his happiness, was rather a barrier 'twixt him and his bride. Though it was sweet to kiss her through it, to look at her through it with loving eyes, yet there were times when it incommoded him with its mockery. Could he but put it from him! yet, that, of course, could not be. He must wear it all his life. And so, as days went by he grew reconciled to his mask. No longer did he feel it jarring on his face. It seemed to become an integral part of him, and, for all its rigid material, it did forsooth express the one emotion that filled him, true love. The face, for whose sake Jenny gave him her heart, could not but be dear to this George Heaven, also.

Every day chastened him with its joy. They lived a very simple life, he and Jenny. They rose betimes, like the birds, for whose goodness they both had so sincere a love. Bread and honey and little strawberries were their morning fare, and in the evening they had seed cake and dewberry wine. Jenny herself made the wine and her husband drank it, in strict moderation, never more than two glasses. He thought it tasted far better than the Regent's cherry brandy, or the Tokay at Brooks's. Of these treasured topes he had, indeed, nearly forgotten the taste. The wine made from wild berries by his little bride was august enough for his palate. Sometimes, after they had dined thus, he would play the flute to her upon the moonlit lawn, or tell her of the great daisy chain he was going to make for her on the morrow, or sit silently by her side, listening to the nightingale, till bedtime. So admirably simple were their days.

One morning, as he was helping Jenny to water the flowers, he said to her suddenly, "Sweetheart, we had forgotten!"

"What was there we should forget?" asked Jenny, looking up from her task.

"'Tis the mensiversary of our wedding," her husband answered gravely. "We must not let it pass without some celebration."

"No, indeed," she said, "we must not. What shall we do?"

Between them they decided upon an unusual feast. They would go into the village and buy a bag of beautiful buns and eat them in the afternoon. So soon, then, as all the flowers were watered, they set forth to Herbert's shop, bought the buns and returned home in very high spirits, George bearing a paper bag that held no less than twelve of the wholesome delicacies. Under the plane tree on the lawn Jenny sat her down, and George stretched himself at her feet. They were loth to enjoy their feast too soon. They dallied in childish anticipation. On the little rustic table Jenny built up the buns, one above the other, till they looked like a tall pagoda. When, very gingerly, she had crowned the structure with the twelfth bun, her husband looking on with admiration, she clapped her hands and danced about it. She laughed so loudly (for, though she was only sixteen years old, she had a great sense of humor), that the table shook, and alas! the pagoda tottered and fell to the lawn. Swift as a kitten, Jenny chased the buns, as they rolled, hither and thither, over the grass, catching them deftly with her hand. Then she came back, flushed and merry under her tumbled hair, with her arm full of buns. She began to put them back in the paper bag.

"Dear husband," she said, looking down to him, "why do not you smile too at my folly? Your grave face rebukes me. Smile, or I shall think I vex you. Please smile a little."

But the mask could not smile, of course. It was made for a mirror of true love, and it was grave and immobile. "I am very much amused, dear," he said, "at the fall of the buns, but my lips will not curve to a smile. Love of you has bound them in spell."

"But I can laugh, though I love you. I do not understand."

And she wondered. He took her hand in his and stroked it gently, wishing it were possible to smile. Some day, perhaps, she would tire of this monotonous gravity, this rigid sweetness. It was not strange that she should long for a little facile expression. They sat silently.

"Jenny, what is it?" he whispered suddenly. For Jenny, with wide-open eyes, was gazing over his head, across the lawn. "Why do you look frightened?"

"There is a strange woman smiling at me across the palings," she said. "I do not know her."

Her husband's heart sank. Somehow, he dared not turn his head to the intruder. He dreaded who she might be.

"She is nodding to me," said Jenny. "I think she is foreign, for she has an evil face."

"Do not notice her," he whispered. "Does she look evil?"

"Very evil and very dark. She has a pink parasol. Her teeth are like ivory."

"Do not notice her. Think! It is the mensiversary of our wedding, dear!"

"I wish she would not smile at me. Her eyes are like bright blots of ink."

"Let us eat our beautiful buns!"

"Oh, she is coming in!" George heard the latch of the gate jar. "Forbid her to come in!" whispered Jenny, "I am afraid!" He heard the jar of heels on the gravel path. Yet he dared not turn. Only he clasped Jenny's hand more tightly, as he waited for the voice. It was La Gambogi's.

"Pray, pray, pardon me! I could not mistake the back of so old a friend."

With the courage of despair, George turned and faced the woman.

"Even," she smiled, "though his face has changed marvelously."

"Madam," he said, rising to his full height and stepping between her and his bride, "begone, I command you, from the garden. I do not see what good is to be served by the renewal of our acquaintance."

"Acquaintance!" murmured La Gambogi, with an arch of her beetle-brows. "Surely we were friends, rather, nor is my esteem for you so dead that I would crave estrangement."

"Madam," rejoined Lord George, with a tremor in his voice, "you see me happy, living very peacefully with my bride—"

"To whom, I beseech you, old friend, present me."

"I would not," he said hotly, "desecrate her sweet name by speaking it with so infamous a name as yours."

"Your choler hurts me, old friend," said La Gambogi, sinking composedly upon the garden seat and smoothing the silk of her skirts.

"Jenny," said George, "then do you retire, pending this lady's departure, to the cottage." But Jenny clung to his arm. "I were less frightened at your side," she whispered. "Do not send me away!"

"Suffer her pretty presence," said La Gambogi. "Indeed I am come this long way from the heart of the town, that I may see her, no less than you, George. My wish is only to befriend her. Why should she not set you a mannerly example, giving me welcome? Come and sit by me, little bride, for I have things to tell you. Though you reject my friendship, give me, at least, the slight courtesy of audience. I will not detain you overlong, will be gone very soon. Are you expecting guests, George? *On dirait une masque champêtre!*" She eyed the couple critically. "Your wife's mask," she said, "is even better than yours."

"What does she mean?" whispered Jenny. "Oh, send her away!"

"Serpent," was all George could say, "crawl from our Eden, ere you poison with your venom its fairest denizen."

La Gambogi rose. "Even *my* pride," she cried passionately, "knows certain bounds. I have been forebearing, but even in my zeal for friendship I will not be called 'serpent.' I will indeed begone from this rude place. Yet, ere I go, there is a boon I will deign to beg. Show me, oh show me but once again, the dear face I have so often caressed, the lips that were dear to me!"

George started back.

"What does she mean?" whispered Jenny.

"In memory of our old friendship," continued La Gambogi, "grant me this piteous favor. Show me your own face but for one instant, and I vow I will never again remind you that I live. Intercede for me, little bride. Bid him unmask for me. You have more authority over him than I. Doff his mask with your own uxorious fingers."

"What does she mean?" was the refrain of poor Jenny.

"If," said George, gazing sternly at his traitress, "you do not go now, of your own will, I must drive you, man though I am, violently from the garden."

"Doff your mask and I am gone."

George made a step of menace towards her.

"False saint!" she shrieked, "then *I* will unmask you."

Like a panther she sprang upon him and clawed at his waxen cheeks. Jenny fell back, mute with terror. Vainly did George try to free himself from the hideous assailant, who writhed round and round him, clawing, clawing at what Jenny fancied to be his face. With a wild cry, Jenny fell upon the furious creature and tried, with all her childish strength, to release her dear one. The combatives swayed to and fro, a revulsive trinity. There was a loud pop, as though some great cork had been withdrawn, and La Gambogi recoiled. She had torn away the mask. It lay before her upon the lawn, upturned to the sky.

George stood motionless. La Gambogi stared up into his face, and her dark flush died swiftly away. For there, staring back at her, was the man she had unmasked, but, lo! his face was even as his mask had been. Line for line, feature for feature, it was the same. 'Twas a saint's face.

"Madam," he said, in the calm voice of despair, "your cheek may well blanch, when you regard the ruin you have brought upon me. Nevertheless do I pardon you. The gods have avenged, through you, the imposture I wrought upon one who was dear to me. For that unpardonable sin I am punished. As for my poor bride, whose love I stole by the means of that waxen semblance, of her I cannot ask pardon. Ah, Jenny, Jenny, do not look at me. Turn your eyes from the foul reality that I dissembled." He shuddered and hid his face in his hands. "Do not look at me. I will go from the garden. Nor will I ever curse you with the odious spectacle of my face. Forget me, forget me."

But, as he turned to go, Jenny laid her hands upon his wrists and besought him that he would look at her. "For indeed," she said, "I am bewildered by your strange words. Why did you woo me under a mask? And why do you imagine I could love you less dearly, seeing your own face?"

He looked into her eyes. On their violet surface he saw the tiny reflection of his own face. He was filled with joy and wonder.

"Surely," said Jenny, "your face is even dearer to me, even fairer, than the semblance that hid it and deceived me. I am not angry. 'Twas well that you veiled from me the full glory of your face, for indeed I was not worthy to behold it too soon. But I am your wife now. Let me look always at your own face. Let the time of my probation be over. Kiss me with your own lips."

So he took her in his arms, as though she had been a little child, and kissed her with his own lips. She put her arms round his neck, and he was happier than he had ever been. They were alone in the garden now. Nor lay the mask any longer upon the lawn, for the sun had melted it.

FOR DISCUSSION

1. "The Happy Hypocrite" is a short story that has elements of fable in it. Beerbohm carefully includes some fabulous details to provide an appropriate background for the strange plot. How do the Dwarf and his actions and the mask of Apollo each contribute to this fablelike atmosphere?

2. In order to get what he wanted, Lord George acted deceitfully, and through this deceit, he becomes good. This seems immoral; yet the result is a true morality. Is this contradictory, or even impossible? Whatever your answer, explain clearly the reasoning that led to it.

3. Lord George's repentance is not merely a matter of saying, "I'm sorry." What actions does he take to prove his repentance? Does this have anything to do with his final transformation?

4. In one word, what is Lord George's road to heaven? Is this perhaps the only road to heaven? Explain.

INTRODUCTION

If actions are important to our getting to heaven or hell, what part does intent play? In "The Happy Hypocrite" Beerbohm seemed to suggest that both intent and action are necessary. In this narrative poem, John Davidson insists that intent is all-important. Although the ballad form is not the ideal vehicle for conveying a value judgment, Davidson succeeds in his purpose. And he does so without sacrificing the major characteristics of the ballad: the near-melodramatic sentiment, the personification, the perfidious treachery, and the triumphant ending. The young woman in this poem has a task equally as difficult as the poet's, and she too succeeds. Deliberately she sets forth on the road to hell, but heaven is her destination.

A Ballad of Hell

John Davidson

"A letter from my love today!
　　Oh, unexpected, dear appeal!"
She struck a happy tear away
　　And broke the crimson seal.

"My love, there is no help on earth,　　　　　5
　　No help in heaven; the dead man's bell
Must toll our wedding; our first hearth
　　Must be the well-paved floor of hell."

The color died from out her face,
　　Her eyes like ghostly candles shone;　　　10
She cast dread looks about the place,
　　Then clenched her teeth, and read right on.

"I may not pass the prison door;
   Here must I rot from day to day,
Unless I wed whom I abhor,
   My cousin, Blanche of Valencay.   15

"At midnight with my dagger keen
   I'll take my life; it must be so.
Meet me in hell tonight, my queen,
   For weal and woe."   20

She laughed although her face was wan,
   She girded on her golden belt,
She took her jewelled ivory fan,
   And at her glowing missal knelt.

Then rose, "And am I mad?" she said,   25
   She broke her fan, her belt untied;
With leather girt herself instead,
   And stuck a dagger at her side.

She waited, shuddering in her room,
   Till sleep had fallen on all the house.   30
She never flinched; she faced her doom:
   They two must sin to keep their vows.

Then out into the night she went
   And stooping, crept by hedge and tree;
Her rose bush flung a snare of scent,   35
   And caught a happy memory.

She fell, and lay a minute's space;
   She tore the sward in her distress;
The dewy grass refreshed her face;
   She rose and ran with lifted dress.   40

She started like a morn-caught ghost
   Once when the moon came out and stood
To watch; the naked road she crossed,
   And dived into the murmuring wood.

The branches snatched her streaming cloak;   45
    A live thing shrieked; she made no stay!
She hurried to the trysting-oak—
    Right well she knew the way.

Without a pause she bared her breast
    And drove her dagger home and fell,   50
And lay like one that takes her rest,
    And died and wakened up in hell.

She bathed her spirit in the flame,
    And near the center took her post;
From all sides to her ears there came   55
    The dreary anguish of the lost.

The devil started at her side,
    Comely, and tall, and black as jet.
"I am young Malespina's bride;
    Has he come hither yet?"   60

"My poppet, welcome to your bed."
    "Is Malespina here?"
"Not he!   Tomorrow he must wed
    His cousin Blanche, my dear!"

"You lie; he died with me tonight."   65
    "Not he!   It was a plot."   "You lie."
"My dear, I never lie outright."
    "We died at midnight, he and I."

The devil went.   Without a groan
    She, gathered up in one fierce prayer,   70
Took root in hell's midst all alone,
    And waited for him there.

She dared to make herself at home,
    Amidst the wail, the uneasy stir.

The blood-stained flame that filled the dome,   75
    Scentless and silent, shrouded her.

How long she stayed I cannot tell;
    But when she felt his perfidy,
She marched across the floor of hell;
    And all the damned stood up to see.   80

The devil stopped her at the brink;
    She shook him off; she cried, "Away!"
"My dear, you have gone mad, I think."
    "I was betrayed: I will not stay."

Across the weltering deep she ran—   85
    A stranger thing was never seen:
The damned stood silent to a man;
    They saw the great gulf set between.

To her it seemed a meadow fair;
    And flowers sprang up about her feet;   90
She entered heaven; she climbed the stair;
    And knelt down at the mercy seat.

Seraphs and saints with one great voice
    Welcomed that soul that knew not fear;
Amazed to find it could rejoice,   95
    Hell raised a hoarse half-human cheer.

FOR DISCUSSION

1. The fifth stanza of this poem spells out the infernal bargain
    rather clearly. Why will the two participants meet in hell?
2. "My dear, I never lie outright," says the devil. What does
    he mean? How is this devil different from "typical" devils?
3. The young heroine wears a kind of invisible, but magic, robe.
    What kind of magic robe is it, and how does it affect the
    noise and flames of hell?

4. A great gulf separates heaven from hell; yet as the betrayed bride flees, the ground beneath her feet is fair and firm. Why is she permitted to make the perilous journey that "none can make"? What is her road to heaven?
5. The last two lines both startle and provoke. They startle because they are unexpected. They provoke because they give us new insight into the character of the damned. Explain these statements.

Bargains with the Devil

CHAPTER THREE

To dream is to move beyond our limitations. To dream is to have money, fame, power—anything we wish. Unfortunately dreams end, and when we wake, like Caliban, we "cry to dream again."

A lucky few grasp their dreams and force them to come alive in the real world. The rest of us go on dreaming. But from time to time one of us will say: "Satan, if you ‚are listening, take my soul and give me now my dream."

[The devil likes bargains, and he is liberal. He yields gold freely, provides power, offers fame, and all have but one price tag— a human soul. For the person who would rule the world, it is not an unreasonable price; for the nonbeliever, there is really no cost at all.] For these people, the price is right, the bargain is made, the dream comes true—until it's time to pay.

This trade in souls is no modern innovation. It is too much a part of human nature to belong to one age. It began with the creation of humankind, and Eve was the first to enter into an infernal bargain. To her, the serpent offered the pure and perfect knowledge of the Almighty God. How dazzling a dream! How could one resist such an offer? The price, that first time, was immortality. For herself and for her descendants, Eve accepted mortality. And this acceptance led naturally to curiosity and dread of an afterworld. For without death, there would be no life after death as we envision it now. The price was steep, but no more so than in Satan's usual bargain.

Eve's questionable fortune did little to discourage people from trying to buy their dreams. A bargain with the devil is still attractive. The devil is evil, and to worst him in a trade is exemplary. The devil is sly, and his craft challenges ours. The devil is grotesque, and the grotesque is amusing.

Traffic with the devil is never far from our consciousness. Our vocabulary betrays us. Angrily we advise an enemy to "go to the devil!" Less frequently—but still often enough—we say: "I'd sell my soul to the devil if I could have that new car (or diamond ring or political office)." We say it casually, not really meaning it, using the allusion to describe the greatness of our desire. There are other phrases: "Give the devil his due"; "The Devil takes care of his own"; and "Speak of the devil." They all have one thing in common: they allow us to rationalize our hostilities and justify our actions.

Thus the devil makes a nice scapegoat. It is easier to say that the child has a devil in him than to correct his behavior. It was more expedient, three centuries ago, for people to accuse a woman of being a witch and working with the devil, than to admit that she might be superior to or be more knowledgeable than they. It was easier a few decades ago to label our enemies "foreign devils" than to consider soberly the causes of war and the means to peaceful alternatives. It is easier today, as we recognize a possibly innate tendency toward evil, to turn to demonism—devil-worship—than to wrestle, rationally and persistently, with the evil within ourselves.

Deals with the devil have been around for thousands of years, but they were given a clear-cut form only with the origin of the Faust story. It all began in 1525 when Magister Georgius Sabellicus Faustus, Junior was carried off by the devil. Faustus's contemporaries considered him a mountebank and a fool, or simply a charlatan. Philipp Begardi in 1539 considered him one of the "wicked, cheating, useless and unlearned doctors." Manlius, a few years later, described him as "a disgraceful beast and sewer of many devils." And Johann Weiher in 1563 noted that Faustus had studied magic and had practised "this beautiful art shamelessly up and down Germany, with unspeakable deceit, many lies and with great effect."

Notice the development of the legend. Faustus started off as a fool, went on to become an illiterate cheat, then a beast, and finally a magician in league with the devil. The true roots of the legend lie in the far distant past; certainly Faustus was not the first to strike up a bargain with Satan. But the time was ripe in the sixteenth century for the story of Faustus to become popular. It captured the imaginations of commoner and intellectual. The first Faust book, *Historia von D. Johann Fausten,* was published in 1587 by Johann Spies at Frankfurt. It was an immediate best seller; additional printings and revised editions were in demand for the next 150 years.

The Faust legend—the story of a man who sold his soul to the devil for power, wealth, and knowledge—had solidified. What had been oral tradition became now a literary source. It could be versified, dramatized, or narrated. It could be changed. It could—and did—become a vehicle for a dozen opposing philosophies.

Before we go on to some examples of the Faust legend, one more element should be considered. In a deal with the devil, we believe it is possible for the human being to win. There's something right and splendid and daring about challenging him. Anyway, no one really expects to pay the devil off. All challengers believe, deep down, that somehow, someway, they'll find a loophole or prove craftier than Satan himself. They rationalize, thinking that there is no hell, or that the Blessed Virgin can be appealed to, or that some decent, fearless fellow human will in the end assist. There is no fun in a battle that can have only one end, but there is endless fun in a battle that one might win against superior forces. The greater the odds, the greater the reward.

INTRODUCTION

This ballad is one of the first literary results of the Faust legend. It appeared in around 1588. Its complete title is "The Judgment of God showed upon one John Faustus, Doctor in Divinity," and like most ballads of the time, it was meant to be sung. It describes briefly but effectively the complete Faustus story.

Ballad of Faustus

Anonymous

All Christian men, give ear a while to me,
How I am plunged in pain, but cannot die.
I lived a life the like did none before,
Forsaking Christ; and I am damned therefore.

At Wittenberg, a town in Germany,   5
There was I born and bred of good degree;
Of honest stock, which afterwards I shamed;
Accurst therefore, for Faustus was I named.

In learning, lo, my uncle brought up me,
And made me Doctor in Divinity;   10
And, when he died, he left me all his wealth
Whose cursed gold did hinder my soul's health.

Then did I shun the holy Bible-book,
Nor on God's word would ever after look;
But studied accursed conjuration,   15
Which was the cause of my utter damnation.

The devil in friar's weeds appeared to me,
And straight to my request he did agree,
That I might have all things at my desire:
I gave him soul and body for his hire.   20

Twice did I make my tender flesh to bleed,
Twice with my blood I wrote the devil's deed,
Twice wretchedly I soul and body sold,
To live in pleasure and do what things I would.

For four and twenty years this bond was made,   25
And at the length my soul was truly paid.
Time ran away, and yet I never thought
How dear my soul our Savior Christ had bought.

Would I had first been made a beast by kind!
Then had not I so vainly set my mind;   30
Or would, when reason first began to bloom,
Some darksome den had been my deadly tomb!

Woe to the day of my nativity!
Woe to the time that once did foster me!
And woe unto the hand that sealed the bill!   35
Woe to myself, the cause of all my ill!

The time I passed away, with much delight,
Among princes, peers, and many a worthy knight:
I wrought such wonders by my magic skill
That all the world may talk of Faustus still.   40

The devil he carried me up into the sky,
Where I did see how all the world did lie;
I went about the world in eight days' space
And then returned unto my native place.

What pleasure I did wish to please my mind   45
He did perform, as bond and seal did bind;
The secrets of the stars and planets told,
Of earth and sea, with wonders manifold.

When four and twenty years were almost run,
I thought of all things that were past and done: 50
How that the devil would soon claim his right
And carry me to everlasting night.

Then all too late I cursed my wicked deed,
The dread whereof doth make my heart to bleed;
All days and hours I mourned wondrous sore,   55
Repenting me of all things done before.

I then did wish both sun and moon to stay,
All times and seasons never to decay.
Then had my time near come to dated end,
Nor soul and body down to hell descend.   60

At last, when I had but one hour to come,
I turned my glass, for my last hour to run,
And called in learned men to comfort me;
But faith was gone, and none could comfort me.

By twelve o'clock my glass was almost out: 65
My grieved conscience then began to doubt.
I wished the students stay in chamber by;
But, as they stayed, they heard a dreadful cry.

Then presently they came into the hall,
Whereas my brains were cast against the wall;   70
Both arms and legs in pieces torn, they see,
My bowels gone: this was an end of me.

You conjurors and damned witches all,
Example take by my unhappy fall.
Give not your souls and bodies unto hell,   75
See that the smallest hair you do not sell.

But hope that Christ his kingdom you may gain,
Where you shall never fear such mortal pain;
Forsake the devil and all his crafty ways,
Embrace true faith that never more decays.   80

FOR DISCUSSION

1. This is one of the earliest versions of the Faust bargain. Using
   the information given in the ballad, draw up a contract between Faustus and the devil. Include what Faustus is to pay,
   what he is to receive, and the length of time involved.

2. Explain the possible significance of the ideas expressed in the following quotations; note especially the italicized words.
   a. "The devil *in friar's weeds* appeared to me"
   b. "*Twice* with my *blood* I wrote the devil's deed"
3. Let your imagination run free. If the devil approached you and offered you anything you wanted in exchange for your soul, what would you ask for? Project yourself twenty-four years into the future. How would you feel at the end of the twenty-four years? Would the payment you had received be worth an eternity of damnation?

INTRODUCTION

Tradition holds that men from New Hampshire are stern and silent, and incredibly shrewd in driving a bargain. As far as being silent was concerned, Daniel Webster was an exception. By the time he was eighteen years old he was delivering resounding speeches to his fellow citizens. His study in law and his practice before juries rapidly contributed to his oratorical skill.

When Jabez Stone sought a lawyer to meet the devil on legal grounds, he naturally chose the renowned Webster. The devil is silver-tongued, shrewd, and absolutely ruthless, but he didn't know the meaning of a hard bargain until he came up against a couple of New Hampshire men.

The Devil and Daniel Webster

Stephen Vincent Benét

It's a story they all tell in the border country, where Massachusetts joins Vermont and New Hampshire.

Yes, Dan'l Webster's dead—or, at least, they buried him. But every time there's a thunderstorm around Marshfield, they say you can hear his rolling voice in the hollows of the sky. And they say that if you go to his grave and speak loud and clear, "Dan'l Webster —Dan'l Webster!" the ground'll begin to shiver and the trees begin to shake. And after a while you'll hear a deep voice saying, "Neighbor, how stands the Union?" Then you better answer the Union stands as she stood, rock-bottomed and copper-sheathed, one and indivisible, or he's liable to rear right out of the ground. At least, that's what I was told when I was a youngster.

You see, for a while, he was the biggest man in the country. He never got to be President, but he was the biggest man. There were thousands that trusted in him right next to God Almighty, and they told stories about him and all the things that belonged to him that were like the stories of patriarchs and such. They said when he stood up to speak stars and stripes came right out in the sky, and once he spoke against a river and made it sink into the ground. They said when he walked the woods with his fishing rod, Killall, the trout would jump out of the streams right into his pockets, for they knew it was no use putting up a fight against him; and, when he argued a case, he could turn on the harps of the blessed and the shaking of the earth underground. That was the kind of man he was, and his big farm up at Marshfield was suitable to him. The chickens he raised were all white meat down through the drumsticks, the cows were tended like children, and the big ram he called Goliath had horns with a curl like a morning glory vine and could butt through an iron door. But Dan'l wasn't one of your gentlemen farmers; he knew all the ways of the land, and he'd be up by candle-light to see that the chores got done. A man with a mouth like a mastiff, a brow like a mountain, and eyes like burning anthracite—that was Dan'l Webster in his prime. And the biggest case he argued never got written down in the books, for he argued it against the devil, nip and tuck, and no holds barred. And this is the way I used to hear it told:

There was a man named Jabez Stone, lived at Cross Corners, New Hampshire. He wasn't a bad man to start with, but he was an unlucky man. If he planted corn, he got borers; if he planted potatoes, he got blight. He had good-enough land, but it didn't prosper him; he had a decent wife and children, but the more children he had, the less there was to feed them. If stones cropped up in his neighbor's field, boulders boiled up in his; if he had a horse with the spavins, he'd trade it for one with the staggers and give something extra. There's some folks bound to be like that, apparently. But one day Jabez Stone got sick of the whole business.

He'd been plowing that morning and he'd just broke the plowshare on a rock that he could have sworn hadn't been there yesterday. And, as he stood looking at the plowshare, the off horse began to cough—that ropy kind of cough that means sickness and horse doctors. There were two children down with the measles, his wife was ailing, and he had a whitlow on his thumb. It was about the last straw for Jabez Stone. "I vow," he said, and he looked around him kind of desperate—"I vow it's enough to make a man want to sell his soul to the devil! And I would, too, for two cents!"

Then he felt a kind of queerness come over him at having said what he'd said; though, naturally, being a New Hampshireman, he wouldn't take it back. But, all the same, when it got to be evening and, as far as he could see, no notice had been taken, he felt relieved in his mind, for he was a religious man. But notice is always taken, sooner or later, just like the Good Book says. And, sure enough, the next day, about suppertime, a soft-spoken, dark-dressed stranger drove up in a handsome buggy and asked for Jabez Stone.

Well, Jabez told his family it was a lawyer, come to see him about a legacy. But he knew who it was. He didn't like the looks of the stranger, nor the way he smiled with his teeth. They were white teeth, and plentiful—some say they were filed to a point, but I wouldn't vouch for that. And he didn't like it when the dog took one look at the stranger and ran away howling, with his tail between his legs. But having passed his word, more or less, he stuck to it, and they went out behind the barn and made their bargain. Jabez Stone had to prick his finger to sign, and the stranger lent him a silver pen. The wound healed clean, but it left a little white scar.

After that, all of a sudden, things began to pick up and prosper for Jabez Stone. His cows got fat and his horses sleek, his crops were the envy of the neighborhood, and lightning might strike all over the valley, but it wouldn't strike his barn. Pretty soon, he was one of the prosperous people of the county; they asked him to stand for selectman, and he stood for it; there began to be talk of running him for state senate. All in all, you might say the Stone family was as happy and contented as cats in a dairy. And so they were, except for Jabez Stone.

He'd been contented enough, the first few years. It's a great thing when bad luck turns; it drives most other things out of your head. True, every now and then, especially in rainy weather, the little white scar on his finger would give him a twinge. And once a year, punctual as clockwork, the stranger with the handsome buggy would come driving by. But the sixth year, the stranger lighted, and, after that, his peace was over for Jabez Stone.

The stranger came up through the lower field, switching his

boots with a cane—they were handsome black boots, but Jabez Stone never liked the look of them, particularly the toes. And, after he'd passed the time of day, he said, "Well, Mr. Stone, you're a hummer! It's a very pretty property you've got here, Mr. Stone."

"Well, some might favor it and others might not," said Jabez Stone, for he was a New Hampshireman.

"Oh, no need to decry your industry!" said the stranger, very easy, showing his teeth in a smile. "After all, we know what's been done, and it's been according to contract and specifications. So when—ahem—the mortgage falls due next year, you shouldn't have any regrets."

"Speaking of that mortgage, mister," said Jabez Stone, and he looked around for help to the earth and the sky, "I'm beginning to have one or two doubts about it."

"Doubts?" said the stranger, not quite so pleasantly.

"Why, yes," said Jabez Stone. "This being the U.S.A. and me always having been a religious man." He cleared his throat and got bolder. "Yes, sir," he said, "I'm beginning to have considerable doubts as to that mortgage holding in court."

"There's courts and courts," said the stranger, clicking his teeth. "Still, we might as well have a look at the original document." And he hauled out a big black pocketbook, full of papers. "Sherwin, Slater, Stevens, Stone," he muttered. "I, Jabez Stone, for a term of seven years—Oh, it's quite in order, I think."

But Jabez Stone wasn't listening, for he saw something else flutter out of the black pocketbook. It was something that looked like a moth, but it wasn't a moth. And as Jabez Stone stared at it, it seemed to speak to him in a small sort of piping voice, terrible small and thin, but terrible human.

"Neighbor Stone!" it squeaked. "Neighbor Stone! Help me! For God's sake, help me!"

But before Jabez Stone could stir hand or foot, the stranger whipped out a big bandanna handkerchief, caught the creature in it, just like a butterfly, and started tying up the ends of the bandanna.

"Sorry for the interruption," he said. "As I was saying—"

But Jabez Stone was shaking all over like a scared horse.

"That's Miser Stevens' voice!" he said, in a croak. "And you've got him in your handkerchief!"

The stranger looked a little embarrassed.

"Yes, I really should have transferred him to the collecting box," he said with a simper, "but there were some rather unusual specimens there and I didn't want them crowded. Well, well, these little contretemps will occur."

"I don't know what you mean by contertan," said Jabez Stone, "but that was Miser Stevens' voice! And he ain't dead! You can't tell me he is! He was just as spry and mean as a woodchuck, Tuesday!"

"In the midst of life—" said the stranger, kind of pious. "Listen!" Then a bell began to toll in the valley, and Jabez Stone listened, with the sweat running down his face. For he knew it was tolled for Miser Stevens and that he was dead.

"These long-standing accounts," said the stranger with a sigh; "one really hates to close them. But business is business."

He still had the bandanna in his hand, and Jabez Stone felt sick as he saw the cloth struggle and flutter.

"Are they all as small as that?" he asked hoarsely.

"Small?" said the stranger. "Oh, I see what you mean. Why, they vary." He measured Jabez Stone with his eyes, and his teeth showed. "Don't worry, Mr. Stone," he said. "You'll go with a very good grade. I wouldn't trust you outside the collecting box. Now, a man like Dan'l Webster, of course—well, we'd have to build a special box for him, and even at that, I imagine the wing spread would astonish you. He'd certainly be a prize. I wish we could see our way clear to him. But, in your case, as I was saying—"

"Put that handkerchief away!" said Jabez Stone, and he began to beg and to pray. But the best he could get at the end was a three years' extension, with conditions.

But till you make a bargain like that, you've got no idea of how fast four years can run. By the last months of those years, Jabez Stone's known all over the state and there's talk of running him for governor—and it's dust and ashes in his mouth. For every day, when he gets up, he thinks, "There's one more night gone," and every night when he lies down, he thinks of the black pocketbook and the soul of Miser Stevens, and it makes him sick at heart. Till, finally, he can't bear it any longer, and, in the last days of the last year, he hitches up his horse and drives off to seek Dan'l Webster. For Dan'l Webster was born in New Hampshire, only a few miles

168

from Cross Corners, and it's well known that he has a particular soft spot for old neighbors.

It was early in the morning when he got to Marshfield, but Dan'l was up already, talking Latin to the farm hands and wrestling with the ram, Goliath, and trying out a new trotter and working up speeches to make against John C. Calhoun. But when he heard a New Hampshireman had come to see him, he dropped everything else he was doing, for that was Dan'l's way. He gave Jabez Stone a breakfast that five men couldn't eat, went into the living history of every man and woman in Cross Corners, and finally asked him how he could serve him.

Jabez Stone allowed that it was a kind of mortgage case.

"Well, I haven't pleaded a mortgage case in a long time, and I don't generally plead now, except before the Supreme Court," said Dan'l, "but if I can, I'll help you."

"Then I've got hope for the first time in ten years," said Jabez Stone, and told him the details.

Dan'l walked up and down as he listened, hands behind his back, now and then asking a question, now and then plunging his eyes at the floor, as if they'd bore through it like gimlets. When Jabez Stone had finished, Dan'l puffed out his cheeks and blew. Then he turned to Jabez Stone, and a smile broke over his face like the sunrise over Monadnock.

"You've certainly given yourself the devil's own row to hoe, Neighbor Stone," he said, "but I'll take your case."

"You'll take it?" said Jabez Stone, hardly daring to believe.

"Yes," said Dan'l Webster. "I've got about seventy-five other things to do and the Missouri Compromise to straighten out, but I'll take your case. For if two New Hampshiremen aren't a match for the devil, we might as well give the country back to the Indians."

Then he shook Jabez Stone by the hand and said, "Did you come down here in a hurry?"

"Well, I admit I made time," said Jabez Stone.

"You'll go back faster," said Dan'l Webster, and he told 'em to hitch up Constitution and Constellation to the carriage. They were matched grays with one white forefoot, and they stepped like greased lightning.

Well, I won't describe how excited and pleased the whole Stone family was to have the great Dan'l Webster for a guest, when they finally got there. Jabez Stone had lost his hat on the way, blown off when they overtook a wind, but he didn't take much account of that. But after supper he sent the family off to bed, for he had most particular business with Mr. Webster. Mrs. Stone wanted them to sit in the front parlor, but Dan'l Webster knew front parlors and said he preferred the kitchen. So it was there they sat, waiting for the stranger, with a jug on the table between them and a bright fire on the hearth—the stranger being scheduled to show up on the stroke of midnight, according to specification.

Well, most men wouldn't have asked for better company than Dan'l Webster and a jug. But with every tick of the clock Jabez Stone got sadder and sadder. His eyes roved round, and though he sampled the jug you could see he couldn't taste it. Finally, on the stroke of 11:30 he reached over and grabbed Dan'l Webster by the arm.

"Mr. Webster, Mr. Webster!" he said, and his voice was shaking with fear and a desperate courage. "For God's sake, Mr. Webster, harness your horses and get away from this place while you can!"

"You've brought me a long way, neighbor, to tell me you don't like my company," said Dan'l Webster, quite peaceable, pulling at the jug.

"Miserable wretch that I am!" groaned Jabez Stone. "I've brought you a devilish way, and now I see my folly. Let him take me if he wills. I don't hanker after it, I must say, but I can stand it. But you're the Union's stay and New Hampshire's pride! He mustn't get you, Mr. Webster! He mustn't get you!"

Dan'l Webster looked at the distracted man, all gray and shaking in the firelight, and laid a hand on his shoulder.

"I'm obliged to you, Neighbor Stone," he said gently. "It's kindly thought of. But there's a jug on the table and a case in hand. And I never left a jug or a case half-finished in my life."

And just at that moment there was a sharp rap on the door.

"Ah," said Dan'l Webster, very coolly, "I thought your clock was a trifle slow, Neighbor Stone." He stepped to the door and opened it. "Come in!" he said.

The stranger came in—very dark and tall he looked in the

firelight. He was carrying a box under his arm—a black, japanned box with little air holes in the lid. At the sight of the box, Jabez Stone gave a low cry and shrank into a corner of the room.

"Mr. Webster, I presume," said the stranger, very polite, but with his eyes glowing like a fox's deep in the woods.

"Attorney of record for Jabez Stone," said Dan'l Webster, but his eyes were glowing too. "Might I ask your name?"

"I've gone by a good many," said the stranger carelessly. "Perhaps Scratch will do for the evening. I'm often called that in these regions."

Then he sat down at the table and poured himself a drink from the jug. The liquor was cold in the jug, but it came steaming into the glass.

"And now," said the stranger, smiling and showing his teeth, "I shall call upon you, as a law-abiding citizen, to assist me in taking possession of my property."

Well, with that the argument began—and it went hot and heavy. At first, Jabez Stone had a flicker of hope, but when he saw Dan'l Webster being forced back at point after point, he just sat scrunched in his corner, with his eyes on that japanned box. For there wasn't any doubt as to the deed or the signature—that was the worst of it. Dan'l Webster twisted and turned and thumped his fist on the table, but he couldn't get away from that. He offered to compromise the case; the stranger wouldn't hear of it. He pointed out the property had increased in value, and state senators ought to be worth more; the stranger stuck to the letter of the law. He was a great lawyer, Dan'l Webster, but we know who's the King of Lawyers, as the Good Book tells us, and it seemed as if, for the first time, Dan'l Webster had met his match.

Finally, the stranger yawned a little. "Your spirited efforts on behalf of your client do you credit, Mr. Webster," he said, "but if you have no more arguments to adduce, I'm rather pressed for time—" and Jabez Stone shuddered.

Dan'l Webster's brow looked dark as a thundercloud. "Pressed or not, you shall not have this man!" he thundered. "Mr. Stone is an American citizen, and no American citizen may be forced into the service of a foreign prince. We fought England for that in '12 and we'll fight all hell for it again!"

"Foreign?" said the stranger. "And who calls me a foreigner?"

"Well, I never yet heard of the dev—of your claiming American citizenship," said Dan'l Webster with surprise.

"And who with better right?" said the stranger, with one of his terrible smiles. "When the first wrong was done to the first Indian, I was there. When the first slaver put out for the Congo, I stood on her deck. Am I not in your books and stories and beliefs, from the first settlements on? Am I not spoken of, still, in every church in New England? 'Tis true the North claims me for a Southerner, and the South for a Northerner, but I am neither. I am merely an honest American like yourself—and of the best descent—for, to tell the truth, Mr. Webster, though I don't like to boast of it, my name is older in this country than yours."

"Aha!" said Dan'l Webster, with the veins standing out in his forehead. "Then I stand on the Constitution! I demand a trial for my client!"

"The case is hardly one for an ordinary court," said the stranger, his eyes flickering. "And, indeed, the lateness of the hour—"

"Let it be any court you choose, so it is an American judge and an American jury!" said Dan'l Webster in his pride. "Let it be the quick or the dead; I'll abide the issue!"

"You have said it," said the stranger, and pointed his finger at the door. And with that, and all of a sudden, there was a rushing of wind outside and a noise of footsteps. They came, clear and distinct, through the night. And yet, they were not like the footsteps of living men.

"In God's name, who comes by so late?" cried Jabez Stone, in an ague of fear.

"The jury Mr. Webster demands," said the stranger, sipping at his boiling glass. "You must pardon the rough appearance of one or two; they will have come a long way."

And with that the fire burned blue and the door blew open and twelve men entered, one by one.

If Jabez Stone had been sick with terror before, he was blind with terror now. For there was Walter Butler, the loyalist, who spread fire and horror through the Mohawk Valley in the times of the Revolution; and there was Simon Girty, the renegade, who saw white men burned at the stake and whooped with the Indians to see them burn. His eyes were green, like a catamount's, and the stains on his hunting shirt did not come from the blood of the deer. King Philip was there, wild and proud as he had been in life, with the great gash in his head that gave him his death wound, and cruel Governor Dale, who broke men on the wheel. There was Morton of Merry Mount, who so vexed the Plymouth Colony, with his flushed, loose, handsome face and his hate of the godly. There was Teach, the bloody pirate, with his black beard curling on his breast. The Reverend John Smeet, with his strangler's hands and his Geneva gown, walked as daintily as he had to the gallows. The red print of the rope was still around his neck, but he carried a perfumed handkerchief in one hand. One and all, they came into the room with the fires of hell still upon them, and the stranger named their names and their deeds as they came, till the tale of twelve was told. Yet the stranger had told the truth—they had all played a part in America.

"Are you satisfied with the jury, Mr. Webster?" said the stranger mockingly, when they had taken their places.

The sweat stood upon Dan'l Webster's brow, but his voice was clear.

"Quite satisfied," he said. "Though I miss General Arnold from the company."

"Benedict Arnold is engaged upon other business," said the stranger, with a glower. "Ah, you asked for a justice, I believe."

He pointed his finger once more, and a tall man, soberly clad in Puritan garb, with the burning gaze of the fanatic, stalked into the room and took his judge's place.

"Justice Hathorne is a jurist of experience," said the stranger. "He presided at certain witch trials once held in Salem. There were others who repented of the business later, but not he."

"Repent of such notable wonders and undertakings?" said the stern old justice. "Nay, hang them—hang them all!" And he muttered to himself in a way that struck ice into the soul of Jabez Stone.

Then the trial began, and, as you might expect, it didn't look anyways good for the defense. And Jabez Stone didn't make much of a witness in his own behalf. He took one look at Simon Girty and screeched, and they had to put him back in his corner in a kind of swoon.

It didn't halt the trial, though; the trial went on, as trials do. Dan'l Webster had faced some hard juries and hanging judges in his time, but this was the hardest he'd ever faced, and he knew it. They sat there with a kind of glitter in their eyes, and the stranger's smooth voice went on and on. Every time he'd raise an objection, it'd be "Objection sustained," but whenever Dan'l objected, it'd be "Objection denied." Well, you couldn't expect fair play from a fellow like this Mr. Scratch.

It got to Dan'l in the end, and he began to heat, like iron in the forge. When he got up to speak he was going to flay that stranger with every trick known to the law, and the judge and jury too. He didn't care if it was contempt of court or what would happen to him for it. He didn't care any more what happened to Jabez Stone. He just got madder and madder, thinking of what he'd say. And yet, curiously enough, the more he thought about it, the less he was able to arrange his speech in his mind.

Till, finally, it was time for him to get up on his feet, and he did so, all ready to bust out with lightnings and denunciations. But before he started he looked over the judge and jury for a moment, such being his custom. And he noticed the glitter in their eyes was twice as strong as before, and they all leaned forward. Like hounds just before they get the fox, they looked, and the blue mist of evil in the room thickened as he watched them. Then he saw what he'd been about to do, and he wiped his forehead, as a man might who's just escaped falling into a pit in the dark.

For it was him they'd come for, not only Jabez Stone. He read it in the glitter of their eyes and in the way the stranger hid his mouth with one hand. And if he fought them with their own weapons, he'd fall into their power; he knew that, though he couldn't have told you how. It was his own anger and horror that burned in their eyes; and he'd have to wipe that out or the case was lost. He stood there for a moment, his black eyes burning like anthracite. And then he began to speak.

He started off in a low voice, though you could hear every word. They say he could call on the harps of the blessed when he chose. And this was just as simple and easy as a man could talk. But he didn't start out by condemning or reviling. He was talking about the things that make a country a country, and a man a man.

And he began with the simple things that everybody's known

and felt—the freshness of a fine morning when you're young, and the taste of food when you're hungry, and the new day that's every day when you're a child. He took them up and he turned them in his hands. They were good things for any man. But without freedom, they sickened. And when he talked of those enslaved, and the sorrows of slavery, his voice got like a big bell. He talked of the early days of America and the men who had made those days. It wasn't a spread-eagle speech, but he made you see it. He admitted all the wrong that had ever been done. But he showed how, out of the wrong and the right, the suffering and the starvations, something new had come. And everybody had played a part in it, even the traitors.

Then he turned to Jabez Stone and showed him as he was—an ordinary man who'd had hard luck and wanted to change it. And, because he'd wanted to change it, now he was going to be punished for all eternity. And yet there was good in Jabez Stone, and he showed that good. He was hard and mean, in some ways, but he was a man. There was sadness in being a man, but it was a proud thing too. And he showed what the pride of it was till you couldn't help feeling it. Yes, even in hell, if a man was a man, you'd know it. And he wasn't pleading for any one person any more, though his voice rang like an organ. He was telling the story and the failures and the endless journey of mankind. They got tricked and trapped and bamboozled, but it was a great journey. And no demon that was ever foaled could know the inwardness of it—it took a man to do that.

The fire began to die on the hearth and the wind before morning to blow. The light was getting gray in the room when Dan'l Webster finished. And his words came back at the end to New Hampshire ground, and the one spot of land that each man loves and clings to. He painted a picture of that, and to each one of that jury he spoke of things long forgotten. For his voice could search the heart, and that was his gift and his strength. And to one, his voice was like the forest and its secrecy, and to another like the sea and the storms of the sea; and one heard the cry of his lost nation in it, and another saw a little harmless scene he hadn't remembered for years. But each saw something. And when Dan'l Webster finished he didn't know whether or not he'd saved Jabez Stone. But he knew he'd done a miracle. For the glitter was gone from the eyes of judge and jury, and, for the moment, they were men again, and knew they were men.

"The defense rests," said Dan'l Webster, and stood there like a mountain. His ears were still ringing with his speech, and he didn't hear anything else till he heard Judge Hathorne say, "The jury will retire to consider its verdict."

Walter Butler rose in his place and his face had a dark, gay pride on it.

"The jury has considered its verdict," he said, and looked the stranger full in the eye. "We find for the defendant, Jabez Stone."

With that, the smile left the stranger's face, but Walter Butler did not flinch.

"Perhaps 'tis not strictly in accordance with the evidence," he said, "but even the damned may salute the eloquence of Mr. Webster."

With that, the long crow of a rooster split the gray morning sky, and judge and jury were gone from the room like a puff of smoke and as if they had never been there. The stranger turned to Dan'l Webster, smiling wryly. "Major Butler was always a bold man," he said. "I had not thought him quite so bold. Nevertheless, my congratulations, as between two gentlemen."

"I'll have that paper first, if you please," said Dan'l Webster, and he took it and tore it into four pieces. It was queerly warm to the touch. "And now," he said, "I'll have you!" and his hand came down like a bear trap on the stranger's arm. For he knew that once you bested anybody like Mr. Scratch in fair fight, his power on you was gone. And he could see that Mr. Scratch knew it too.

The stranger twisted and wriggled, but he couldn't get out of that grip. "Come, come, Mr. Webster," he said, smiling palely. "This sort of thing is ridic—ouch!—is ridiculous. If you're worried about the costs of the case, naturally, I'd be glad to pay—"

"And so you shall!" said Dan'l Webster, shaking him till his teeth rattled. "For you'll sit right down at that table and draw up a document, promising never to bother Jabez Stone nor his heirs or assigns nor any other New Hampshireman till doomsday! For any hades we want to raise in this state, we can raise ourselves, without assistance from strangers."

"Ouch!" said the stranger. "Ouch! Well, they never did run very big to the barrel, but—ouch!—I agree!"

So he sat down and drew up the document. But Dan'l Webster kept his hand on his coat collar all the time.

"And, now, may I go?" said the stranger, quite humble, when Dan'l'd seen the document was in proper and legal form.

"Go?" said Dan'l, giving him another shake. "I'm still trying to figure out what I'll do with you. For you've settled the costs of the case, but you haven't settled with me. I think I'll take you back to Marshfield," he said, kind of reflective. "I've got a ram there named Goliath that can butt through an iron door. I'd kind of like to turn you loose in his field and see what he'd do."

Well, with that the stranger began to beg and to plead. And he begged and he pled so humble that finally Dan'l, who was naturally kindhearted, agreed to let him go. The stranger seemed terrible grateful for that and said, just to show they were friends, he'd tell Dan'l's fortune before leaving. So Dan'l agreed to that, though he didn't take much stock in fortune-tellers ordinarily.

But, naturally, the stranger was a little different. Well, he pried and he peered at the lines in Dan'l's hands. And he told him one thing and another that was quite remarkable. But they were all in the past.

"Yes, all that's true, and it happened," said Dan'l Webster. "But what's to come in the future?"

The stranger grinned, kind of happily, and shook his head. "The future's not as you think it," he said. "It's dark. You have a great ambition, Mr. Webster."

"I have," said Dan'l firmly, for everybody knew he wanted to be President.

"It seems almost within your grasp," said the stranger, "but you will not attain it. Lesser men will be made President and you will be passed over."

"And, if I am, I'll still be Daniel Webster," said Dan'l. "Say on."

"You have two strong sons," said the stranger, shaking his head. "You look to found a line. But each will die in war and neither reach greatness."

"Live or die, they are still my sons," said Dan'l Webster. "Say on."

"You have made great speeches," said the stranger. "You will make more."

"Ah," said Dan'l Webster.

"But the last great speech you make will turn many of your own against you," said the stranger. "They will call you Ichabod; they will call you by other names. Even in New England some will say you have turned your coat and sold your country, and their voices will be loud against you till you die."

"So it is an honest speech, it does not matter what men say," said Dan'l Webster. Then he looked at the stranger and their glances locked.

"One question," he said. "I have fought for the Union all my life. Will I see that fight won against those who would tear it apart?"

"Not while you live," said the stranger, grimly, "but it will be won. And after you are dead, there are thousands who will fight for your cause, because of words that you spoke."

"Why, then, you long-barreled, slab-sided, lantern-jawed, fortune-telling note-shaver!" said Dan'l Webster, with a great roar of laughter, "be off with you to your own place before I put my mark on you! For, by the thirteen original colonies I'd go to the Pit itself to save the Union!"

And with that he drew back his foot for a kick that would have stunned a horse. It was only the tip of his shoe that caught the stranger, but he went flying out of the door with his collecting box under his arm.

"And now," said Dan'l Webster, seeing Jabez Stone beginning to rouse from his swoon, "let's see what's left in the jug, for it's dry work talking all night. I hope there's pie for breakfast, Neighbor Stone."

But they say that whenever the devil comes near Marshfield, even now, he gives it a wide berth. And he hasn't been seen in the state of New Hampshire from that day to this. I'm not talking about Massachusetts or Vermont.

FOR DISCUSSION

1. What are the terms of the contract as described in this story? Consider the payment to be received, the payment to be made, the length of the contract, and the reason for Jabez Stone's entering into the contract. Compare and contrast these terms with those accepted by Faustus.

2. Daniel Webster is a folk hero as well as a prominent figure in American history. Show how the author blended mythical anecdotes with historical facts. Why is the result more interesting than it would be if the story were built on mythical anecdotes only? On historical facts only?

3. According to Benét, how does the devil keep the souls he has already harvested? Is this method more or less horrible than the old stories of fire and brimstone? Why?

4. When Daniel Webster rose to make his concluding speech to the jury, what kind of speech was he planning to make? How would this have played into the devil's hands? What kind of speech did Webster finally make?

5. The author says of Daniel Webster, "For his voice could search the heart, and that was his gift and his strength." What exactly does this sentence mean in relation to the devil's jury?

INTRODUCTION

The devil is, above all, a gambler, though naturally he prefers to gamble on sure things. With his power and wiliness, he usually wins his bets. One day he met Sam Shay, a man who loved betting more than he loved anything else—except perhaps his sweetheart, Shannon. Shay could no more resist making three bets with the devil than he could resist breathing. At the end of their three bets Satan lost his temper, and even the devil can't afford that luxury. Shay's weapons were his good heart and his quick wit, but even they wouldn't have sufficed if the devil hadn't lost his cool.

Satan and Sam Shay

Robert Arthur

I am told that sin has somewhat declined since Satan met Sam Shay. I cannot vouch for this, but they say that production has definitely fallen off since that evening when Sam Shay won three wagers from the Devil. And this is the tale of it.

Sam Shay, you'll understand, was a bold rascal with Irish blood in his veins, though Yankee-born and bred. Six feet he stood, with wide shoulders and a grin and dark hair with a touch of curl to it. Looking at his hands and his brawn you'd hardly have guessed he'd never done an honest day's labor in his life. But it was true. For Sam was a gambling man, and since he was a boy, matching coppers or playing odd-and-even with his fellows, every penny passing through his fingers had been the fruit of wagering. And he was now approaching his thirtieth year.

Do not think to his discredit, however, that Sam Shay was a flinty-hearted professional, betting only on things that were sure or at odds much tipped in his favor. He bet not mathematically but by intuition, and the betting was as important as the winning. Were you to have given him the money he would not have taken it; there would have been no savor to it. He must win it by his wits to enjoy it, and he could find fun in losing a good wager, too.

So it was a sad thing to Sam that the one girl of his heart, Shannon Malloy, should be dead set against gambling. But the late Malloy had squandered all his earnings in just such divertissements as Sam Shay enjoyed, and the Widow Malloy had brought her daughter up most strictly to abjure men who loved the sound of rolling dice, the riffle of the cards or the quickening of the pulse that comes as the horses turn into the homestretch and stream for the finish line.

In the early days of their acquaintance, Shannon Malloy, who was small, with dark eyes that held a glow in their depths, had over-looked Sam's failing, feeling that Sam would mend his ways for love of her. And indeed Sam promised. But he could no more live without betting than he could without eating—less, for he could go a day without food undistressed, but in twenty years no sun had set without his making a wager of some kind, however small, just to keep his hand in.

Frequently, therefore, Sam Shay found himself in disgrace, while Shannon, more in sorrow than in anger, pleaded with him. And each time Sam once again promised to reform, knowing in his heart that once again he would fail. Inevitably, then, there came the time when Shannon, putting aside the veils that love cast upon her vision, saw with sad clarity that Sam Shay was Sam Shay and naught would alter him. She loved him, but her convictions were as adamant. So she gave him back the ring she had accepted from him when his resolves had been less tarnished.

"I'm sorry, Sam," she had said, this very evening, and her words rang knell-like in Sam's ears now as he strode homeward through the soft evening dusk that lay across the park. "I'm sorry," and her voice had broken. "But today I heard your name spoken. By some men. And they were saying you are a born gambler who could make three bets with Satan and win them all. And if that is true, I can't marry you. Not feeling as I do. Not until you change."

And Sam, knowing that only some force far stronger than himself could turn him from his wagering, took the ring and went with only one backward glance. That glance showed him Shannon Malloy weeping but resolute, and he was as proud of her resolution as disconsolate that she should feel so strongly about his little weakness.

The ring was in his pocket and his fingers touched it sadly as he walked. It was a circlet cold to the touch, a metal zero that summed the total of his chances for having Shannon Malloy to wife. The twilight lay upon the park, and it was queerly hushed, as if something was impending. But, lost in his thoughts, he strode along taking no notice.

It was as he came abreast an ancient oak that the shadow of the tree, athwart the sidewalk, with great unexpectedness solidified into a pillar of blackness church-steeple high, which condensed swiftly into a smallish individual with flowing white locks and a benign countenance.

The individual who had so unconventionally placed himself in Sam's path was clad in garments of sober cut, an old-fashioned cape slung over his shoulders and a soft dark hat upon his white hair. He smiled with innocent engagingness at Samuel Shay, and spoke in a voice both mild and friendly.

"Good evening, Sam," he said, as one might to an acquaintance not seen in a great while. "I'll bet you don't know who I am."

But Sam Shay, his right hand gripping the stout thorn stick he liked to carry about with him, was not to be trapped. He had seen the shadow of an oak tree change into a man, and this, to say the least, was unusual.

"Why," he proclaimed boldly, "I have a hundred dollars in my pocket, and I'll lay it against one that you are Satan."

Satan—for Sam's intuition had not failed him—let an expression of displeasure cross the benign countenance he had assumed for this visit. For he too had heard the report Shannon Malloy had quoted to Sam—that he could make three bets with Satan and win them all. And, his curiosity aroused, the Devil had come to test Sam's prowess, for he was fond of gambling, though a bad loser.

But the expression was gone in an instant and the gentle smile resumed its place. The old gentleman reached beneath his cloak and brought out a wallet which bulged pleasingly, although it was of a leather whose appearance Sam did not care for.

"That may be, Sam," Satan replied genially. "And if I am, I owe you a dollar. But I have another hundred here says you can't prove it."

And he waited, well pleased, for this was a wager that had stumped many eminent philosophers in centuries past. But Sam Shay was a man of action, not of words.

"Taken," he agreed at once, and raised his thorn stick above

182

his head. "I'll just bash you a time or two over the pate. If you're an honest citizen I'll take your wallet, and if you're Satan I'll win the wager. For you could not let a mortal man trounce you so and still look yourself in the eye—an accomplishment quite individually yours. So—"

And Sam brought the stick down in a whistling blow.

A sulphurous sheet of flame cracked out from the heart of the oak tree, and the thorn stick was riven into a thousand splinters that hissed away through the air. A strong pain shot up Sam's arm, a tingling, numbing sensation that extended to the shoulder. But, rubbing his wrist, he was well satisfied.

Not so Satan. In his anger the little old gentleman had shot upward until he loomed twelve feet high now, and looked far more terrifying than benign.

"You win, Sam Shay," Satan told him sourly. "But there's a third bet yet to come." Which Sam knew to be true, for on any such occasion as this when the Devil showed himself to a mortal, the unhappy man must win three wagers from him to go free. "And this time we'll increase the stakes. Your soul against the contents of this wallet that you can't win from me again."

Sam did not hesitate. For he must wager, whether he would or not.

"Taken," he answered. "But I must name the bet, since you named the others and it is my turn now."

Satan it was who hesitated, but right and logic were with Sam, so he nodded.

"Name it, then," he directed, and his voice was like grumbling thunder beyond the skyline.

"Why, as to that," Sam told him with an impudent grin, "I am betting that you do not intend for me to win this wager."

Hardly were the words out of his mouth before Satan, in uncontrolled rage, had shot up to a tremendous height, his black cloak flowing from him like night itself draping over the city. For Sam had caught him neatly. If he responded that he did intend for Sam to win, then Sam perforce must go free. And if he responded that he had not so intended, then Sam won anyway.

Glaring down from his great height, Satan directed an awful gaze upon Sam Shay.

"This is an ill night's work you have done!" he cried, in a voice that shook with rage, so that the skyscrapers nearby trembled a bit, and the next day's papers carried an item concerning a small earthquake. "Hear me well, Sam Shay! From this moment onward, never shall you win another wager! All the forces of hell will be marshalled to prevent you."

Then, while Sam still gaped upward in dismay, the great figure faded from sight. A vast blast of hot air fanned past Sam, singeing the leaves of the nearest trees. He heard a distant clanging sound, as of a metal gate closing. After that all was quiet as it had been before.

Sam Shay stood in thought for several minutes, and then realized he still was fingering the ring Shannon Malloy had returned to him. He laughed, in something of relief.

"Glory!" he said aloud. "I've been standing here dreaming, while my mind wandered. If I'm to have nightmares, I'd best have them in bed."

And he hurried homeward, stopping by the way only long enough to buy the next day's racing form.

By morning Sam had half forgotten his queer bemusement of the evening before. But Shannon had dismissed him and returned his ring he remembered all too well. The bit of gold seemed heavy in his pocket as the weight that lay on his heart, so that he set about choosing his wagers for the day's racing with a gloomy mind.

It was perhaps this gloom that made it harder than was customary for him to make a choice. Usually his intuition made quick decision. But today he labored long, and was only half satisfied when he had finished marking down his picks.

Then, having breakfasted, with Shannon Malloy's face coming betwixt him and his coffee, he rode out to the track. Today he desired action, crowds, noise, excitement to take his mind off Shannon's rejection of him. So that the pushing throngs about the mutuel windows, the crowd murmur that rose to a shrill ululation as the horses burst from the barrier, the heart-tightening sensation as they turned into the homestretch all fitted well into his mood.

And he was feeling better when, his tickets tucked inside his pocket, he stood with the rest and watched the leaders in the first swing 'round the turn. He was well pleased to note his choice to the fore by half a dozen lengths, when something happened. Perhaps the nag put its hoof into a pocket in the track. Perhaps it broke stride, or merely tired. At all events it faltered, slowed as though the Devil himself had it by the tail—now why had that precise comparison flashed across his mind then, Sam Shay wondered—and was beaten to the finish by a neck.

Sam tore up his tickets and scattered them to the breeze. He was not distressed. There were six races yet to come, and his pockets were well filled with money.

But when in the second his pick threw its jockey rounding the three-quarter pole and in the lead, and when in the third a saddle girth broke just as the jockey was lifting his mount for a winning surge, Sam Shay began to whistle a bit beneath his breath.

It was queer. It was decidedly queer, and he did not like it in the least. And when in the fourth, just as it was in the clear, his choice swerved and cut across the nag behind it, thus being disqualified, Sam's whistle grew more tuneless. He sniffed, and sniffed again. Yes, it was there—the faintest whiff of sulphur somewhere about. In a most meditative mood Sam purchased a single two-dollar ticket for the fifth.

The ticket, as he had been unhappily convinced would be the case, proved a poor investment, his horse throwing a shoe at the far turn and pulling up last, limping badly.

Sam's whistle dropped until it was quite inaudible. He made his way toward the paddock and stood close as they led the winded horses out. As his choice passed he sniffed, strongly. And this time there was the slightest touch of brimstone mixed with the smell of sulphur.

Walking with a slow pace that did not in any way reflect the churning of his thoughts, Sam Shay returned to the grandstand and in the minutes before the next race was run reflected fast and furiously. Already his pockets, so thickly lined but an hour before, were well-nigh empty. And apprehension was beginning to sit, a tiny cloud, on Sam's brow.

This time he bought no ticket. But he sought out an individual with whom he had had dealings, and stood beside him as the race was run. The ponies were streaming around the three-quarter pole and into the stretch, with forty lengths and half a dozen horses separating the first nag from the last, when Sam spoke suddenly.

"Ten dollars," said he to his acquaintance, "to a dime that Seven doesn't win."

The bookie gave him an odd glance. For Seven was the trailer, forty lengths behind and losing distance steadily. Any mortal eye could see she couldn't win, and it came to him Sam might be daft.

"Twenty dollars!" said Samuel Shay. "To a five-cent piece!"

They were odds not to be resisted, and the bookie nodded.

"Taken!" he agreed, and the words were scarce out of his mouth before Seven put on a burst of speed. She seemed to rise into the air with the very rapidity of her motion. Her legs churned. And she whisked forward so fast her astonished jockey was but an ace from being blown out of the saddle by the very rush of air. Closing the gap in a manner quite unbelievable, she came up to the leaders and, with a scant yard to the finish, shot ahead to win.

The crowd was too dazed even to roar. The judges gathered at once in frowning conference. But nothing amiss with Seven's equipment could be found—no electric batteries or other illegal contrivances—so at last her number was posted.

Sam Shay paid over the twenty dollars, while his acquaintance goggled at him. He would have asked questions, but Sam was in no mood for conversation. He moved away and sought a seat. There he pondered.

There could no longer be any doubt. His dream of the evening before had been no dream. It was Satan himself he had met face to face in the park, and Satan was having his vengeance for being bested. Sam could not call to mind the name of any other man in history who had outwitted the Devil without rueing it, and it was plain he was not to be the exception.

Wagering was Sam's life and livelihood, as Satan had well known. And if Sam was never to win another bet—he swallowed hard at the thought. Not only would he have lost Shannon Malloy for naught, but he would even be forced to the indignity of earning his living by the strength of his hands, he who had lived by his wits so pleasantly for so long.

It was a sobering reflection. But for the moment no helpful scheme would come. Just before the warning bell for the last race of the day, however, Sam rose with alacrity. He counted his money. Aside from car fare back to town, he had just fourteen dollars upon him. Seven two-dollar tickets—and in the last there was a field of seven!

Sam chuckled and bought seven tickets to win, one on each of the entries. Then, feeling somewhat set up, he found a position of vantage. Now, he said beneath his breath, let's see the Devil himself keep you from having a winning ticket this time, Samuel Shay! And complacently he watched his seven horses get off to a good start.

The race proceeded normally towards the half, and then to the three-quarters, with nothing untoward come about. Sam chuckled some more, for if he cashed a ticket on this race, then Satan had been bested again, and his curse on Sam's wagering broken.

But the chuckle came too soon. As the seven turned into the stretch, into a sky that had been cerulean blue leaped a storm cloud purple and black. From the cloud a bolt of lightning sped downward, in a blinding flash, to strike among the branches of an ancient elm which stood beside the grandstand near the finish line. A horrid thunderclap deafened the throng. The elm tottered. Then it toppled and fell across the track, so that the seven jockeys were just able to pull up their mounts in time to avoid plunging into it.

And as sudden as it had come, the storm cloud was gone.

But obviously there could be no winner of the last race. The perplexed and shaken stewards hurriedly declared it no race, and announced that all bets would be refunded. Sam received his money back—but that was not winning. And with the bills thrust into his coat he gloomily returned to his lodgings to devote more thought to this matter. For it was plain the Devil had meant what he had said—Sam would never win another wager. And with all the myriad hosts of hell arrayed against him, Sam did not see what he could do about it.

But the Shays were never a quitter stock. Though Beelzebub and all his myrmidons opposed him, Sam was of no mind to turn to honest labor without giving the Devil a run for his money. So in the days that followed, Sam, with dogged resolution, did not cease his efforts to make a wager he could win. And his endeavors were a source of some concern in hell.

It was on an afternoon two weeks perhaps after the fateful meeting between Satan and Sam Shay that the Devil recalled the matter to his mind and pressed a button summoning his chief lieutenant to make report. Whisking from his private laboratory, where he was engaged in a delicate experiment leading towards the creation of a brand new and improved form of sin, his head assistant covered seven million miles in no time at all and deposited himself in Satan's presence, still scorching from the speed at which he had come.

The Devil, seated behind a desk of basalt, frowned upon him.

"I wish," he stated, "to know if my orders concerning the mortal y-clept Sam Shay have been carried out."

"To the letter, Infernal Highness," his lieutenant replied, with a slight air of reserve.

"He has not won a wager since I pronounced my curse upon him?"

"Not of the most inconsequential kind."

"He is thoroughly miserable?"

"Completely so."

"He is in such despair he might even commit suicide, and so place himself in our hands?"

The other was silent. Satan's voice took on sharpness.

"He is *not* in despair?"

"He is in a very low frame of mind indeed," his chief assistant replied with reluctance. "But there is no notion of suicide in his mind. He is defiant. And troublesome in the extreme, I must add."

"Troublesome?" The three-million-bulb chandelier overhead rattled. "How can a mere mortal be troublesome to the hosts of hell? Kindly explain yourself."

The tips of his lieutenant's bat wings quivered with inward nervousness, and absently he plucked a loose scale from his chest. But summoning his resolution, he answered.

"He is a persistent mortal, this Sam Shay," he replied humbly. "Although your infernal curse has been passed upon him, he refuses to be convinced he cannot evade it. He is constantly scheming to get around the fiat by means of trickery and verbal quibbling. And I have had to assign a good many of my best and most resourceful workers to keep a twenty-four-hour watch on Sam Shay to see he does not succeed. Let me explain.

"Last week, having already tried some hundreds of wagers of various kinds, he offered to bet an acquaintance it would not rain before noon. The wager was the merest quibble of a bet, for it then lacked but ten seconds of the hour, the sun was shining in a cloudless sky, and in addition the Weather Bureau had actually predicted storm.

"Sam Shay, however, got his gamble accepted by promising to spend double his winnings, if he won, on strong drink for his companion. A completely specious wager if ever one was made. Nevertheless, had it not rained before the hour of noon, technically he would have been the winner of a bet, and so the letter of your hellish curse would have been violated.

"So, upon the notice of merest seconds, I had to call two hundred and eighty workers away from urgent duty in Proselytizing, to borrow on an instant's notice another hundred from Punishment, to take a score of my best laboratory technicians off Research, and rush them all to the spot. Between them they managed to divert a storm that was raging over Ohio and scheduled to cause a flood estimated to produce for us a job lot of a hundred and eighty souls, whisking it to cover New England within the time limit.

"But the affair caused widespread comment, threw us off schedule and has disrupted my entire force, due to the necessity for keeping a large emergency squad upon twenty-four-hour duty in constant readiness for any other such calls. And there have been dozens of them. Simply dozens!"

A drop of sweat rolled down the unhappy demon's brow, dissolving in steam.

"That's only a sample," he said earnestly. "This Sam Shay has scores of such tricks up his sleeves. Only yesterday he was attempting to win a wager at the race track, and his efforts kept us busy the entire afternoon. In the fifth race he made such a complicated series of bets as to the relative positions in which the various horses would finish that my most trusted aide completely lost track of them. He had to call on me personally at the last moment, and since one of the wagers was that the race itself wouldn't be finished, the only solution I could hit upon in time was to have all the horses finish in a dead heat, save for the one Sam Shay had bet upon to win.

"This one, in order to confound the fellow, I was forced to remove entirely from the race and set down in Australia, so that none of Shay's various stipulations concerning it could come true.

But the talk caused by a seven-horse dead heat, together with the complete disappearance of one of the beasts and its jockey, caused a considerable stir.

"Taken in conjunction with the storm I had to arrange, and a number of similar matters, it has started a religious revival. People are flocking into the churches, undoing some of our best work. So, Your Infernal Highness, if only we could overlook one or two of Sam Shay's more difficult wagers, it would make things much easier to—"

The crash of Satan's hooves upon the adamantine tiling cut him short.

"Never! I have put my curse upon this Shay! It must be carried out to the letter. 'Tend to it!"

"Yes, Prince of Evil," his head assistant squeaked, and being a prudent demon hurled himself away and across the seven million miles of space to his laboratory so swiftly that he struck with such force at the other end he was lame for a month. And never again did he dare mention the matter.

But of all this Sam Shay had no inkling. He was immersed in his own problems. Having failed in every wager he had made, however difficult to lose, he was in a depressed state of mind.

His resources were coming to an end. There were but a few dollars left in his pockets and none in his bank account. Shannon Malloy refused to see him. He had not won a wager since the night he had met the Devil, and he was so low in his mind that several times he had caught himself glancing through the Help Wanted sections of the papers.

Upon this particular day he was so sunk in despair that it was the middle of the afternoon, and he had not once tried the Devil's mettle to see if this time he could slip a winning wager past the demonic forces on watchful guard all about him. It was a day cut and tailored to his mood. The sky was lowering gray and rain whipped down out of the north as if each drop had personal anger against the earth upon which it struck. And Sam Shay sat in his room, staring out at the storm, as close to despair as it had ever been his misfortune to come.

At last he bestirred himself; it was not in the blood of a Shay to sit thus forever wrapped in gray gloom. He found his hat and ulster, and with heavy step made his way out and down the street to a cozy bar and grill where perhaps a cheery companion might lighten his mood.

Ensconced in a corner where a fireplace glowed he found Tim Malloy, who was by way of being Shannon's brother, a round, merry little man who was the merrier because a mug of dark stood upon the table before him. Tim Malloy greeted him with words of cheer and Sam sat himself down, answering as nearly in kind as he might. He ordered himself a mug of dark too, and made inquiry concerning Shannon.

"Why, as to that," Tim Malloy said, draining off half his mug, "sometimes of a night I hear her crying behind her locked door. And—" he drained off the rest of his dark—"she never did that before she gave you back your ring, Sam."

"Have another," Sam invited, feeling, suddenly, somewhat heartened. "Then mayhap she might take back the ring if I asked her, you think?" he asked, hope in his tone.

Tim Malloy accepted the dark, but after dipping into it shook his head, a moustache of foam on his lip.

"Never while you're a betting man, Sam, and that'll be forever," he said, "unless some wondrous force stronger than she is makes her do it. Not though she's unhappy the rest of her life from sending you away."

Sam sighed.

"Would it make any difference if she knew I lost all the wagers I make now?" he asked.

"Not so much as a pinpoint of difference," Tim Malloy answered. "Not so much as a pinpoint. To change the subject, how long will it keep raining, would you say?"

"All day, I suppose," Sam said, in a gloom again. "And all night too. I've no doubt. Though I could stop it raining in five minutes if I'd a mind to."

"Could you so?" Tim Malloy said, interested. "Let's see how it goes, Sam. Just for curiosity's sake."

Sham Shay shrugged.

"Bet me a dollar it'll stop raining within five minutes," he said. "And I'll bet the same it'll not. But since it'll be costing me a dollar to show, you must promise to spend it back again treating me."

"Fair's fair," Tim Malloy answered prompt. "And I promise. Then, Sam, I bet you a dollar it'll stop raining inside five minutes."

Lackadaisically Sam accepted and they laid their wagers out upon the table. And sure enough, within the five minutes the storm clouds overhead abruptly whisked away. The blue sky appeared, the sun shone, and it was as if the storm had never been.

"Now that's a curious thing, Sam," Tim Malloy said, eyes wide, as he ordered up more dark. "And if you could do that any time you wished, your fortune would be made."

"Oh, I can do it," Sam sighed, disinterested. "Fair to storm and storm to fair, I need but wager on it to make it come the opposite of my bet. For that matter, any event I make a gamble on will come out the opposite, be it what it may. It's a curse laid upon me, Tim."

"Is it now?" said Tim Malloy, and his eyes grew wider. "And by whom would the curse be laid, Sam Shay?"

Sam leaned forward and whispered in his ear, and Tim Malloy's eyes bade fair to start from their sockets.

"Draw in a deep breath," Sam said, nodding. "Sniff hard, Tim. You'll see."

Tim Malloy sniffed long and deep, and awe crept upon his features.

"Sulphur!" he whispered. "Sulphur and brimstone!"

Sam but nodded and went on drinking his dark. Tim Malloy, though, stretched out a hand and put it upon his arm.

"Sam," he said, voice hoarse, "you have never heard that there's people willing to pay good money to insure the weather'll be as they want it upon a certain day? Have you never heard of insuring against storms, Sam, and against accidents, sickness, twins and such misfortunes? And insuring isn't really betting. It's but a business—a legitimate, money-making business."

Sam stopped drinking his dark. He put his mug upon the table with a bang, and upon his face there came a look.

"So it is," he said, struck by the sudden thought. "So it is!"

"Sam," Tim Malloy said, emotion in his tone, "let us take but a single example. This Sunday coming the Loyal Sons of Saint Patrick parade. Suppose, then, the Loyal Sons said to you, 'Sam, we want to insure it does not storm this Sunday coming. Here's twenty dollars insurance money against rain. If it storms, now, you must pay us five hundred, but if it's fair, you keep the twenty.'

"And then suppose, Sam, you came to me and, 'Tim,' you'd say,

'I want to make a bet. And the bet is one dollar against another dollar that this Sunday coming it will rain.' Whereupon I'd say to you, 'Sam, I accept the wager. One dollar to one dollar that it does not rain this Sunday coming.'

"And as you are doomed to lose your gamble, it does not rain; you keep the twenty dollars paid you by the Loyal Sons, and your profit, Sam, your fair profit on a straightforward business deal which no one could call gambling would be—"

"Nineteen dollars!" Sam said, much moved. "Nineteen dollars profit, Tim, and no wager involved. And you say there are many people wanting such insurance?"

"Thousands of them," said Tim Malloy. "Thousands upon thousands of them. And there's no reason why you shouldn't insure them against anything they wish—seeing as you're backed, one might say, by all the resources of a tremendous big firm."

Sam Shay stood up, and in his eyes there was a light.

"Tim," he said, in a voice that rang, "here is twenty dollars. Rent me an office and have a sign painted saying Samuel Shay, Insurance. The biggest sign that can be managed. And here, Tim, is a dollar. That dollar I bet you Shannon will not say 'yes' to me a moment hence when I call upon her. Do you take the wager?"

"I take it, Sam," agreed Tim Malloy, but already Sam was striding out, and in scarce a minute was standing in the Malloy living room, large and masterful, while Shannon, who had tried to hold the door shut against him, stared at him with blazing eyes.

"Sam Shay," she cried hotly, "I won't see you!"

"You cannot help seeing me," Sam replied with tenderness, "for I am standing here before you."

"Then I won't look at you!" cried Shannon, and shut her eyes.

"In that case you must take the consequences," said Sam, and stepping forward, kissed her so that Shannon's eyes flew open again.

"Sam Shay," she exclaimed, "I—"

"I'll bet a dollar," Sam interrupted her, "you're going to say you hate me."

It was indeed what Shannon had been about to say, but now some perverse demon seemed to seize her tongue.

"I'm not!" she denied. "I was going to say I love you." And having said it, she stared at Sam as if she could not believe her ears.

"Then, Shannon, darling," Sam Shay asked, "will you take

back my ring and marry me? And I'll bet another dollar you're going to say no."

And "no" it was that Shannon tried to say. But once again it was as if a contrary devil had her tongue.

"Indeed I'm not," she declared, to her own consternation. "For I say yes, and I will."

With which Sam swept her into his arms and kissed her again, so soundly she had no more time to wonder at the way her tongue had twisted. Indeed, she was forced to believe it was some strange power in Sam himself that had drawn the words from her. And on this point Sam wisely refrained from ever correcting her.

Thus they were married, and at this moment Sam Shay's insurance business is prospering beyond belief. Money is flowing in from all sides, and being a prudent man Sam has arranged his affairs in excellent order. He has wagered with Tim Malloy, his junior partner, that he and Shannon will not live in good health to be ninety-nine each, while Tim has wagered they will. Sam has likewise bet that he and Shannon will be desperately unhappy, Tim gambling to the contrary. Finally Sam has gambled that they will not have ten fine, strapping children, six boys and four girls, and Tim has placed his money that they will.

So sin continues to decline as Sam's business grows, and Sam himself sleeps soundly of nights. And if there is sometimes the faintest smell of brimstone and sulphur about the house, as though from much coming and going of harassed demons, no one in the household minds it, not even Dion, youngest of the ten young Shays.

FOR DISCUSSION

1. This is a different kind of bargain with the devil. It is based on an old belief that if a devil appears to a human, the human must win three bets with the devil or lose his soul. What are Sam Shay's three bets and how does he win each one?
2. The devil dislikes being defeated by a mortal. When he lost the three wagers, what curse did he pronounce upon Shay? Describe briefly the immediate effects of the curse on Shay's way of living.
3. Perhaps the most humorous part of this story is the dialogue

between Satan and his chief lieutenant. During the conversation the chief lieutenant announces fearfully that the curse on Shay is indirectly causing a decrease of sin in the world. Explain how and why this is happening.

4. Sam Shay and Tim Malloy at last figure out a way to get around Satan's curse. How do they do this so that the curse actually becomes a blessing?

5. Sam Shay is not a very nice fellow. His only interest is gambling; he's too lazy to do any regular work; and he won't sacrifice even a few bets to win the woman he claims he loves. When he does finally win Shannon, he does so by employing a disgraceful trick. How is it, then, that when all goes well for him in the end, we find ourselves enthusiastically applauding the happy conclusion?

INTRODUCTION

Hell is a land of fire and brimstone, and water is antithetical to fire. When the devil boarded a clipper ship in the Indian Ocean to claim a soul he had purchased twenty years earlier, he should have been more wary. A landlubber can rarely get the better of a seaman, and this is especially true when both are in the latter's domain. This story shows the devil in an alien element, tricked out of his prize by means which are common in the world of a seaman.

The Devil and the Old Man

John Masefield

Up away north, in the old days, in Chester, there was a man who never throve. Nothing he put his hand to ever prospered, and as his state worsened, his friends fell away and he grew desperate. So one night when he was alone in his room, thinking of the rent due in two or three days and the money he couldn't scrape together, he cried out, "I wish I could sell my soul to the devil like that man the old books tell about."

Now just as he spoke the clock struck twelve, and, while it chimed, a sparkle began to burn about the room, and the air, all at once, began to smell of brimstone, and a voice said:

"Will these terms suit you?"

He then saw that someone had just placed a parchment there. He picked it up and read it through; and being in despair, and not knowing what he was doing, he answered, "Yes," and looked round for a pen.

"Take and sign," said the voice again, "but first consider what it is you do; do nothing rashly. Consider."

So he thought awhile; then, "Yes," he said, "I'll sign," and with that he groped for the pen.

"Blood from your left thumb and sign," said the voice.

So he pricked his left thumb and signed.

"Here is your earnest money," said the voice, "nine and twenty silver pennies. This day twenty years hence I shall see you again."

Now early next morning our friend came to himself and felt like one of the drowned. "What a dream I've had," he said. Then he woke up and saw the nine and twenty silver pennies and smelled a faint smell of brimstone.

So he sat in his chair there, and remembered that he had sold his soul to the devil for twenty years of heart's desire; and whatever fears he may had had as to what might come at the end of those twenty years, he found comfort in the thought that, after all, twenty years is a good stretch of time, and that throughout them he could eat, drink, merrymake, roll in gold, dress in silk, and be carefree, heart at ease, and jib-sheet to windward.

So for nineteen years and nine months he lived in great state, having his heart's desire in all things; but, when his twenty years were nearly run through, there was no wretcheder man in all the world than that poor fellow. So he threw up his house, his position, riches, everything, and away he went to the port of Liverpool, where he signed on as A.B., aboard a Black Ball packet, a tea clipper, bound to the China Seas.

They made a fine passage out, and when our friend had only three days more, they were in the Indian Ocean, lying lazy, becalmed.

Now it was his wheel that forenoon, and it being dead calm, all he had to do was just to think of things, the ship of course having no way on her.

So he stood there, hanging onto the spokes, groaning and weeping till, just twenty minutes or so before eight bells were made, up came the captain for a turn on deck.

He went aft of course, took a squint aloft, and saw our friend crying at the wheel. "Hello, my man," he says, "why, what's all this? Ain't you well? You'd best lay aft for a dose o' salts at four bells tonight."

"No, Cap'n," said the man, "there's no salts'll ever cure my sickness."

"Why, what's all this?" says the old man. "You must be sick if it's as bad as all that. But come now; your cheek is all sunk, and

The Devil and the Old Man   197

you look as if you ain't slept well. What is it ails you, anyway? Have you anything on your mind?"

"Captain," he answers very solemn, "I have sold my soul to the devil."

"Oh," said the old man, "why, that's bad. That's powerful bad. I never thought them sort of things ever happened outside a book."

"But," said our friend, "that's not the worst of it, Captain. At this time three days hence the devil will fetch me home."

"Good Lord!" groaned the old man. "Here's a nice hurrah's nest to happen aboard my ship. But come now," he went on, "did the devil give you no chance—no saving clause like? Just think quietly for a moment."

"Yes, Captain," said our friend, "just when I made the deal, there came a whisper in my ear. And," he said, speaking very quietly, so as not to let the mate hear, "if I can give the devil three jobs to do which he cannot do, why, then, Captain," he says, "I'm saved, and that deed of mine is cancelled."

Well, at this the old man grinned and said, "You just leave things to me, my son. *I'll* fix the devil for you. Aft there, one o' you, and relieve the wheel. Now you run forrard, and have a good watch below, and be quite easy in your mind, for I'll deal with the devil for you. You rest and be easy."

And so that day goes by, and the next, and the one after that, and the one after that was the day the devil was due.

Soon as eight bells was made in the morning watch, the old man called all hands aft.

"Men," he said, "I've got an all-hands job for you this forenoon.

"Mr. Mate," he cried, "get all hands onto the main-tops'l halyards and bouse the sail stiff up and down."

So they passed along the halyards and took the turns off, and old John Chantyman piped up:

> "There's a Black Ball clipper
> Comin' down the river."

And away the yard went to the masthead till the bunt robands jammed in the sheave.

"Very well that," said the old man. "Now get my dinghy off o' the half deck and let her drag alongside."

So they did that too.

"Very well that," said the old man. "Now forrard with you, to the chain locker, and rouse out every inch of chain you find there."

So forrard they went, and the chain was lighted up and flaked along the deck all clear for running.

"Now, Chips," says the old man to the carpenter, "just bend the spare anchor to the end of that chain and clear away the fo'c'sle rails ready for when we let go."

So they did this, too.

"Now," said the old man, "get them tubs of slush from the galley. Pass that slush along there, doctor. Very well that. Now turn to, all hands, and slush away every link in that chain a good inch thick in grease."

So they did that, too, and wondered what the old man meant.

"Very well that," cries the old man. "Now get below, all hands! Chips, on to the fo'c'sle head with you and stand by! I'll keep the deck, Mr. Mate! Very well that."

So all hands tumbled down below; Chips took a fill o' 'baccy to the leeward of the capstan, and the old man walked the weather poop, looking for a sign of hellfire.

It was still dead calm—but presently, toward six bells, he raised a black cloud away to leeward and saw the glimmer of the lightning in it; only the flashes were too red and came too quick.

"Now," says he to himself, "stand by."

Very soon that black cloud worked up to windward, right alongside, and there came a red flash, and a strong sulfurous smell, and then a loud peal of thunder as the devil steps aboard.

"Mornin', Cap'n," says he.

"Mornin', Mr. Devil," says the old man, "and what in blazes do you want aboard *my* ship?"

"Why, Captain," said the devil, "I've come for the soul of one of your hands as per signed agreement; and, as my time's pretty full up in these wicked days, I hope you won't keep me waiting for him longer than need be."

"Well, Mr. Devil," says the old man, "the man you come for

is down below, sleeping, just at this moment. It's a fair pity to call him till it's right time. So supposin' I set you them three tasks. How would that be? Have you any objections?"

"Why, no," said the devil, "fire away as soon as you like."

"Mr. Devil," said the old man, "you see that main-tops'l yard? Suppose you lay out on that main-tops'l yard and take in three reefs singlehanded."

"Ay, ay, sir," the devil said, and he ran up the ratlines, into the top, up the topmast rigging, and along the yard.

Well, when he found the sail stiff up and down, he hailed the deck:

"Below there! On deck there! Lower away ya halyards!"

"I will not," said the old man, "nary a lower."

"Come up your sheets, then," cried the devil. "This main-top-sail's stiff up and down. How'm I to take in three reefs when the sail's stiff up and down?"

"Why," said the old man, "*you can't do it.* Come out o' that! Down from aloft, you hoof-footed son. That's one to me."

"Yes," says the devil, when he got on deck again, "I don't deny it, Cap'n. That's one to you."

"Now, Mr. Devil," said the old man, going toward the rail, "suppose you was to step into that little boat alongside there. Will you please?"

"Ay, ay, sir," he said, and he slid down the forrard fall, got into the stern sheets, and sat down.

"Now, Mr. Devil," said the skipper, taking a little salt spoon from his vest pocket, "supposin' you bail all the water on that side the boat on to this side the boat, using this spoon as your dipper."

Well!—the devil just looked at him.

"Say!" he said at length. "Which of the New England states d'ye hail from anyway?"

"Not Jersey, anyway," said the old man. "That's two up, all right; ain't it, sonny?"

"Yes," growls the devil as he climbs aboard. "That's two up. Two to you and one to play. Now, what's your next contraption?"

"Mr. Devil," said the old man, looking very innocent, "you see, I've ranged my chain ready for letting go anchor. Now Chips is forrard there, and when I sing out, he'll let the anchor go. Supposin' you stopper the chain with them big hands o' yourn and keep it from running out clear. Will you, please?"

So the devil takes off his coat and rubs his hands together and gets away forrard by the bitts and stands by.

"All ready, Cap'n," he says.

"All ready, Chips?" asked the old man.

"All ready, sir," replies Chips.

"Then, stand by. Let *go* the anchor," and clink, clink, old Chips knocks out the pin, and away goes the spare anchor and greased chain into a five-mile deep of God's sea. As I said, they were in the Indian Ocean.

Well—there was the devil, making a grab here and a grab there, and the slushy chain just slipping through his claws, and at whiles a bight of chain would spring clear and rap him in the eye.

So at last the cable was nearly clean gone, and the devil ran to the last big link (which was seized to the heel of the foremast), and he put both his arms through it and hung on to it like grim death.

But the chain gave such a *yank* when it came to that the big link carried away, and oh, roll and go, out it went through the hawsehole, in a shower of bright sparks, carrying the devil with it. There is no devil now. The devil's dead.

As for the old man, he looked over the bows, watching the bubbles burst, but the devil never rose. Then he went to the fo'c'sle scuttle and banged thereon with a hand spike.

"Rouse out, there, the Port Watch," he called, "an' get my dinghy inboard."

FOR DISCUSSION

1. What are the terms of the contract as described in this story? Consider the payment to be received, the payment to be made, and the length of the contract. In the "Ballad of Faustus" there is also a contract. How is this contract similar to it? How is it different?

2. The devil gives the man twenty-nine silver pennies. Can you

suggest a reason why exactly twenty-nine silver pennies were given?

3. In "Satan and Sam Shay," Sam had to win three bets from Satan. In this story the Captain must assign the devil three tasks that he cannot complete. Explain why the number three might have special significance.

4. Daniel Webster, in "The Devil and Daniel Webster," was from New Hampshire. Sam Shay was also a Yankee. In this story, after the devil fails to complete two of the three tasks, he turns to the Captain and asks: "Which of the New England states d'ye hail from anyway?" Can you suggest any reason why authors tend to make the men who outwit the devil New Englanders?

INTRODUCTION

The twentieth century has seen not only a renewed interest in the Faust legend, but also a sharpened interest in the devil and devil-worship. John Collier has written voluminously on this subject. He is so familiar with this material that he does not hesitate to write about a child's partnership with Mephistopheles. The bargain between the devil and Small Simon is the ultimate twist of the Faust legend.

Thus I Refute Beelzy

John Collier

"There goes the tea bell," said Mrs. Carter. "I hope Simon hears it."

They looked out from the window of the drawing room. The long garden, agreeably neglected, ended in a waste plot. Here a little summerhouse was passing close by beauty on its way to complete decay. This was Simon's retreat: it was almost completely screened by the tangled branches of the apple tree and the pear tree, planted too close together, as they always are in suburban gardens. They caught a glimpse of him now and then as he strutted up and down, mouthing and gesticulating, performing all the solemn mumbo jumbo of small boys who spend long afternoons at the forgotten ends of long gardens.

"There he is, bless him," said Betty.

"Playing his game," said Mrs. Carter. "He won't play with the other children any more. And if I go down there—the temper! And comes in tired out."

"He doesn't have his sleep in the afternoons?" asked Betty.

"You know what Big Simon's ideas are," said Mrs. Carter. " 'Let him choose for himself,' he says. That's what he chooses, and he comes in as white as a sheet."

"Look. He's heard the bell," said Betty. The expression was

justified, though the bell had ceased ringing a full minute ago. Small Simon stopped in his parade exactly as if its tinny dingle had at that moment reached his ear. They watched him perform ritual sweeps and scratchings with his little stick and come lagging over the hot and flaggy grass toward the house.

Mrs. Carter led the way down to the playroom, or garden room, which was also the tearoom for hot days. It had been the huge scullery of this tall Georgian house. Now the walls were cream-washed; there was coarse blue net in the windows, canvas-covered armchairs on the stone floor, and a reproduction of Van Gogh's *Sunflowers* over the mantelpiece.

Small Simon came drifting in and accorded Betty a perfunctory greeting. His face was an almost perfect triangle, pointed at the chin, and he was paler than he should have been. "The little elf child!" cried Betty.

Simon looked at her. "No," he said.

At that moment the door opened, and Mr. Carter came in, rubbing his hands. He was a dentist and washed them before and after everything he did. "You!" said his wife. "Home already!"

"Not unwelcome, I hope," said Mr. Carter, nodding to Betty. "Two people canceled their appointment; I decided to come home. I said, I hope I am not unwelcome."

"Silly!" said his wife. "Of course not."

"Small Simon seems doubtful," continued Mr. Carter. "Small Simon, are you sorry to see me at tea with you?"

"No, Daddy."

"No, what?"

"No, Big Simon."

"That's right. Big Simon and Small Simon. That sounds more like friends, doesn't it? At one time little boys had to call their father 'sir.' If they forgot—a good spanking. On the bottom, Small Simon! On the bottom!" said Mr. Carter, washing his hands once more with his invisible soap and water.

The little boy turned crimson with shame or rage.

"But now, you see," said Betty, to help, "you can call your father whatever you like."

"And what," asked Mr. Carter, "has Small Simon been doing this afternoon? While Big Simon has been at work."

"Nothing," muttered his son.

"Then you have been bored," said Mr. Carter. "Learn from

experience, Small Simon. Tomorrow do something amusing and you will not be bored. I want him to learn from experience, Betty. That is my way, the new way."

"I have learned," said the boy, speaking like an old, tired man, as little boys so often do.

"It would hardly seem so," said Mr. Carter, "if you sit on your behind all the afternoon, doing nothing. Had *my* father caught me doing nothing I should not have sat very comfortably."

"He played," said Mrs. Carter.

"A bit," said the boy, shifting on his chair.

"Too much," said Mrs. Carter. "He comes in all nervy and dazed. He ought to have his rest."

"He is six," said her husband. "He is a reasonable being. He must choose for himself. But what game is this, Small Simon, that is worth getting nervy and dazed over? There are very few games as good as all that."

"It's nothing," said the boy.

"Oh, come," said his father. "We are friends, are we not? You can tell me. I was a Small Simon once, just like you, and played the same games you play. Of course there were no airplanes in those days. With whom do you play this fine game? Come on, we must all answer civil questions, or the world would never go round. With whom do you play?"

"Mr. Beelzy," said the boy, unable to resist.

"Mr. Beelzy?" said his father, raising his eyebrows inquiringly at his wife.

"It's a game he makes up," she said.

"Not makes up!" cried the boy. "Fool!"

"That is telling stories," said his mother. "And rude as well. We had better talk of something different."

"No wonder he is rude," said Mr. Carter, "if you say he tells lies and then insist on changing the subject. He tells you his fantasy; you implant a guilt feeling. What can you expect? A defense mechanism. Then you get a real lie."

"Like in *These Three*," said Betty. "Only different, of course. *She* was an unblushing little liar."

"I would have made her blush," said Mr. Carter, "in the proper part of her anatomy. But Small Simon is in the fantasy stage. Are you not, Small Simon? You just make things up."

"No, I don't," said the boy.

Thus I Refute Beelzy   205

"You do," said his father. "And because you do, it is not too late to reason with you. There is no harm in a fantasy, old chap. There is no harm in a bit of make-believe. Only you have to know the difference between daydreams and real things, or your brain will never grow. It will never be the brain of a Big Simon. So come on. Let us hear about this Mr. Beelzy of yours. Come on. What is he like?"

"He isn't like anything," said the boy.

"Like nothing on earth?" said his father. "That's a terrible fellow."

"I'm not frightened of him," said the child, smiling. "Not a bit."

"I should hope not," said his father. "If you were, you would be frightening yourself. I am always telling people, older people than you are, that they are just frightening themselves. Is he a funny man? Is he a giant?"

"Sometimes he is," said the little boy.

"Sometimes one thing, sometimes another," said his father. "Sounds pretty vague. Why can't you tell us just what he's like?"

"I love him," said the small boy. "He loves me."

"That's a big word," said Mr. Carter. "That might be better kept for real things, like Big Simon and Small Simon."

"He is real," said the boy passionately. "He's not a fool. He's real."

"Listen," said his father. "When you go down the garden there's nobody there. Is there?"

"No," said the boy.

"Then you think of him, inside your head, and he comes."

"No," said Small Simon. "I have to do something with my stick."

"That doesn't matter."

"Yes, it does."

"Small Simon, you are being obstinate," said Mr. Carter. "I am trying to explain something to you. I have been longer in the world than you have, so naturally I am older and wiser. I am explaining that Mr. Beelzy is a fantasy of yours. Do you hear? Do you understand?"

"Yes, Daddy."

"He is a game. He is a let's-pretend."

206

The little boy looked down at his plate, smiling resignedly.

"I hope you are listening to me," said his father. "All you have to do is to say, 'I have been playing a game of let's-pretend. With someone I make up, called Mr. Beelzy.' Then no one will say you tell lies, and you will know the difference between dreams and reality. Mr. Beelzy is a daydream."

The little boy still stared at his plate.

"He is sometimes there and sometimes not there," pursued Mr. Carter. "Sometimes he's like one thing, sometimes another. You can't really see him. Not as you see me. I am real. You can't touch him. You can touch me. I can touch you." Mr. Carter stretched out his big white dentist's hand and took his little son by the shoulder. He stopped speaking for a moment and tightened his hand. The little boy sank his head still lower.

"Now you know the difference," said Mr. Carter, "between a pretend and a real thing. You and I are one thing; he is another. Which is the pretend? Come on. Answer me. Which is the pretend?"

"Big Simon and Small Simon," said the little boy.

"Don't!" cried Betty, and at once put her hand over her mouth, for why should a visitor cry "Don't!" when a father is explaining things in a scientific and modern way?

"Well, my boy," said Mr. Carter, "I have said you must be allowed to learn from experience. Go upstairs. Right up to your room. You shall learn whether it is better to reason or to be perverse and obstinate. Go up. I shall follow you."

"You are not going to beat the child?" cried Mrs. Carter.

"No," said the little boy. "Mr. Beelzy won't let him."

"Go on up with you!" shouted his father.

Small Simon stopped at the door. "He said he wouldn't let anyone hurt me," he whimpered. "He said he'd come like a lion, with wings on, and eat them up."

"You'll learn how real he is!" shouted his father after him. "If you can't learn it at one end, you shall learn it at the other. I'll have your breeches down. I shall finish my cup of tea first, however," he said to the two women.

Neither of them spoke. Mr. Carter finished his tea and unhurriedly left the room, washing his hands with his invisible soap and water.

Mrs. Carter said nothing. Betty could think of nothing to say. She wanted to be talking; she was afraid of what they might hear.

Suddenly it came. It seemed to tear the air apart. "Good God!" she cried. "What was that? He's hurt him." She sprang out of her chair, her silly eyes flashing behind her glasses. "I'm going up there!" she cried, trembling.

"Yes, let us go up," said Mrs. Carter. "Let us go up. That was not Small Simon."

It was on the second-floor landing that they found the shoe, with the man's foot still in it, like that last morsel of a mouse which sometimes falls from the jaws of a hasty cat.

FOR DISCUSSION

1. Big Simon is the most interesting character in this story. In very few words the author depicts him as a thoroughly disagreeable man. Find five incidents that illustrate his character.

2. Throughout the story there are several clues pointing to the identity of Mr. Beelzy. List as many of these clues as you can.

3. After Big Simon has tried to explain the difference between the real and the make-believe, he says to his son: "You and I are one thing; he is another. Which is the pretend?" And Small Simon answers: "Big Simon and Small Simon." Big Simon's feelings are hurt by the answer, but he fails to see the real horror behind his son's words. What is the boy really saying?

4. Would this story be just as effective if the conflict were between husband and wife instead of between father and small son? Explain. How does the active participation of a child contribute to the final horror?

5. In the earlier stories in this unit, definite contracts with definite terms were made. In this story, there is no reference to a formal contract; but a contract of sorts must have been drawn up. On the basis of information given in the story, try to determine what some of the contract terms must have been.

6. Refute means to prove that an argument or a person is wrong. With this in mind, explain the not-so-delicate irony of the title.

INTRODUCTION

In recent decades many psychologists and sociologists have tried to persuade themselves and the world that no one is innately evil or wicked. The thief is the stepchild of poverty; the murderer is the orphan bereft of love.

In this story, set in the future, society has carried this theory to its natural conclusion: "a villain is just a sick hero." If this is true, then what of the arch-villain of all time, the devil? The devil works desperately to make a deal with Acleptos, but Acleptos doesn't believe in the devil and isn't interested in the devil's terms. It's the devil's last try, and the result is the strangest "infernal bargain" in literature.

The Devil Was Sick

Bruce Elliott

It had been aeons since a really violent patient had been forcibly carried across the threshold of the Sane Asylum. So much time had passed that the eye of the beholder no longer paused to read the words cast in the endlessly enduring crystometal that ran across the entrance. Once a brave challenge to the unknown, time had changed them to a cliché. *A villain is just a sick hero.* The motto had been proved true and therefore it was no longer worth consideration. But the words stayed on ... until the day that Acleptos took chisel in hand and changed two of them.

It began because the problem of finding a new subject for a thesis had become harder to solve than getting a degree. Acleptos had, by dint of a great deal of research, found three subjects which he thought the Machine might accept as being original.

He gulped a little as he presented his list to the all-seeing eye of the calculator. The list read, *Activated sludge and what the ancients did about it. The downfall of democracy and why it came about. Devils, demons and demonology.*

The Machine barely paused before it said: "In 4357 Jac Bard

wrote the definitive work on activated sludge. Two hundred years later the last unknown component in regard to the downfall of democracy was analyzed to the utmost by the historian Hermios." There was a tiny wait. Acleptos held his breath. If his last subject had been collected, annotated and written about in its entirety it might mean another twenty years' work finding some more possible subjects. The Machine said: "There are two aspects of devils and demons that have not been presented to me so far. These are, were they real or hallucinatory, and if real, what were they. If hallucinatory, how brought about."

New life and hope surged through Acleptos. He braced his narrow shoulders and walked away from the Machine. At last, after so many years he now had a chance. Of course—the thought brought him up short—of course, there was still a chance that he might not be able to throw any new light on the problem of the reality of devils and demons. But that was something he could work on. The years spent at the reels, the work he had done going through almost all provinces of human knowledge had at last paid off.

A decade ago, the last time he had presented a list to the Machine, he had been so sure that he had found a subject when he had discovered reference in some old reels to something or someone who was known as God. It had been the capitalization of the "g" that had caught his eye in the first place. But the Machine had given him an endless number of theses about the subject finishing up with one written about a thousand years prior, that had proved once and for all the nonexistence of such a being. This thesis, the Machine felt, had ended all future speculations on the subject.

Out of curiosity, Acleptos had checked the reference and was in complete accord, as he always was, with the Machine's summation.

It had been a stroke of genius thinking of the antithesis to God. Acleptos grinned to himself. Now he could go ahead. He would do his research, get his degree and then—then there would be no holding him back. He would be able to leave Earth and go on to his next step. He threw his head back and looked at the sky. That was the way it went. You were Earth-bound until you had done some original piece of research, but with that finished you were allowed to migrate anywhere you wanted to go.

There was a planet out back of Alpha Centauri that she had chosen. And she had promised that no matter how long the time, she would wait until he came. He didn't think he had ever been so depressed in his long life as he had been on the day that the Machine had passed on her thesis. For a long, long while it had seemed as if he had lost her completely. But now the years no longer seemed endless. His search had been fruitful.

Whistling, he entered the reel room and started to work. Pressing the button that was lettered d-e-m to d-e-v he waited until the intricate relay system had performed its function and with a low hum the needed reels popped out of the pneumatic tube.

Three weeks later he felt that he had as much knowledge on the subject of demons, devils and "long-legged beasties that go boomp in the night" as any human had ever had. He shook his head. To think that man had ever been so low in the scale as to believe such things.

He had been forced to work the translating machine over-time. Latin had been the language of a lot of the lore. To think after all his years of studying he had never even heard of the language before.

What garbage! He was indignant when he realized that there had ever been a time when Homo sapiens had believed such trash. Incredible, but then, it was far away and long ago.

He shrugged. Time to get to work on the basic problem. His closest friend, Ttom, walked into the research lab. He had been so busy he had not even checked with him. He hadn't even told him of his success in finding a subject!

"What in . . ." Ttom looked around the spotless green room. On the crystal table a stuffed alligator eyed him unblinkingly. Resting against its horny hide were oddly shaped glass vessels; surrounding the saurian were boxes, trays of powders and on the wall a weather machine was saying, "The moon will be full tonight and . . ." Acleptos switched it off.

"You've come just in time to watch!" he said jubilantly.

"Watch what?" Ttom's round face puckered up like a fat baby's. He said, "You've done it! You've found a subject! Acleptos! I'm so glad!"

"Thanks." Acleptos forced himself to ask, "And you?"

"Still nothing." But Ttom was too happy for his friend to

remain dejected. He asked, "What in the universe did you stumble on?"

"Devils and demons," Acleptos said and went back to mixing some of the powders on the table.

"What are they?"

"A primitive superstition. My job is to find out if they were real, if they were just another name for bad, or sick people, or just exactly what the ancients meant by the words."

"How are you going to do it? What are all those odds and ends?" Ttom asked, pointing to the objects on the table.

"I'm just going to follow the formulas in some old manuscripts and see what happens!"

He had worked hard getting together all the bizarre things that the manuscript called for. He looked at the table and saw that he had everything that he needed. Tonight, at midnight, with the moon full . . . Aloud he said, "A lot of elements went into the 'conjuration of demons.' If you want to wait around and watch, you may find it interesting."

"Sure. I've got nothing to do. I thought I had a lead but as usual someone else had beaten me to it. Acleptos," Ttom asked, "what's going to happen when there are no more fields of human knowledge, when there are no new subjects to explore, when no more theses can be written?"

"I wondered about that, often, until I discovered demons. But I think it's a long way off in the future and I'm sure the Machine will take care of the eventuality when it arises."

"I'm beginning to think that the time is now. Really, Acleptos, you're the first one who's found a subject in five years!" Ttom tried to keep any note of bitterness out of his voice.

"I know what the Machine would say, Ttom." Acleptos poured some red liquid into a tube and added some violet powder to it. "The Machine would say that if I found a subject so can you."

Ttom groaned. "I guess you're right. However, let's forget about me. What happens now?"

"Nothing till midnight. Then, when the moon is full, I chant certain words, light those fatty things there—they're called candles —and then I wait for a devil or a demon to appear."

They both laughed.

At midnight, with smiles still pulling at the corners of their mouths, Ttom sat outside the peculiar design that Acleptos had drawn on the floor. It was called a pentacle. Acleptos had placed a black candle in each of the angles. He had burned the foul-smelling chemicals and he was now chanting in some gibberish that Ttom could not make even an attempt to understand.

It was amusing at first. As time dragged on both men became impatient. Nothing happened. Acleptos stopped chanting and said, "Well, I know the answer to the Machine's first question. Demons are hallucinatory and not real."

That was when it happened.

There was a sudden smell in the room much worse than the chemicals. Then a sort of gray luminescence coalesced near the diagram on the floor.

Acleptos yelled, "Ttom, I forgot. The old books say that you have to be inside the pentacle to be protected from—whatever that is!"

Leaping to his feet, Ttom jumped for the line nearest him. Long before he got there the thing had become solid. It raised its folded lids and when its eyes hit him there was such concentrated malevolence in the glance that Ttom felt something he had never experienced before. It was only because of his reading that he knew that the sensation was something called fear.

The thing said, "Finally."

Even its voice grated on the nerves. Acleptos was stunned. He had performed the experiment because that was the way one found out things, but that it should be successful was beyond his wildest imaginings.

The thing rubbed its odd fingers which had far too many joints for comfort and said, "All those thousands of years. Waiting ... Waiting in the grayness for a call that never came. At first I thought that He had won ... but if that had been the case, I would not have been."

It shrugged its scaly shoulders and opened its red eyes even fuller. They were fascinating. The strange pupils alternately waxed and waned like little crimson moons. It looked from Acleptos to Ttom and said, "So nothing has changed. The adept and the sacrifice, just the way it used to be." Its chuckle was quite unseemly.

"And what reward," the thing looked at Acleptos, "do you want in exchange for this present?"

Ttom had never been called a present before and he found that he did not care for it particularly.

It did not wait for Acleptos to answer. Instead it rubbed its too long fingers together. The grating sound was the only one in the room. It eyed Acleptos and said, "I see. Nothing has changed. A woman. Very well. Here she is."

It made an odd series of gestures in the air and before Acleptos could clear his throat to say no, she was there. She looked frightened. Her hair was as lovely as he remembered it. So was her body. She was naked, as he would have predicted, since the planet she had chosen was a warm one. There was no shame in her pose, just fear.

"Send her back! How dare you drag her across interstellar space! You fool! You might have killed her!" He had no fear of the thing now. His only fear was for his beloved.

She vanished as she had appeared.

The thing grumbled. "I didn't see that you loved her. Thought it was just sex you wanted." It turned its eyes back toward Acleptos. "Gold? They always want gold..." It began to make the stereotyped series of gestures again.

Acleptos realized that he had lost control of the situation, which was ridiculous. He cleared his throat and said, "Enough!"

The thing paused in its occupation and if it had been able to show expression it would have looked surprised. It said, "Now what? How can I get gold for you if you keep interrupting?"

Acleptos was angry. It, like the fear that had preceded it, was a new emotion. He said, "Stand perfectly still. I am the master and you the slave." That was in the directions he had read. He didn't know what a master or a slave was, but the book had seemed to specify these words.

The thing hungrily held its misshapen head still but its eyes wandered hungrily over Ttom's body.

Controlling his new emotion Acleptos said, "You don't seem to understand. I don't want gold, whatever that is."

Ttom said, "I remember that word from my reading. The ancients used to change it into lead or some valuable metal like that."

Acleptos went on, "And I certainly don't want her dragged back from Alpha Centauri."

"Power!" the thing said and this time it almost seemed to grin.

"That never fails. If they're too old for sex and too rich for gold, they always want power." Its hands began to move again.

"*Stop!*" Acleptos yelled for the first time in his life.

The thing froze.

Acleptos said, "Don't do that again. It annoys me! I don't want power and don't tell me what it is because I'm not interested. Now just stand there and answer some questions."

The thing seemed to shrink a little. It said almost querulously, "But—what did you summon me for? If you don't want anything from me, I can't take anything from you . . ." It rolled its eyes at Ttom. Its green tongue licked its scarlike lips.

"I just want some information. How long do you crea— devils live?"

"Live? Forever, of course."

"And what is your function?"

"To tempt man from the path of righteousness."

The words came out quickly enough but Acleptos just couldn't understand what they meant. However, it was all being recorded so he would be able to go back over it and find the sense later.

"Why would you want to do that?" Acleptos asked.

The demon peered at him as though doubting his sanity. It said, "In order that man have free will, of course. He must be able to choose between good and evil."

"What are they, those words, good and evil?"

The demon sat down on its heels disregarding the spurs that sank into its own buttocks. It said, "All those years . . . sitting in the grayness and to be summoned for this." It shook its head. Suddenly it seemed to come to some kind of decision. Springing to its feet, it made a dash for Ttom.

Acleptos raised the force gun he had kept by his side. He pressed the button. The creature froze and then fell face forward on the floor.

Ttom gulped. He said, "I thought you were never going to use that. I'll call the Sane Asylum and have them send for this poor sick creature right away."

Nodding, Acleptos said, "This has turned out to be much more interesting than I would have predicted." He sat thoughtfully until the ambu-bus arrived. It was the first hurry call the Asylum had had in a century but the machines functioned perfectly.

Ttom and Acleptos watched the robots pick up the thing and

cradle it in their metal arms. They went along as the androids placed it in the ambu-bus and flew towards the Asylum.

Halfway there Acleptos spoke for the first time. He said, "Do you see the terrible irony implicit in all this?"

"What do you mean?" Ttom still stared at the thing which lay stretched out as though in death.

"These devils, do you realize what they are?" The words spilled out of Acleptos. "They're just other-dimensional beings. Somehow, some time, a human, back in the dark ages, stumbled on the mathematics of causing them to cross the dimensions. Not knowing what he was doing, shrouded in superstition, he thought that the mumbo jumbo was what called them up, instead of realizing that the diagram and the heat of the candles and the words of the chant all combined to make a key to open the lock of that other dimension."

"It sounds reasonable but where is there any irony in that?"

Acleptos sounded ready to weep. He said, "Don't you see, here was humanity struggling through the dark ages when all the time they had darker brothers right near them who were immortal, who could conquer space by merely setting their hands in the right pattern, and, man, blinded by his superstitious beliefs, was unable to learn from these 'devils.' The worst irony is, however, that the 'devils' couldn't help man because they are idiots . . ."

Ttom nodded. "An almost imbecile race with incredible talents living right next door to us and we never knew it. The Machine is right, there is much for us to learn. I was wrong in thinking that all things are known."

Either the force gun was not set heavily enough or the devil had amazing recuperative powers, Acleptos thought, for as they got out of the ambu-bus the creature unfroze. It screamed as the robots tried to carry it across the threshold of the Sane Asylum.

It struggled so that even the metal ribbons that animated the robots were strained. Acleptos saw its hands suddenly begin to move in that pattern.

He yelled to the robots who were restraining it, "Hold its hands!"

The metallic hands folded over the madly writhing many-jointed fingers and the thing stopped its struggling. Ahead a door opened and one of the doctors walked towards them.

He said, "What in the world is that?" As Acleptos explained,

216

Ttom ran his fingers over the words of the motto on the door. He saw the words, his fingers felt them, but he had seen them too often. They didn't register on his mind.

When Acleptos finished, the doctor said, "I see. Well, we'll have it straightened out in no time. It'll be quite a challenge trying to bring an other-dimensional creature to its senses!"

Acleptos asked, "Do you think it's sick or just stupid?"

The doctor smiled. "Sick, I'm sure. No well being would behave the way you have described its actions. Would you like to watch?"

"Of course, I am more than interested." Acleptos linked his arm in Ttom's. "Imagine," he said, "if we can cure this one it will mean communication with a whole race of the creatures. Isn't it wonderful?"

"Acleptos," Ttom sounded worried, "there's one thing we haven't considered. In all my reading, in all the data we have on the whole universe and all its strange creatures, I have never before heard of any that are immortal. Had you considered that?"

"Sure, but it's just another proof of how right the Machine is in its knowledge that we don't know everything. This is so exciting! I can't wait till I can tell her about it. Won't she be surprised when she finds that it was no dream that she came to my lab, but that she really was there, warped through space and time by a sick creature which has lived forever . . ."

In the operating room there were no scalpels, no sponges, no clamps. The doctor stretched the thing out on the table. The robots kept hold of its hands.

The doctor picked up an instrument. A pulsing light came from its S-shaped lens. The doctor bathed the thing in the light. He said, "This will only take a moment. That is, if it's going to work. If not, there are many other things to do."

Suddenly his voice failed him. Acleptos backed away from the table until the wall stopped him. Ttom gasped. Only the robots were unimpressed.

For the thing was changing. Wherever the lambent light touched it, the scales fell away.

The doctor whispered to the robots, "Release your hold!"

As they did so the creature arose in glory. A golden light played around its soft sweet face. It stepped to the window and the smile that played around its lips was like a valedictory. It poised on the windowsill for a moment before it spread its huge white wings.

It said, *"Pax vobiscum."* The wings swirled and it was gone, wrapped in serenity.

That is why Acleptos changed the words of the motto in front of the Sane Asylum. They now read: *A devil is just a sick angel.*

Of course, the Machine has stopped. For its basis and its strength was infallibility. And it was wrong about the thesis relative to the existence of God with a capital G.

FOR DISCUSSION

1. What is Acleptos's attitude toward demons when he begins his research on this subject?

2. The devil becomes frustrated when he cannot find a suitable type of payment for Acleptos. What are the three things he offers Acleptos? What was Acleptos's answer in each case, and how does each answer reflect an attitude that is essentially different from a contemporary viewpoint?

3. According to the devil, what is the main goal of devils, and why do they try to achieve this goal?

4. After taking the devil to the Sane Asylum, Acleptos comes up with a new theory about who devils really are. It is especially fascinating today now that we have taken the first steps toward interplanetary exploration. Describe and evaluate Acleptos's theory.

5. Go back in the story to the first appearance of the devil. Note some of his physical characteristics. Now reread, in the last part of the story, the description of the angel that appears after the devil has been bathed in pulsing light. Note some of the physical characteristics of this devil-turned-angel. Can you draw any conclusions now about good and evil?

6. How does the sentence, "A devil is just a sick angel," lead directly to the last paragraph? What do you think the last paragraph means? Can you think of more than one possible interpretation?

Reward
and
Retribution

CHAPTER FOUR

Plato spent a large part of his lifetime trying to define the word "just." What, he wondered, is a just person, a just state? Most of us have simplified the problem considerably by equating just with fair. The latter term is not new: it is one of the first evaluating words the child learns. "It isn't fair!" the toddler cries; and what he means is that, in his opinion, there is an undesirable disparity between the act and the result.

What is true of the toddler is true of the adult. Criminals will attempt to avoid punishment, but if it comes, they are probably not outraged because they know they are guilty. Contrast that attitude with the innocent person's. An innocent person wrongly accused of a crime and punished for it will react violently, or sink into despair. It is simply not fair, not just.

This demand for justice, this demand that there be a correlation between act and result, is one of the most basic tenets in the human code. With it, life makes sense; without it, life becomes confusing and irrational. For instance, how do people who are born in the ghetto and are unable to improve their lot, no matter what they do, feel? What does the person born without sight or with deformed limbs think?

In some cases there is a kind of compensation. Occasionally the blind person has an acute sense of hearing that gives him a deeper appreciation of song than is possible for the rest of us. But in many cases, indeed in most, there seems to be no compensation. Some are born rich, some poor; some healthy, some sick; some with an abundance of talent, some with none. Aware of this apparent injustice, how can one human being look another in the eye and insist complacently that all things balance out, that all men are equal in the end? How can any thinking individual examine an institution for mentally or emotionally disturbed children and prattle still of compensation?

Because there are no simple answers to these questions, people have often turned to religion for answers. Christianity spelled it out in resounding terms in Matthew VI:19–21: humans are reminded not to accumulate treasures on earth but to "lay up to yourselves treasures in heaven." But how does one do this? The eight beatitudes explained: be meek, for the meek shall possess the land; mourn, for the mournful shall be comforted; hunger and thirst after justice, for it shall be granted.

It all became marvelously clear. True justice exists when one combines life on earth with life after death. Inequities now will be erased later. The wicked will be punished and the good will be rewarded after death. Sociologists might wince, and social reformers cry aloud in anger; but the sense of justice is satisfied, at least a little, and that alone makes life tolerable for the majority.

For centuries it seemed sufficient that heaven rewarded and hell punished. Balance was attained, justice achieved. Then new questions arose. Are there not degrees of goodness, degrees of wickedness? Should not then rewards and punishments be administered by degrees? Also, are there not different kinds of goodness, different kinds of wickedness? Should there not then be different kinds of rewards and different kinds of punishment? These questions posed philosophical and creative problems.

Let us look first at a truly retributive heaven. Most of us crave love and security, and we never have enough of either. Freud said that we all want to return to the womb. Surely heaven will be that return, assuring warmth, closeness, and total trust. But beyond that, most of us also find happiness in ordinary things —in a good dinner, a fishing trip, a letter from a friend. Each of us has a unique concept of happiness. Therefore, not one heaven is necessary, but many—each geared to a particular vision.

Even more complex and fascinating is the truly retributive hell. Imagine a hell in which every sin has a punishment that is appropriate in kind and in degree. Such a hell offers all kinds of attractive by-products: a neat asset-debit plan that can be propounded at Sunday service; a sop to save the self-esteem of lesser sinners; a hobbyhorse that can be mounted in succession by a hundred faddists.

And how marvelous is such a hell for artists of all kinds. One can paint or write about fire and brimstone only a limited number of times. But if the punishment fits the crime, endless variety becomes possible. A painter can show a glutton encased in a huge, fractured stomach, or a bawdy listener crushed beneath a pair of monstrous ears. A writer can describe a hypocrite clad in a beautiful robe, weighed down by the unseen but heavy lead lining. And each amateur philosopher can draw up his or her own value system, complete with appropriate and ingenious torments.

In short, the retributive hell, like the retributive heaven, assures a selective and meticulous justice which appeals to both saints and sinners. Together they help human beings to make sense in a world that too often seems the pawn of non-sense.

INTRODUCTION

It is hard to accept the finality of death, especially when death snatches away one you love. In this Indian legend, a young brave, powered by love and virtue, pursues his beloved into the world beyond. He learns, as all must learn, that there is no such thing as "heaven-on-demand." He learns, too, that humans traveling the same road will travel in different ways and arrive at different ends. He learns the rules by which he must live if he is to be reunited with his loved one. Above all, he learns that permanent entry into the land of souls is determined by an implacable law: the law of reward and retribution.

The White Stone Canoe

John Bierhorst

There was once a very beautiful young girl, who died suddenly on the day she was to have been married to a handsome young man. He was also brave, but his heart was not strong enough to endure this loss. From the hour she was buried, there was no more joy or peace for him. He would often visit the spot where the women had buried her and sit there dreaming.

Some of his friends thought he should try to forget his sorrow by hunting or by following the warpath. But war and hunting had lost their charms for him. His heart was already dead within him. He pushed aside both his war club and his bow and arrows.

He had heard the old people say there was a path that led to the land of souls, and he made up his mind to follow it. One morning, after having made his preparations for the journey, he picked up his bow and arrows, called to his dog, and started out. He hardly knew which way to go. He was only guided by the tradition that he must go south. As he walked along, he could see at first no change in the face of the country. Forests and hills and valleys and streams had the same look which they wore in his native place. There was snow on the ground, and sometimes it was even piled and matted on the thick trees and bushes. But after a long while it began to diminish, and finally disappeared. The forest took on a more cheerful appearance, the leaves put forth their buds, and before he was aware of the completeness of the change, he found himself surrounded by spring.

He had left behind him the land of snow and ice. The clouds of winter had rolled away from the sky. The air became mild. A pure field of blue was above him. As he went along he saw flowers beside his path and heard the songs of birds. By these signs he knew that he was going the right way, for they agreed with the traditions of his tribe.

At length he spied a path. It led him through a grove, then up a long, high ridge, on the very top of which there stood a lodge. At the door was an old man with white hair, whose eyes, though deeply sunken, had a fiery brilliance. He had a long robe of skins thrown loosely around his shoulders and a staff in his hands.

The young man began to tell his story. But the old chief stopped him before he had spoken ten words. "I have expected you," he said, "and had just risen to welcome you to my lodge. She whom you seek passed here only a few days ago, and being tired from her journey, rested herself here. Enter my lodge and be seated. I will then answer your questions and give you directions for the remainder of your journey."

When this was accomplished, the old chief brought the young man back out through the door of the lodge. "You see yonder lake," said he, "and the wide-stretching blue plains beyond. It is the land of souls. You now stand upon its borders, and my lodge is at the gate of entrance. But you cannot take your body along. Leave it here with your bow and arrows and your dog. You will find them safe on your return."

So saying, he went back into the lodge, and the traveler bounded forward, as if his feet had suddenly been given the power of wings. But all things retained their natural colors and shapes. The woods and leaves, the streams and lakes, were only brighter and more beautiful than before. Animals bounded across his path with a freedom and confidence that seemed to tell him there was no bloodshed here. Birds of beautiful plumage lived in the groves and sported in the waters.

There was one thing, however, that struck him as peculiar. He noticed that he was not stopped by trees or other objects. He seemed to walk directly through them. They were, in fact, merely the souls or shadows of real trees. He became aware that he was in a land of shadows.

When he had traveled half a day's journey, through a country which grew more and more attractive, he came to the banks of a broad lake, in the center of which was a large and beautiful island. He found a canoe of shining white stone tied to the shore. He was now sure that he had followed the right path, for the aged man had told him of this. There were also shining paddles. He immediately got into the canoe, and had just taken the paddles in his hands when, to his joy and surprise, he beheld the object of his search in another canoe, exactly like his own in every respect. She had exactly imitated his motions, and they were side by side.

At once they pushed out from the shore and began to cross the lake. Its waves seemed to be rising, and at a distance looked ready to swallow them up. But just as they came to the whitened edge of the first great wave, it seemed to melt away, as if it had been merely a shadow or a reflection. No sooner did they pass through one wreath of foam, however, than another still more threatening rose up. They were in constant fear. Moreover, through the clear water they could see the bones of many men who had perished, strewn on the bottom of the lake.

The Master of Life had decreed that the two of them should pass safely through, for they had both led good lives on earth. But they saw many others struggling and sinking in the waves. There were old men and young men, and women too. Some passed safely through, and some sank. But it was only the little children whose canoes seemed to meet no waves at all. Finally every difficulty was passed, as if in an instant, and they both leaped out on the happy island.

They felt that the air was food. It strengthened and nourished them. They wandered over the blissful fields, where everything was made to please the eye and the ear. There were no storms. There was no ice, no chilly wind. No one shivered for want of warm clothes. No one suffered from hunger, no one mourned the dead. They saw no graves. They heard of no wars. There was no hunting for animals, for the air itself was food.

226

Gladly would the young warrior have remained there forever, but he was obliged to go back for his body. He did not see the Master of Life, but he heard his voice in a soft breeze. "Go back," said the voice, "to the land where you came from. Your time has not yet come. The duties for which I made you, and which you are to perform, are not yet finished. Return to your people and accomplish the duties of a good man. You will be the ruler of your tribe for many days. The rules you must observe will be told you by my messenger who keeps the gate. When he gives you back your body, he will tell you what to do. Listen to him, and you shall one day rejoin the spirit whom you must now leave behind. She has been accepted, and will be here always, as young and as happy as she was when I first called her from the land of snows."

When the voice had ceased, the young man awoke. It had been only a dream, and he was still in the bitter land of snows, and hunger, and tears.

FOR DISCUSSION

1. A legend is a romanticized story, often dealing with a historical person or event. Like a myth, it may attempt to explain the inexplicable. Using specific details from the text, prove that this story is a legend.
2. Souls, of course, are spirits. They are not composed of matter. How does this explain the instructions given to the young man at the entrance to the land of souls? How does it explain his first observations within the land of souls?
3. The most significant part of this story is the action that occurs on the lake. What does the crossing of the lake symbolize? How is the theme of reward and retribution exemplified in this incident?
4. In the previous unit, all the selections described bargains with the devil. Explain the nature of the bargain in this selection. How is this bargain different from the bargains in the previous unit?

INTRODUCTION

If love and security are universal human needs, how much more urgently they must be needed by those people who seldom know either. In this poem, Johnson uses overtones from the Bible and from the Negro spiritual and combines them to construct the only kind of heaven that would make sense to Sister Caroline. Here she rests on "the loving breast of Jesus," receiving her reward —the love and security which were denied her in her life on earth.

Go Down, Death!

A Funeral Sermon

James Weldon Johnson

Weep not, weep not,
She is not dead;
She's resting in the bosom of Jesus.
Heart-broken husband—weep no more;
Grief-stricken son—weep no more;   5
Left-lonesome daughter—weep no more;
She's only just gone home.

Day before yesterday morning,
God was looking down from His great, high Heaven,
Looking down on all His children,   10
And His eye fell on Sister Caroline,
Tossing on her bed of pain.
And God's big heart was touched with pity,
With the everlasting pity.

And God sat back on His throne,   15
And He commanded that tall, bright angel standing at
    His right hand,

228

Call me Death!
And that tall, bright angel cried in a voice
That broke like a clap of thunder,
Call Death!   Call Death! 20
And the echo sounded down the streets of Heaven
Till it reached away back to that shadowy place
Where Death waits with his pale, white horses.

And Death heard the summons,
And he leaped on his fastest horse, 25
Pale as a sheet in the moonlight.
Up the golden street Death galloped,
And the hoofs of his horse struck fire from the gold,
But they didn't make no sound.
Up Death rode to the great, white throne, 30
And waited for God's command.

And God said, Go down, Death, go down,
Go down to Savannah, Georgia,
Down in Yamacraw,
And find Sister Caroline. 35
She's borne the burden and heat of the day,
She's labored long in my vineyard,
And she's tired—
She's weary—
Go down, Death, and bring her to me. 40

And Death didn't say a word,
But he loosed the reins on his pale, white horse,
And he clamped the spurs to his bloodless sides,
And out and down he rode,
Through Heaven's pearly gates, 45
Past suns and moons and stars.
On Death rode,
And the foam from his horse was like a comet in the sky;
On Death rode,
Leaving the lightning's flash behind, 50
Straight on down he came.

While we were watching round her bed,
She turned her eyes and looked away,
She saw what we couldn't see;
She saw old Death. She saw old Death,   55
Coming like a falling star.
But Death didn't frighten Sister Caroline;
He looked to her like a welcome friend.
And she whispered to us, I'm going home,
And she smiled and closed her eyes.   60

And Death took her up like a baby,
And she lay in his icy arms,
But she didn't feel no chill.
And Death began to ride again—
Up beyond the evening star,   65
Out beyond the morning star,
Into the glittering light of glory,
On to the great white throne.
And there he laid Sister Caroline
On the loving breast of Jesus.   70

And Jesus took His own hand and wiped away her tears,
And He smoothed the furrows from her face,
And the angels sang a little song,
And Jesus rocked her in His arms,
And kept a-saying, Take your rest,   75
Take your rest, take your rest!

Weep not—weep not,
She is not dead;
She's resting in the bosom of Jesus.

FOR DISCUSSION

1. Here, a poem about death is turned into a paean—a hymn of
    joy. It is not dread of the unknown that dominates the poem,
    but total trust. List a few phrases that illustrate the perfect
    trust possessed both by Sister Caroline and by the poet.

2. Reward rather than retribution is the theme of this p[oem],
and the reward, from stanza to stanza, is individually pa[t]-
terned for Sister Caroline. In the fifth stanza, for example,
Sister Caroline is tired from the hard manual labor she has
done all her life, and God calls Death to release her and give
her rest. Find three other examples of how Sister Caroline's
reward was designed for her and is especially suited to her
needs.

3. James Weldon Johnson often used a style that was influenced
equally by the old Negro spiritual and by the Bible. This
style is marked by (a) repetition, (b) parallel structure, and
(c) simple diction. In the poem, find an example of each of
these stylistic techniques, and explain how each contributes
to the overall effect.

man who has best understood the true meaning of
rworld is Dante, the Italian poet, who in the year
a "journey" through hell, purgatory, and heaven.
s afterworld is thoughtfully constructed. Hell, for
example, is composed of nine circles. A specific type of sinner is
confined in each circle. Each sinner is assigned a specific and related
punishment. Hence, gluttons find themselves wallowing in garbage
in the third center of hell. And they are a kind of garbage themselves, being devoured by Cerberus, the three-headed dog of the
underworld. Violent people find themselves in the seventh circle,
steeped in the boiling blood they spilled and assailed by arrows
they shot at others.

We should not think of this journey as limited to the afterworld. Dante himself reminds us that it is also a journey through
life, in which good is distinguished from evil, and in which both
good and evil are measured and ranked according to degree.

Here in "Canto V" Dante describes Circle Two, the home of
carnal sinners. Lust was frowned upon in 1300, but it was not
considered as evil as treachery or violence. As you read "Canto V,"
note the logical relationship between the sin and the assigned
punishment.

From the Inferno

Dante

Canto V

CIRCLE TWO   *The Carnal*

So we went down to the second ledge alone;
    a smaller circle of so much greater pain
    the voice of the damned rose in a bestial moan.

There Minos sits, grinning, grotesque, and hale.
   He examines each lost soul as it arrives   5
   and delivers his verdict with his coiling tail.

That is to say, when the ill-fated soul
   appears before him it confesses all,
   and that grim sorter of the dark and foul

decides which place in Hell shall be its end,   10
   then wraps his twitching tail about himself
   one coil for each degree it must descend.

The soul descends and others take its place:
   each crowds in its turn to judgment, each confesses,
   each hears its doom and falls away through space.   15

"O you who come into this camp of woe,"
   cried Minos when he saw me turn away
   without awaiting his judgment, "watch where you go

once you have entered here, and to whom you turn!
   Do not be misled by that wide and easy passage!"   20
   And my Guide to him: "That is not your concern;

it is his fate to enter every door.
   This has been willed where what is willed must be,
   and is not yours to question.   Say no more."

Now the choir of anguish, like a wound,   25
   strikes through the tortured air.   Now I have come
   to Hell's full lamentation, sound beyond sound.

I came to a place stripped bare of every light
   and roaring on the naked dark like seas
   wracked by a war of winds.   Their hellish flight   30

of storm and counterstorm through time foregone,
   sweeps the souls of the damned before its charge.
   Whirling and battering it drives them on,

and when they pass the ruined gap of Hell
    through which we had come, their shrieks begin anew.   35
    There they blaspheme the power of God eternal.

And this, I learned, was the never ending flight
    of those who sinned in the flesh, the carnal and lusty
    who betrayed reason to their appetite.

As the wings of wintering starlings bear them on   40
    in their great wheeling flights, just so the blast
    wherries these evil souls through time foregone.

Here, there, up, down, they whirl and, whirling, strain
    with never a hope of hope to comfort them,
    not of release, but even of less pain.   45

As cranes go over sounding their harsh cry,
    leaving the long streak of their flight in air,
    so come these spirits, wailing as they fly.

And watching their shadows lashed by wind, I cried:
    "Master, what souls are these the very air   50
    lashes with its black whips from side to side?"

"The first of these whose history you would know,"
    he answered me, "was Empress of many tongues.
    Mad sensuality corrupted her so

that to hide the guilt of her debauchery   55
    she licensed all depravity alike,
    and lust and law were one in her decree.

She is Semiramis of whom the tale is told
    how she married Ninus and succeeded him
    to the throne of that wide land the Sultans hold.   60

The other is Dido; faithless to the ashes
    of Sichaeus, she killed herself for love.
    The next whom the eternal tempest lashes

is sense-drugged Cleopatra. See Helen there,
    from whom such ill arose. And great Achilles,   65
    who fought at last with love in the house of prayer.

And Paris. And Tristan." As they whirled above
    he pointed out more than a thousand shades
    of those torn from the mortal life by love.

I stood there while my Teacher one by one   70
    named the great knights and ladies of dim time;
    and I was swept by pity and confusion.

At last I spoke: "Poet, I should be glad
    to speak a word with those two swept together
    so lightly on the wind and still so sad."   75

And he to me: "Watch them. When next they pass,
    call to them in the name of love that drives
    and damns them here. In that name they will pause."

Thus, as soon as the wind in its wild course
    brought them around, I called: "O wearied souls!   80
    if none forbid it, pause and speak to us."

As mating doves that love calls to their nest
    glide through the air with motionless raised wings,
    borne by the sweet desire that fills each breast—

Just so those spirits turned on the torn sky   85
    from the band where Dido whirls across the air;
    such was the power of pity in my cry.

"O living creature, gracious, kind, and good,
    going this pilgrimage through the sick night,
    visiting us who stained the earth with blood,   90

were the King of Time our friend, we would pray His peace
    on you who have pitied us. As long as the wind
    will let us pause, ask of us what you please.

The town where I was born lies by the shore
  where the Po descends into its ocean rest   95
  with its attendant streams in one long murmur.

Love, which in gentlest hearts will soonest bloom
  seized my lover with passion for that sweet body
  from which I was torn unshriven to my doom.

Love, which permits no loved one not to love,   100
  took me so strongly with delight in him
  that we are one in Hell, as we were above.

Love led us to one death.   In the depths of Hell
  Caïna waits for him who took our lives."
  This was the piteous tale they stopped to tell.   105

And when I had heard those world-offended lovers
  I bowed my head.   At last the Poet spoke:
  "What painful thoughts are these your lowered brow covers?"

When at length I answered, I began: "Alas!
  What sweetest thoughts, what green and young desire   110
  led these two lovers to this sorry pass."

Then turning to those spirits once again,
  I said: "Francesca, what you suffer here
  melts me to tears of pity and of pain.

But tell me: in the time of your sweet sighs   115
  by what appearances found love the way
  to lure you to his perilous paradise?"

And she: "The double grief of a lost bliss
  is to recall its happy hour in pain.
  Your Guide and Teacher knows the truth of this.   120

But if there is indeed a soul in Hell
  to ask of the beginning of our love
  out of his pity, I will weep and tell:

236

On a day for dalliance we read the rhyme
   of Lancelot, how love had mastered him.   125
   We were alone with innocence and dim time.

Pause after pause that high old story drew
   our eyes together while we blushed and paled;
   but it was one soft passage overthrew

our caution and our hearts. For when we read   130
   how her fond smile was kissed by such a lover,
   he who is one with me alive and dead

breathed on my lips the tremor of his kiss.
   That book, and he who wrote it, was a pander.
   That day we read no further." As she said this,   135

the other spirit, who stood by her, wept
   so piteously, I felt my senses reel
   and faint away with anguish. I was swept

by such a swoon as death is, and I fell,
as a corpse might fall, to the dead floor of Hell.   140

FOR DISCUSSION

1.   The first five circles of hell, according to Dante, form upper
     hell and are reserved for those who committed sins of incon-
     tinence: the lustful, the gluttonous, the miserly and the waste-
     ful, the wrathful and the sullen. Lower hell is reserved for
     those who committed far more serious sins: sins of violence,
     fraud, and treachery. Why are sins of incontinence usually
     considered the less serious sins? How is lust (the sin pun-
     ished in Circle Two) a sin of incontinence?

2.   One of Dante's greatest skills as a poet is his ability to depict
     graphically a concept that is fairly abstract. A fine example
     of this is his description of the judging process. According
     to Dante, how is each soul made aware of the circle of hell

he is condemned? Why is Dante's technique here
ve?
he souls in Circle Two are Cleopatra, Helen, Paris,
nd Dido. Select three of these people and explain
has been condemned to Circle Two.

4. The story of Paolo and Francesca has been made famous by
its inclusion in *The Inferno*. How was their relationship
sinful? What was the immediate cause of their sin? How
did it happen that they arrived together in Circle Two?

5. Later in *The Inferno* Dante shows a fortune-teller with his
head on backwards, able to look only to the past. It is a
retributive punishment directly related to the sin. In life the
fortune-teller wrongfully tried to see the future, now in death
he can see only the past. Describe the punishment of the
lustful in Circle Two, and show as completely as possible the
retributive quality of this punishment.

INTRODUCTION

Like many of Washington Irving's stories, "The Devil and Tom Walker" is based on early nineteenth century folklore. In this case the setting is Massachusetts, and the characters are a greedy pair who worship money and have no use for goodness or compassion. Irving never shows us hell proper, but he does portray a vestibule of hell which is magnificently revealing. Few readers will ever forget the great trees which reflect the condition of the souls they represent; or the remains of Tom's wife who met an end she surely deserved; or Tom's own ironic capture. But best of all is the neat touch of retribution at the end, when hell reaches up and leaves its mark on earth.

The Devil and Tom Walker

Washington Irving

A few miles from Boston in Massachusetts, there is a deep inlet, winding several miles into the interior of the country from Charles Bay, and terminating in a thickly wooded swamp or morass. On one side of this inlet is a beautiful dark grove; on the opposite side the land rises abruptly from the water's edge into a high ridge, on which grow a few scattered oaks of great age and immense size. Under one of these gigantic trees, according to old stories, there was a great amount of treasure buried by Kidd the pirate. The inlet allowed a facility to bring the money in a boat secretly and at night to the very foot of the hill; the elevation of the place permitted a good lookout to be kept that no one was at hand; while the remarkable trees formed good landmarks by which the place might easily be found again. The old stories add, moreover, that the devil presided at the hiding of the money, and took it under his guardianship; but this, it is well known, he always does with buried treasure, particularly when it has been ill-gotten. Be that as it may, Kidd never returned to recover his wealth; being shortly after seized at Boston, sent out to England, and there hanged for a pirate.

About the year 1727, just at the time that earthquakes were prevalent in New England, and shook many tall sinners down upon their knees, there lived near this place a meager, miserly fellow, of the name of Tom Walker. He had a wife as miserly as himself: they were so miserly that they even conspired to cheat each other. Whatever the woman could lay hands on, she hid away; a hen could not cackle but she was on the alert to secure the new-laid egg. Her husband was continually prying about to detect her secret hoards, and many and fierce were the conflicts that took place about what ought to have been common property. They lived in a forlorn-looking house that stood alone, and had an air of starvation. A few straggling savin trees, emblems of sterility, grew near it; no smoke ever curled from its chimney; no traveler stopped at its door. A miserable horse, whose ribs were as articulate as the bars of a gridiron, stalked about a field where a thin carpet of moss, scarcely covering the ragged beds of pudding stone, tantalized and balked his hunger; and sometimes he would lean his head over the fence, look piteously at the passerby, and seem to petition deliverance from this land of famine.

The house and its inmates had altogether a bad name. Tom's wife was a tall termagant, fierce of temper, loud of tongue, and strong of arm. Her voice was often heard in wordy warfare with her husband; and his face sometimes showed signs that their conflicts were not confined to words. No one ventured, however, to interfere between them. The lonely wayfarer shrank within himself at the horrid clamor and clapperclawing, eyed the den of discord askance, and hurried on his way, rejoicing, if a bachelor, in his celibacy.

One day that Tom Walker had been to a distant part of the neighborhood, he took what he considered a short cut homeward, through the swamp. Like most short cuts, it was an ill-chosen route. The swamp was thickly grown with great gloomy pines and hemlocks, some of them ninety feet high, which made it dark at noonday, and a retreat for all the owls of the neighborhood. It was full of pits and quagmires, partly covered with weeds and mosses, where the green surface often betrayed the traveler into a gulf of black, smothering mud; there were also dark and stagnant pools, the abodes of the tadpole, the bullfrog, and the water snake, where the trunks of pines and hemlocks lay half drowned, half rotting, looking like alligators sleeping in the mire.

Tom had long been picking his way cautiously through this treacherous forest; stepping from tuft to tuft of rushes and roots, which afforded precarious footholds among deep sloughs; or pacing carefully, like a cat, along the prostrate trunks of trees; startled now and then by the sudden screaming of the bittern, or the quacking of a wild duck rising on the wing from some solitary pool. At length he arrived at a firm piece of ground, which ran out like a peninsula into the deep bosom of the swamp. It had been one of the strongholds of the Indians during their wars with the first colonists. Here they had thrown up a kind of fort, which they had looked upon as almost impregnable, and had used as a place of refuge for their squaws and children. Nothing remained of the old Indian fort but a few embankments, gradually sinking to the level of the surrounding earth, and already overgrown in part by oaks and other forest trees, the foliage of which formed a contrast to the dark pines and hemlocks of the swamp.

It was late in the dusk of evening when Tom Walker reached the old fort, and he paused there awhile to rest himself. Anyone but he would have felt unwilling to linger in this lonely, melancholy place, for the common people had a bad opinion of it, from the stories handed down from the time of the Indian wars, when it was asserted that the savages held incantations here, and made sacrifices to the evil spirit.

Tom Walker, however, was not a man to be troubled with any fears of the kind. He reposed himself for some time on the trunk of a fallen hemlock, listening to the boding cry of the tree toad, and delving with his walking staff into a mound of black mold at his feet. As he turned up the soil unconsciously, his staff struck against something hard. He raked it out of the vegetable mold and lo! a cloven skull, with an Indian tomahawk buried deep in it, lay before him. The rust on the weapon showed the time that had elapsed since this deathblow had been given. It was a dreary memento of the fierce struggle that had taken place in this last foothold of the Indian warriors.

"Humph!" said Tom Walker, as he gave it a kick to shake the dirt from it.

"Let that skull alone!" said a gruff voice. Tom lifted up his eyes, and beheld a great black man seated directly opposite him, on the stump of a tree. He was exceedingly surprised, having neither heard nor seen anyone approach; and he was still more perplexed on observing, as well as the gathering gloom would permit, that the stranger was neither Negro nor Indian. It is true he was dressed in a rude half-Indian garb, and had a red belt or sash swathed round his body; but his face was neither black nor copper-color, but swarthy and dingy, and begrimed with soot, as if he had been accustomed to toil among fires and forges. He had a shock of coarse black hair, that stood out from his head in all directions, and bore an ax on his shoulder.

He scowled for a moment at Tom with a pair of great red eyes.

"What are you doing on my grounds?" said the black man, with a hoarse growling voice.

"Your grounds!" said Tom, with a sneer, "no more your grounds than mine; they belong to Deacon Peabody."

"Deacon Peabody be d——d," said the stranger, "as I flatter myself he will be, if he does not look more to his own sins and less to those of his neighbors. Look yonder, and see how Deacon Peabody is faring."

Tom looked in the direction that the stranger pointed, and beheld one of the great trees, fair and flourishing without, but rotten at the core, and saw that it had been nearly hewn through, so that the first high wind was likely to blow it down. On the bark of the tree was scored the name of Deacon Peabody, an eminent man, who had waxed wealthy by driving shrewd bargains with the Indians. He now looked around, and found most of the tall trees marked with the name of some great man of the colony, and all more or less scored by the ax. The one on which he had been seated, and which had evidently just been hewn down, bore the name of Crowninshield; and he recollected a mighty rich man of that name, who made a vulgar display of wealth, which it was whispered he had acquired by buccaneering.

"He's just ready for burning!" said the black man, with a growl of triumph. "You see I am likely to have a good stock of firewood for winter."

"But what right have you," said Tom, "to cut down Deacon Peabody's timber?"

"The right of a prior claim," said the other. "This woodland

242

belonged to me long before one of your white-faced race put foot upon the soil."

"And pray, who are you, if I may be so bold?" said Tom.

"Oh, I go by various names. I am the wild huntsman in some countries; the black miner in others. In this neighborhood I am known by the name of the black woodsman. I am he to whom the red men consecrated this spot, and in honor of whom they now and then roasted a white man, by way of sweet-smelling sacrifice. Since the red men have been exterminated by you white savages, I amuse myself by presiding at the persecutions of Quakers and Anabaptists; I am the great patron and prompter of slave dealers, and the grand master of the Salem witches."

"The upshot of all which is that, if I mistake not," said Tom, sturdily, "you are he commonly called Old Scratch."

"The same, at your service!" replied the black man, with a half-civil nod.

Such was the opening of this interview, according to the old story; though it has almost too familiar an air to be credited. One would think that to meet with such a singular personage, in this wild, lonely place, would have shaken any man's nerves; but Tom was a hard-minded fellow, not easily daunted, and he had lived so long with a termagant wife that he did not even fear the devil.

It is said that after this commencement they had a long and earnest conversation together, as Tom returned homeward. The black man told him of great sums of money buried by Kidd the pirate, under the oak trees on the high ridge, not far from the morass. All these were under his command, and protected by his power, so that none could find them but such as propitiated his favor. These he offered to place within Tom Walker's reach, having conceived an especial kindness for him; but they were to be had only on certain conditions. What these conditions were may be easily surmised, though Tom never disclosed them publicly. They must have been very hard, for he required time to think of them, and he was not a man to stick at trifles when money was in view. When they had reached the edge of the swamp, the stranger paused. "What proof have I that all you have been telling me is true?" said Tom. "There's my signature," said the black man, pressing his finger on Tom's forehead. So saying, he turned off among the thickets of the swamp, and seemed, as Tom said, to go down,

down, down, into the earth, until nothing but his head and shoulders could be seen, and so on, until he totally disappeared.

When Tom reached home, he found the black print of a finger burnt, as it were, into his forehead, which nothing could obliterate.

The first news his wife had to tell him was the sudden death of Absalom Crowninshield, the rich buccaneer. It was announced in the papers with the usual flourish, that "a great man had fallen in Israel."

Tom recollected the tree which his black friend had just hewn down, and which was ready for burning. "Let the freebooter roast," said Tom, "who cares!" He now felt convinced that all he had heard and seen was no illusion.

He was not prone to let his wife into his confidence; but as this was an uneasy secret, he willingly shared it with her. All her avarice was awakened at the mention of hidden gold, and she urged her husband to comply with the black man's terms, and secure what would make them wealthy for life. However Tom might have felt disposed to sell himself to the devil, he was determined not to do so to oblige his wife; so he flatly refused, out of the mere spirit of contradiction. Many and bitter were the quarrels they had on the subject; but the more she talked, the more resolute was Tom not to be damned to please her.

At length she determined to drive the bargain on her own account and, if she succeeded, to keep all the gain to herself. Being of the same fearless temper as her husband, she set off for the old Indian fort toward the close of a summer's day. She was many hours absent. When she came back, she was reserved and sullen in her replies. She spoke something of a black man, whom she had met about twilight hewing at the root of a tall tree. He was sulky, however, and would not come to terms: she was to go again with a propitiatory offering, but what it was she forbore to say.

The next evening she set off for the swamp, with her apron heavily laden. Tom waited and waited for her, but in vain; midnight came, but she did not make her appearance: morning, noon, night returned, but still she did not come. Tom now grew uneasy for her safety, especially as he found she had carried off in her apron the silver teapot and spoons, and every portable article of value. Another night elapsed, another morning came, but no wife. In a word, she was never heard of more.

What was her real fate nobody knows, in consequence of so many pretending to know. It is one of those facts which have become confounded by a variety of historians. Some asserted that she lost her way among the tangled mazes of the swamp, and sank into some pit or slough; others, more uncharitable, hinted that she had eloped with the household booty, and made off to some other province; while others surmised that the tempter had decoyed her into a dismal quagmire, on the top of which her hat was found lying. In confirmation of this, it was said a great black man, with an ax on his shoulder, was seen late that very evening coming out of the swamp, carrying a bundle tied in a checked apron, with an air of surly triumph.

The most current and probable story, however, observes that Tom Walker grew so anxious about the fate of his wife and his property that he set out at length to seek them both at the Indian fort. During a long summer's afternoon he searched about the gloomy place, but no wife was to be seen. He called her name repeatedly, but she was nowhere to be heard. The bittern alone responded to his voice, as he flew screaming by; or the bullfrog croaked dolefully from a neighboring pool. At length, it is said, just in the brown hour of twilight, when the owls began to hoot, and the bats to flit about, his attention was attracted by the clamor of carrion crows hovering about a cypress tree. He looked up, and beheld a bundle tied in a checked apron and hanging in the branches of the tree, with a great vulture perched hard by, as if keeping watch upon it. He leaped with joy; for he recognized his wife's apron, and supposed it to contain the household valuables.

"Let us get hold of the property," said he, consolingly to himself, "and we will endeavor to do without the woman."

As he scrambled up the tree, the vulture spread its wide wings, and sailed off, screaming, into the deep shadows of the forest. Tom seized the checked apron, but, woeful sight! found nothing but a heart and liver tied up in it!

Such, according to this most authentic old story, was all that was to be found of Tom's wife. She had probably attempted to deal with the black man as she had been accustomed to deal with her husband; but though a female scold is generally considered a match for the devil, yet in this instance she appears to have had the worst of it. She must have died game, however; for it is said Tom noticed many prints of cloven feet deeply stamped about the tree, and found handfuls of hair, that looked as if they had been plucked from the coarse black shock of the woodman. Tom knew his wife's prowess by experience. He shrugged his shoulders, as he looked at the signs of a fierce clapperclawing. "Egad," said he to himself, "Old Scratch must have had a tough time of it!"

Tom consoled himself for the loss of his property with the loss of his wife, for he was a man of fortitude. He even felt something like gratitude toward the black woodman, who, he considered, had done him a kindness. He sought, therefore, to cultivate a further acquaintance with him, but for some time without success; the old blacklegs played shy, for, whatever people may think, he is not always to be had for calling for; he knows how to play his cards when pretty sure of his game.

At length, it is said, when delay had whetted Tom's eagerness to the quick, and prepared him to agree to anything rather than not gain the promised treasure, he met the black man one evening in his usual woodman's dress, with his ax on his shoulder, sauntering along the swamp, and humming a tune. He affected to receive Tom's advances with great indifference, made brief replies, and went on humming his tune.

By degrees, however, Tom brought him to business, and they began to haggle about the terms on which the former was to have the pirate's treasure. There was one condition which need not be mentioned, being generally understood in all cases where the devil grants favors; but there were others about which, though of less importance, he was inflexibly obstinate. He insisted that the money found through his means should be employed in his service. He proposed, therefore, that Tom should employ it in the black traffic; that is to say, that he should fit out a slave ship. This, however, Tom resolutely refused; he was bad enough in all conscience; but the devil himself could not tempt him to turn slave trader.

Finding Tom so squeamish on this point, he did not insist upon it, but proposed, instead, that he should turn usurer; the devil being extremely anxious for the increase of usurers, looking upon them as his peculiar people.

To this no objections were made, for it was just to Tom's taste.

"You shall open a broker's shop in Boston next month," said the black man.

"I'll do it tomorrow, if you wish," said Tom Walker.

"You shall lend money at two percent a month."

"Egad, I'll charge four!" replied Tom Walker.

"You shall extort bonds, foreclose mortgages, drive the merchants to bankruptcy—"

"I'll drive them to the d——l," cried Tom Walker.

"You are the usurer for my money!" said blacklegs with delight. "When will you want the rhino?"

"This very night."

"Done!" said the devil.

"Done!" said Tom Walker.

So they shook hands and struck a bargain.

A few days' time saw Tom Walker seated behind his desk in a countinghouse in Boston.

His reputation for a ready-moneyed man, who would lend money out for a good consideration, soon spread abroad. Everybody remembers the time of Governor Belcher, when money was particularly scarce. It was a time of paper credit. The country had been deluged with government bills; the famous Land Bank had been established; there had been a rage for speculating; the people had run mad with schemes for new settlements; for building cities in the wilderness; landjobbers went about with maps of grants, and townships, and El Dorados, lying nobody knew where, but which everybody was ready to purchase. In a word, the great speculating fever which breaks out every now and then in the country had raged to an alarming degree, and everybody was dreaming of making sudden fortunes from nothing. As usual the fever had subsided; the dream had gone off, and the imaginary fortunes with it; the patients were left in doleful plight, and the whole country resounded with the consequent cry of "hard times."

At this propitious time of public distress did Tom Walker set up as usurer in Boston. His door was soon thronged by customers. The needy and adventurous; the gambling speculator; the dreaming landjobber; the thriftless tradesman; the merchant with cracked credit; in short, everyone driven to raise money by desperate means and desperate sacrifices hurried to Tom Walker.

Thus Tom was the universal friend of the needy, and acted like a "friend in need"; that is to say, he always exacted good pay and good security. In proportion to the distress of the applicant was the highness of his terms. He accumulated bonds and mortgages, gradually squeezed his customers closer and closer: and sent them at length, dry as a sponge, from his door.

In this way he made money hand over hand; became a rich and mighty man, and exalted his cocked hat upon 'Change. He built himself, as usual, a vast house, out of ostentation; but left the greater part of it unfinished and unfurnished, out of parsimony. He even set up a carriage in the fullness of his vainglory, though he nearly starved the horses which drew it; and as the ungreased wheels groaned and screeched on the axletrees, you would have thought you heard the souls of the poor debtors he was squeezing.

As Tom waxed old, however, he grew thoughtful. Having secured the good things of this world, he began to feel anxious about those of the next. He thought with regret on the bargain he had made with his black friend, and set his wits to work to cheat him out of the conditions. He became, therefore, all of a sudden, a violent churchgoer. He prayed loudly and strenuously, as if heaven were to be taken by force of lungs. Indeed, one might always tell when he had sinned most during the week, by the clamor of his Sunday devotion. The quiet Christians who had been modestly and steadfastly traveling Zionward were struck with self-reproach at seeing themselves so suddenly outstripped in their career by this new-made convert. Tom was as rigid in religious as in money matters; he was a stern supervisor and censurer of his neighbors, and seemed to think every sin entered up to their account became a credit on his own side of the page. He even talked of the expediency of reviving the persecution of Quakers and Anabaptists. In a word, Tom's zeal became as notorious as his riches.

Still, in spite of all this strenuous attention to forms, Tom had a lurking dread that the devil, after all, would have his due. That he might not be taken unawares, therefore, it is said he always carried a small Bible in his coat pocket. He had also a great folio Bible on his countinghouse desk, and would frequently be found reading it when people called on business; on such occasions he would lay his green spectacles in the book, to mark the place, while he turned round to drive some usurious bargain.

Some say that Tom grew a little crackbrained in his old days, and that, fancying his end approaching, he had his horse new-shod, saddled and bridled, and buried with his feet uppermost; because he supposed that at the last day the world would be turning upside down; in which case he should find his horse standing ready for mounting, and he was determined at the worst to give his old friend a run for it. This, however, is probably a mere old wives' fable. If he really did take such a precaution, it was totally superfluous; at least so says the authentic old legend, which closes this story in the following manner.

One hot summer afternoon in the dog days, just as a terrible black thunder-gust was coming up, Tom sat in his countinghouse, in his white linen cap and India silk morning gown. He was on the point of foreclosing a mortgage, by which he could complete the ruin of an unlucky land speculator for whom he had professed the greatest friendship. The poor landjobber begged him to grant a few months' indulgence. Tom had grown testy and irritated, and refused another day.

"My family will be ruined, and brought upon the parish," said the landjobber.

"Charity begins at home," replied Tom; "I must take care of myself in these hard times."

"You have made so much money out of me," said the speculator.

Tom lost his patience and his piety. "The devil take me," said he, "if I have made a farthing!"

Just then there were three loud knocks at the street door. He stepped out to see who was there. A black man was holding a black horse, which neighed and stamped with impatience.

"Tom, you're come for," said the black fellow, gruffly. Tom shrank back, but too late. He had left his little Bible at the bottom of his coat pocket, and his big Bible on the desk buried under the mortgage he was about to foreclose: never was sinner taken more unawares. The black man whisked him like a child into the saddle, gave the horse the lash, and away he galloped, with Tom on his back, in the midst of the thunderstorm. The clerks stuck their pens behind their ears, and stared after him from the windows. Away went Tom Walker, dashing down the streets; his white cap bobbing up and down; his morning gown fluttering in the wind, and his steed striking fire out of the pavement at every bound. When the clerks turned to look for the black man, he had disappeared.

Tom Walker never returned to foreclose the mortgage. A

countryman, who lived on the border of the swamp, reported that in the height of the thunder-gust he had heard a great clattering of hoofs and a howling along the road, and running to the window caught sight of a figure, such as I have described, on a horse that galloped like mad across the fields, over the hills, and down into the black hemlock swamp toward the old Indian fort; and that shortly after a thunderbolt falling in that direction seemed to set the whole forest in a blaze.

The good people of Boston shook their heads and shrugged their shoulders, but had been so much accustomed to witches and goblins, and tricks of the devil, in all kinds of shapes, from the first settlement of the colony, that they were not so much horror-struck as might have been expected. Trustees were appointed to take charge of Tom's effects. There was nothing, however, to administer upon. On searching his coffers, all his bonds and mortgages were found reduced to cinders. In place of gold and silver, his iron chest was filled with chips and shavings; two skeletons lay in his stable instead of his half-starved horses, and the very next day his great house took fire and was burnt to the ground.

Such was the end of Tom Walker and his ill-gotten wealth. Let all griping money brokers lay this story to heart. The truth of it is not to be doubted. The very hole under the oak trees, whence he dug Kidd's money, is to be seen to this day; and the neighboring swamp and old Indian fort are often haunted in stormy nights by a figure on horseback, in morning gown and white cap, which is doubtless the troubled spirit of the usurer. In fact, the story has resolved itself into a proverb, and is the origin of that popular saying, so prevalent throughout New England, of "The Devil and Tom Walker."

FOR DISCUSSION

1. Tom Walker is so greedy that at first he refuses to sell his soul to the devil because his wife will also profit from the deal. Find three other incidents that emphasize Tom's extreme greediness.
2. Does Tom's religious conversion near the end of the story contradict or reinforce his basic character? Explain your point of view.

3. Through satire, Irving manages to mock and expose several of the faults of his society. For example, Deacon Peabody's perilous moral condition is the result of hypocrisy, which permits a sinner to hide under the mask of false piety. Describe how Irving satirizes two other defects of his society.

4. Near the end of the story, the author notes that when the good people of Boston saw the devil run off with Tom, they "were not so much horror-struck as might have been expected." How does Irving explain their lack of horror? Thinking over the story as a whole, can you suggest another reason for their reaction?

5. In real life, retribution occurs frequently, but rarely with the pointed irony that it possesses in this short story. Show how the retribution is exactly appropriate for each of the following:
   a. the end of Tom Walker's wife
   b. the end of Tom Walker
   c. the end of Tom Walker's possessions

INTRODUCTION

The simplest theory of retribution—and, today, the most difficult one to accept—holds that our life on earth is balanced and complete in itself. Our evil deeds have within them the germs of chastisement, and our good deeds of themselves send forth flowers of reward. It is a theory that we want to embrace, but the obvious cruel inequities make such adoption impossible.

It was not impossible, though, to Hesiod, the Greek poet of the 8th century B.C. Hesiod grew up, a happy child, in a rural village at the base of Mount Helicon. When his younger brother Perses cheated him of his portion of their father's estate, Hesiod grieved more for the effect the crime would have on Perses than for his own loss. Amazingly he was right. For Perses, impractical and lazy, squandered both his own and his brother's shares and ended in hopeless poverty; while Hesiod, a conscientious farmer, prospered. Doubtless Hesiod remembered this when he wrote "Right and Wrong," a description of the most direct retribution of all.

Right and Wrong

Hesiod

"Wrong, if he yield to its abhorred control,
Shall pierce like iron to the poor man's soul:
Wrong weighs the rich man's conscience to the dust,
When his foot stumbles on the way unjust.
Far different is the path, a path of light,   5
That guides the feet to equitable right:
The end of righteousness, enduring long,
Exceeds the short prosperity of wrong.
The fool by suffering his experience buys;
The penalty of folly makes him wise.   10
But they who never from the right have strayed,
Who as the citizen the stranger aid,

They and their cities flourish: genial Peace
Dwells in their borders; and their youth increase:
Nor Jove, whose radiant eyes behold afar,   15
Hangs forth in heaven the signs of grievous war.
Nor scathe nor famine on the righteous prey;
Feasts, strewn by earth, employ their easy day:
Rich are their mountain oaks; the topmost trees
With clustering acorns full, the trunks with hiving bees.   20
Still flourish they, nor tempt with ships the main;
The fruits of earth are poured from every plain.
   But o'er the wicked race, to whom belong
The thought of evil, and the deed of wrong,
Saturnian Jove, of wide beholding eyes,   25
Bids the dark signs of retribution rise.
The god sends down his angry plagues from high,
Famine and pestilence: in heaps they die.
Again, in vengeance of his wrath he falls
On their great hosts, and breaks their tottering walls;   30
Arrests their navies on the ocean's plain,
And whelms their strength with mountains of the main."

FOR DISCUSSION

1.   Near the beginning of this poem Hesiod says, "Wrong weighs the rich man's conscience to the dust." Does this belief seem true in the second half of the twentieth century? Before you answer, review carefully all you have read and heard about the very wealthy.

2.   According to Hesiod, what are the earthly rewards enjoyed by the righteous? What are the earthly tribulations suffered by the wicked?

3.   Tradition says that in one poetical contest Hesiod edged out Homer for first prize. After considering the subject matter of this poem, can you suggest one possible reason for Hesiod's popularity in his own time?

4.   Hesiod's primary message in "Right and Wrong" is that the good are rewarded and the wicked punished right here on earth. Do you agree or disagree? Support your answer.

INTRODUCTION

The Greek farmer Hesiod insisted that retribution was the natural and inevitable end of our own actions; 2,800 years later, a New England farmer, Robert Frost, questioned whether retribution existed at all. Frost pondered the biblical Job—a good man who suffered through illness, the death of his loved ones, and every kind of material disaster. Why? the poet asked. Job did not bring these evils upon himself; he did not earn them by his own words or deeds. Why, then, must he endure them? Is his life, part of a larger pattern, intended to merge with other lives into a yet unknown but ultimate good? Or is his life but a casual move in a cosmic game of Chinese checkers?

In *A Masque of Reason,* a verse-drama that is both comedy and tragedy, Frost gropes for an answer.

A Masque of Reason

Robert Frost

A fair oasis in the purest desert.
A man sits leaning back against a palm.
His wife lies by him looking at the sky.

MAN. You're not asleep?
WIFE.   No, I can hear you. Why?
MAN. I said the incense tree's on fire again.   5
WIFE. You mean the Burning Bush?
MAN.   The Christmas Tree.
WIFE. I shouldn't be surprised.
MAN.   The strangest light!
WIFE. There's a strange light on everything today.
MAN. The myrrh tree gives it. Smell the rosin burning?
      The ornaments the Greek artificers   10
      Made for the Emperor Alexius,

254

The Star of Bethlehem, the pomegranates,
The birds, seem all on fire with Paradise.
And hark, the gold enameled nightingales
Are singing.   Yes, and look, the Tree is troubled.   15
Someone's caught in the branches.

WIFE.   So there is.
He can't get out.

MAN.   He's loose!   He's out!

WIFE.   It's God.
I'd know Him by Blake's picture anywhere.
Now what's He doing?

MAN.   Pitching throne, I guess,
Here by our atoll.

WIFE.   Something Byzantine.   20

[*The throne's a plywood flat, prefabricated,*
That GOD *pulls lightly upright on its hinges*
And stands beside, supporting it in place.]

Perhaps for an Olympic Tournament,
Or Court of Love.

MAN.   More likely Royal Court—   25
Or Court of Law, and this is Judgment Day.
I trust it is.   Here's where I lay aside
My varying opinion of myself
And come to rest in an official verdict.
Suffer yourself to be admired, my love,   30
As Waller says.

WIFE.   Or not admired.   Go over
And speak to Him before the others come.
Tell Him He may remember you: you're Job.

GOD.   Oh, I remember well: you're Job, my Patient.
How are you now?   I trust you're quite recovered,   35
And feel no ill effects from what I gave you.

JOB.   Gave me in truth: I like the frank admission.
I am a name for being put upon.
But yes, I'm fine, except for now and then
A reminiscent twinge of rheumatism.   40

A Masque of Reason   255

The letup's heavenly.   You perhaps will tell us
If that is all there is to be of Heaven,
Escape from so great pains of life on earth
It gives a sense of letup calculated
To last a fellow to Eternity.   45

GOD.   Yes, by and by.   But first a larger matter.
I've had you on my mind a thousand years
To thank you someday for the way you helped
      me
Establish once for all the principle
There's no connection man can reason out   50
Between his just deserts and what he gets.
Virtue may fail and wickedness succeed.
'Twas a great demonstration we put on.
I should have spoken sooner had I found
The word I wanted.   You would have supposed   55
One who in the beginning *was* the Word
Would be in a position to command it.
I have to wait for words like anyone.
Too long I've owed you this apology
For the apparently unmeaning sorrow   60
You were afflicted with in those old days.
But it was of the essence of the trial
You shouldn't understand it at the time.
It had to seem unmeaning to have meaning.
And it came out all right.   I have no doubt   65
You realize by now the part you played
To stultify the Deuteronomist
And change the tenor of religious thought.
My thanks are to you for releasing me
From moral bondage to the human race.   70
The only free will there at first was man's,
Who could do good or evil as he chose.
I had no choice but I must follow him
With forfeits and rewards he understood—
Unless I liked to suffer loss of worship.   75
I had to prosper good and punish evil.
You changed all that.   You set me free to reign.
You are the Emancipator of your God,
And as such I promote you to a saint.

256

JOB.	You hear Him, Thyatira: we're a saint. 80
	Salvation in our case is retroactive.
	We're saved, we're saved, whatever else it
	means.
JOB'S WIFE.	Well, after all these years!
JOB.	This is my wife.
JOB'S WIFE.	If You're the deity I assume You are
	(I'd know You by Blake's picture anywhere)— 85
GOD.	The best, I'm told, I ever have had taken.
JOB'S WIFE.	—I have a protest I would lodge with You.
	I want to ask You if it stands to reason
	That women prophets should be burned as
	witches,
	Whereas men prophets are received with
	honor. 90
JOB.	Except in their own country, Thyatira.
GOD.	You're not a witch?
JOB'S WIFE.	No.
GOD.	Have you ever been one?
JOB.	Sometimes she thinks she has and gets herself
	Worked up about it. But she really hasn't—
	Not in the sense of having to my knowledge 95
	Predicted anything that came to pass.
JOB'S WIFE.	The Witch of Endor was a friend of mine.
GOD.	You wouldn't say she fared so very badly.
	I noticed when she called up Samuel
	His spirit had to come. Apparently 100
	A witch was stronger than a prophet there.
JOB'S WIFE.	But she was burned for witchcraft.
GOD.	That is not
	Of record in my Note Book.
JOB'S WIFE.	Well, she was.
	And I should like to know the reason why.
GOD.	There you go asking for the very thing 105
	We've just agreed I didn't have to give.—

[*The throne collapses. But He picks it up
And this time locks it up and leaves it.*]

Where has she been the last half hour or so?

	She wants to know why there is still injustice.	110
	I answer flatly: That's the way it is,
	And bid my will avouch it like Macbeth.
	We may as well go back to the beginning
	And look for justice in the case of Segub.
JOB.	Oh, Lord, let's not go *back* to anything.	115
GOD.	Because your wife's past won't bear looking
	into?—
	In our great moment what did you do, Madam?
	What did you try to make your husband say?
JOB'S WIFE.	No, let's not live things over. I don't care.
	I stood by Job. I may have turned on You.	120
	Job scratched his boils and tried to think what
	he
	Had done or not done to or for the poor.
	The test is always how we treat the poor.
	It's time the poor were treated by the state
	In some way not so penal as the poorhouse.	125
	That's one thing more to put on Your agenda.
	Job hadn't done a thing, poor innocent.
	I told him not to scratch: it made it worse.
	If I said once I said a thousand times,
	Don't scratch! And when, as rotten as his skin,	130
	His tents blew all to pieces, I picked up
	Enough to build him every night a pup tent
	Around him so it wouldn't touch and hurt him.
	I did my wifely duty. I should tremble!
	All You can seem to do is lose Your temper	135
	When reason-hungry mortals ask for reasons.
	Of course, in the abstract high singular
	There isn't any universal reason;
	And no one but a man would think there was.
	You don't catch women trying to be Plato.	140
	Still there must be lots of unsystematic
	Stray scraps of palliative reason
	It wouldn't hurt You to vouchsafe the faithful.
	You thought it was agreed You needn't give
	them.
	You thought to suit Yourself. I've not agreed	145
	To anything with anyone.

JOB.	There, there,
	You go to sleep. God must await events,
	As well as words.
JOB'S WIFE.	I'm serious. God's had
	Aeons of time and still it's mostly women
	Get burned for prophecy, men almost never.	150
JOB.	God needs time just as much as you or I
	To get things done. Reformers fail to see that.—
	She'll go to sleep. Nothing keeps her awake
	But physical activity, I find.
	Try to read to her and she drops right off.	155
GOD.	She's beautiful.
JOB.	Yes, she was just remarking
	She now felt younger by a thousand years
	Than the day she was born.
GOD.	That's about right,
	I should have said. You got your age reversed
	When time was found to be a space dimension	160
	That could, like any space, be turned around in?
JOB.	Yes, both of us: we saw to that at once.
	But, God, I have a question too to raise.
	(My wife gets in ahead of me with hers.)
	I need some help about this reason problem	165
	Before I am too late to be got right
	As to what reasons I agree to waive.
	I'm apt to string along with Thyatira.
	God knows—or rather, You know (God forgive
	me)
	I waived the reason for my ordeal—but—	170
	I have a question even there to ask—
	In confidence. There's no one here but her,
	And she's a woman: she's not interested
	In general ideas and principles.
GOD.	What are her interests, Job?
JOB.	Witch-women's rights. 175
	Humor her there or she will be confirmed
	In her suspicion You're no feminist.
	You have it in for women, she believes.
	Kipling invokes You as Lord God of Hosts.

A Masque of Reason   259

	She'd like to know how You would take a	
	prayer	180
	That started off Lord God of Hostesses.	
GOD.	I'm charmed with her.	
JOB	Yes, I could see You were.	
	But to my question. I am much impressed	
	With what You say we have established,	
	Between us, You and I.	
GOD.	I make you see?	185
	It would be too bad if Columbus-like	
	You failed to see the worth of your achievement.	
JOB.	You call it mine.	
GOD.	We groped it out together.	
	Any originality it showed	
	I give you credit for. My forte is truth,	190
	Or metaphysics, long the world's reproach	
	For standing still in one place true forever;	
	While science goes self-superseding on.	
	Look at how far we've left the current science	
	Of Genesis behind. The wisdom there, though,	195
	Is just as good as when I uttered it.	
	Still, novelty has doubtless an attraction.	
JOB.	So it's important who first thinks of things?	
GOD.	I'm a great stickler for the author's name.	
	By proper names I find I do my thinking.	200
JOB'S WIFE.	God, who invented earth?	
JOB.	What, still awake?	
GOD.	Any originality it showed	
	Was of the Devil. He invented Hell,	
	False premises that are the original	
	Of all originality, the sin	205
	That felled the angels, Wolsey should have said.	
	As for the earth, we groped that out together,	
	Much as your husband, Job, and I together	
	Found out the discipline man needed most	
	Was to learn his submission to unreason;	210
	And that for man's own sake as well as mine,	
	So he won't find it hard to take his orders	
	From his inferiors in intelligence	
	In peace and war—especially in war.	

260

JOB.	So he won't find it hard to take his war.	215
GOD.	You have the idea. There's not much I can tell you.	
JOB.	All very splendid. I am flattered proud	
	To have been in on anything with You.	
	'Twas a great demonstration if You say so.	
	Though incidentally I sometimes wonder	220
	Why it had had to be at my expense.	
GOD.	It had to be at somebody's expense.	
	Society can never think things out:	
	It has to see them acted out by actors,	
	Devoted actors at a sacrifice—	225
	The ablest actors I can lay my hands on.	
	Is that your answer?	
JOB.	No, for I have yet	
	To ask my question. We disparage reason.	
	But all the time it's what we're most concerned with.	
	There's will as motor and there's will as brakes.	230
	Reason is, I suppose, the steering gear.	
	The will as brakes can't stop the will as motor	
	For very long. We're plainly made to go.	
	We're going anyway and may as well	
	Have some say as to where we're headed for;	235
	Just as we will be talking anyway	
	And may as well throw in a little sense.	
	Let's do so now. Because I let You off	
	From telling me Your reason, don't assume	
	I thought You had none. Somewhere back	240
	I knew You had one. But this isn't it	
	You're giving me. You say we groped this out.	
	But if You will forgive me the irreverence,	
	It sounds to me as if You thought it out,	
	And took Your time to it. It seems to me	245
	An afterthought, a long-long-after-thought.	
	I'd give more for one least beforehand reason	
	Than all the justifying ex-post-facto	
	Excuses trumped up by You for theologists.	
	The front of being answerable to no one	250
	I'm with You in maintaining to the public.	

But, Lord, we showed them what.   The audience
Has all gone home to bed.   The play's played
   out.
Come, after all these years—to satisfy me.
I'm curious.   And I'm a grown-up man: 255
I'm not a child for You to put me off
And tantalize me with another "Oh, because."
You'd be the last to want me to believe
All Your effects were merely lucky blunders.
That would be unbelief and atheism.   260
The artist in me cries out for design.
Such devilish ingenuity of torture
Did seem unlike You, and I tried to think
The reason might have been some other person's.
But there is nothing You are not behind.   265
I did not ask then, but it seems as if
Now after all these years You might indulge me.
Why did You hurt me so?   I am reduced
To asking flatly for the reason—outright.

GOD.   I'd tell you, Job—

JOB.   All right, don't tell me, then,   270
If you don't want to.   I don't want to know.
But what is all this secrecy about?
I fail to see what fun, what satisfaction
A God can find in laughing at how badly
Men fumble at the possibilities   275
When left to guess forever for themselves.
The chances are when there's so much pretense
Of metaphysical profundity
The obscurity's a fraud to cover nothing.
I've come to think no so-called hidden value's   280
Worth going after.   Get down into things
It will be found there's no more given there
Than on the surface.   If there ever was,
The crypt was long since rifled by the Greeks.
We don't know where we are, or who we are.   285
We don't know one another; don't know You;
Don't know what time it is.   We don't know,
   don't we?

Who says we don't? Who got up these mis-
    givings?
Oh, we know well enough to go ahead with.
I mean we seem to know enough to act on.   290
It comes down to a doubt about the wisdom
Of having children—after having had them,
So there is nothing we can do about it
But warn the children they perhaps should
    have none.
You could end this by simply coming out   295
And saying plainly and unequivocally
Whether there's any part of man immortal.
Yet, You don't speak. Let fools bemuse them-
    selves
By being baffled for the sake of being.
I'm sick of the whole artificial puzzle.   300

JOB'S WIFE.   You won't get any answers out of God.
GOD.   My kingdom, what an outbreak!
JOB'S WIFE.   Job is right.
Your kingdom, yes, Your kingdom come on
    earth.
Pray tell me what does that mean? Anything?
Perhaps that earth is going to crack someday   305
Like a big egg and hatch a heaven out
Of all the dead and buried from their graves.
One simple little statement from the throne
Would put an end to such fantastic nonsense;
And, too, take care of twenty of the four   310
And twenty freedoms on the party docket.
Or is it only four? My extra twenty
Are freedoms from the need of asking questions.
(I hope You know the game called twenty
    questions.)
For instance, is there such a thing as Progress?   315
Job says there's no such thing as Earth's
    becoming
An easier place for man to save his soul in.
Except as a hard place to save his soul in,

A trial ground where he can try himself
And find out whether he is any good,   320
It would be meaningless. It might as well
Be Heaven at once and have it over with.

GOD.   Two pitching on like this tend to confuse me.
One at a time, please. I will answer Job first.
I'm going to tell Job why I tortured him,   325
And trust it won't be adding to the torture.
I was just showing off to the Devil, Job,
As is set forth in Chapters One and Two.
(JOB *takes a few steps pacing.*) Do you mind?
(*God eyes him anxiously.*)

JOB.   No. No, I mustn't.   330
'Twas human of You. I expected more
Than I could understand and what I get
Is almost less than I can understand.
But I don't mind. Let's leave it as it stood.
The point was it was none of my concern.   335
I stick to that. But talk about confusion!—
How is that for a mix-up, Thyatira?—
Yet I suppose what seems to us confusion
Is not confusion, but the form of forms,
The serpent's tail stuck down the serpent's
        throat,   340
Which is the symbol of eternity
And also of the way all things come round,
Or of how rays return upon themselves,
To quote the greatest Western poem yet.
Though I hold rays deteriorate to nothing: 345
First white, then red, then ultrared, then out.

GOD.   Job, you must understand my provocation.
The tempter comes to me and I am tempted.
I'd had about enough of his derision
Of what I valued most in human nature.   350
He thinks he's smart. He thinks he can con-
        vince me
It is no different with my followers
From what it is with his. Both serve for pay.
Disinterestedness never did exist,

264

And if it did, it wouldn't be a virtue.   355
Neither would fairness.   You have heard the
   doctrine.
It's on the increase.   He could count on no one:
That was his lookout.   I could count on you.
I wanted him forced to acknowledge so much.
I gave you over to him, but with safeguards.   360
I took care of you.   And before you died
I trust I made it clear I took your side
Against your comforters in their contention
You must be wicked to deserve such pain.
That's Browning and sheer Chapel Noncon-
   formism.   365

JOB.   God, please, enough for now.   I'm in no mood
For more excuses.

GOD.   What I mean to say:
Your comforters were wrong.

JOB.   Oh, that committee!

GOD.   I saw you had no fondness for committees.
Next time you find yourself pressed onto one   370
For the revision of the Book of Prayer
Put that in if it isn't in already:
Deliver us from committees.   'Twill remind me.
I would do anything for you in reason.

JOB.   Yes, yes.

GOD.   You don't seem satisfied.

JOB.   I am.   375

GOD.   You're pensive.

JOB.   Oh, I'm thinking of the Devil.
You must remember he was in on this.
We can't leave him out.

GOD.   No.   No, we don't need to.
We're too well off.

JOB.   Someday we three should have
A good old get-together celebration.   380

GOD.   Why not right now?

JOB.   We can't without the Devil.

GOD.   The Devil's never very far away.
He too is pretty circumambient.

He has but to appear. He'll come for me,
Precipitated from the desert air.—   385
Show yourself, son.—I'll get back on my throne
For this I think. I find it always best
To be upon my dignity with him.

        [*The Devil enters like a sapphire wasp
        That flickers mica wings. He lifts a hand*   390
        To brush away a disrespectful smile.
        Job's wife sits up.]

JOB'S WIFE.   Well, if we aren't all here,
Including me, the only Dramatis
Personae needed to enact the problem.
JOB.   We've waked her up.
JOB'S WIFE.   I haven't been asleep.   395
I've heard what you were saying—every word.
JOB.   What did we say?
JOB'S WIFE.   You said the Devil's in it.
JOB.   She always claims she hasn't been asleep.—
And what else did we say?
JOB'S WIFE.   Well, what led up—
Something about—(*The three men laugh.*)   400
—The Devil's being God's best inspiration.
JOB.   Good, pretty good.
JOB'S WIFE.   Wait till I get my Kodak.—
Would you two please draw in a little closer?
No—no, that's not a smile there. That's a grin.
Satan, what ails you? Where's the famous
        tongue,   405
Thou one time Prince of Conversationists?
This is polite society you're in,
Where good and bad are mingled every which
        way,
And ears are lent to any sophistry
Just as if nothing mattered but our manners.   410
You look as if you either hoped or feared
You were more guilty of mischief than you are.

Nothing has been brought out that for my part
I'm not prepared for or that Job himself
Won't find a formula for taking care of.   415

SATAN.   Like the one Milton found to fool himself
About his blindness.

JOB'S WIFE.   Oh, he speaks! He *can* speak!
That strain again!   Give me excess of it!
As dulcet as a pagan temple gong!
He's twitting us.—Oh, by the way, you haven't   420
By any chance a Lady Apple on you?
I saw a boxful in the Christmas market.
How I should prize one personally from you.

GOD.   Don't *you* twit. He's unhappy. Church neglect
And figurative use have pretty well   425
Reduced him to a shadow of himself.

JOB'S WIFE.   *That* explains why he's so diaphanous
And easy to see through.   But where's he off to?
I thought there were to be festivities
Of some kind.   We could have charades.   430

GOD.   He has his business he must be about.
Job mentioned him, and so I brought him in,
More to give his reality its due
Than anything.

JOB'S WIFE.   He's very real to me
And always will be.—Please don't go. Stay, stay   435
But to the evensong, and having played
Together we will go with you along.
There are who won't have had enough of you
If you go now.—Look how he takes no steps!
He isn't really going, yet he's leaving.   440

JOB.   (*Who has been standing dazed with new ideas*)
He's on that tendency that like the Gulf Stream,
Only of sand, not water, runs through here.
It has a rate distinctly different
From the surrounding desert; just today   445
I stumbled over it and got tripped up.

JOB'S WIFE.   Oh, yes, that tendency!—Oh, do come off it.
Don't let it carry you away.   I hate
A tendency.   The minute you get on one

It seems to start right off accelerating. 450
Here, take my hand.

> [*He takes it and alights*
> *In three quick steps as off an escalator.*
> *The tendency, a long, long narrow strip*
> *Of middle-aisle church carpet, sisal hemp,* 455
> *Is worked by hands invisible, offstage.*]

I want you in my group beside the throne—
Must have you.   There, that's just the right
  arrangement.
Now someone can light up the Burning Bush
And turn the gold enameled artificial birds on.
I recognize them.   Greek artificers 460
Devised them for Alexius Comnenus.
They won't show in the picture.   That's too bad.
Neither will I show.   That's too bad moreover.
Now if you three have settled anything
You'd as well smile as frown on the occasion. 465

> [*Here endeth Chapter Forty-three of Job.*]

FOR DISCUSSION

1. This verse-drama was written in 1945. Job and his wife,
   Thyatira, ask questions that reflect some of the problems that
   concerned people at that time.   Describe briefly three of these
   problems.   After each description, note whether the problem
   has been solved or is still of concern today.
2. Through the Bible we learn that Job received compensation
   for each of his trials.   But for the Job in this drama it is not
   enough.   He wants to know God's reason for sending these
   tribulations.   God gives two reasons for his actions.   What are
   they?   Is God serious in giving these reasons?   Do they satisfy
   Job?   Why, or why not?